Debating Nationalism

[Aurobindo, Gandhi, Pal, Tagore and Savarkar]

About the Authors

Anil Dutta Mishra is a distinguished Gandhian scholar and writer. He started his career as Assistant Professor in the Department of Non-violence and Peace Studies, Jain Vishva Bharati University, Ladnun, Rajasthan, became Deputy Director of National Gandhi Museum and Honorary Professor, Centre for Gandhian Philosophy and Human Development, Gayatri Vidya Parishad Degree College [Autonomous], Visakhapatnam and Professor Research, U.P. Rajarshi Tandon Open University, Allahabad. Presently, Treasurer IIPA, Delhi Regional Branch, New Delhi.

Mishra has held the post of General Secretary of Indian Society of Gandhian Studies, Alliance for Sarvodaya, Member Board of Studies, Nagpur and Punjab Universities and is Member of Gandhian Studies Centre of different colleges and universities across India sponsored by UGC. He is author of Reading Gandhi.

Prem Anand Mishra well established Gandhian scholar teaches at Department of Gandhian Studies and Peace Research Centre, Gujarat Vidyapith, Ahmedabad. He has contributed to the renowned Journal Gandhi Marg, Journal of Gandhian Studies and The Indian Journal of Political Science. His latest book is *Hind Swaraj: A Deconstructive Reading*.

DEBATING NATIONALISM

[Aurobindo, Gandhi, Pal, Tagore and Savarkar]

Anil Dutta Mishra
Prem Anand Mishra

CONCEPT PUBLISHING COMPANY PVT. LTD.
NEW DELHI-110059

ISBN-13: 978-93-86682-44-4

First Published in 2018

Published and Printed by

Concept
Since 1974

Concept Publishing Company Pvt. Ltd.
A/15-16, Commercial Block, Mohan Garden,
New Delhi-110059 (INDIA)
T: +91 11 25351460, +91 11 25351794
E: publishing@conceptpub.com, *W*: www.conceptpub.com

Cataloging in Publication Data--Courtesy: D.K. Agencies (P) Ltd. <docinfo@dkagencies.com>

Mishra, Anil Dutta, 1965- **author.**
Debating nationalism : Aurobindo, Gandhi, Pal, Tagore and Savarkar / Anil Dutta Mishra, Prem Anand Mishra.
pages cm
Includes bibliographical references and index.
Includes index.
ISBN 9789386682444

1. Nationalism—India—History. 2. India—Politics and government—20th century 3. Nationalism in literature. 4. Indic prose literature (English)—History and criticism. I. Mishra, Prem Anand, author. II. Title.

LCC DS480.45.M57 2018 DDC 954.035 23

Acknowledgements

"Debating Nationalism" is the result of collaborative efforts of a teacher and a student. This symbolizes how two can be harmonized for a cause of humanity. In India still nationalism like Japan and Germany is missing. We need a Strong nationalistic bond and must feel proud of being Indian. This work is out of our original research on Aurobindo, Pal, Mahatma Gandhi, Tagore and V.D. Savarkar. All of them wanted to transform India and Indians and also for the liberation of motherland from the yoke of colonial power. It is our pleasure to express my gratitude to a large number of people without whom this work would not have been possible. First and foremost, we would like to place our gratitude to Dr. Amrendra Kumar Dubey, IAS, Secretary, Ministry of Youth Affairs, Government of India.

We cannot forget our friends, Mr. Virender Singh, IPS, Mr. Prabhat Ranjan, IRTS, Mr. Atul Tiwari, IAS, Professor P.V. Sarma, Professor ABSV Ranga Rao, Professor Manohar Lal Sharma, Professor Ram Prakash Dwivedi, Professor R.C. Mishra and, who have always stood by us in all our academic endeavours.

We would also like to thank Shri T.N. Chaturvedi, former CAG and former Governor of Karnataka and Kerala and Shri Subodh Kant Sahay, Former Cabinet Minister, for their constant encouragement and blessings in all my academic pursuits. Another person who greatly encouraged us is Professor R.P. Misra, former Vice Chancellor, University of Allahabad.

Within the family we are grateful to Dr. Sweta Mishra, Senior Assistant Professor, Department of Political Science, Gargi College,

University of Delhi and daughters, Sanstuti and Sansriti, for providing us peaceful environment to complete this work.

We take this opportunity to thank our publisher, Shri Ashok K. Mittal, Managing Director, Conecpt Publishing Company Pvt. Ltd., New Delhi for bringing out this book in such a nice form and that too within short span of time.

Anil Dutta Mishra
Prem Anand Mishra

Preface

Nationalism is a modern phenomenon. Nationalism has been considered essential to "the establishment of a modern industrial society" and "the sole vision and rationale of political solidarity today".[1] Nationalism gives legitimacy to the state, and inspires its citizens to feel an emotional attachment towards it. It can be a source of creativity in the arts, and enterprise in the economy. Its power to mobilise political activity is unsurpassed, especially in the vital activity of nation-building.[2]

The manifestations of nationalism are widespread and complex. Very large and contradictory literature on the subject, with works by philosophers, historians, sociologist, writers, activists, freedom-fighters and by political scientists is available, although, there is no integrated theory of the politics of nationalism in India. This is especially needed, as it is politics which gives the most powerful expression to nations and people. In fact nationalism is both an ideology and a form of behaviour. Nationalism is come back with vengeance. The Developed Nations have rejected globalization. We are living in the decay of lunacy, right wing extremism and violence. Humanity is taken a back seat in the name of nationalism and that is too of a particular type. Therefore, it is essential to debate nationalism in Indian context by different ideologues.

Two major dimensions need to be considered when analyzing nationalism. We must look at the ways in which nationalism both shapes and attempts to cope with the rise of the modern state; and because the study of nationalism cannot be limited to its political character, we have to also acknowledge fully the role nationalism plays as one of the major sources of identity for contemporary individuals.[3] Nationalism originated from the assumption that nations are the primary focus of political allegiance. The spread of nationalism has been the result of Europeanization and modernization of non-western and pre-modern societies. Its rise is linked to numerous phenomena, important among these are: "origins of popular sovereignty; the theory of government by the active 'consent' of the governed; the growth of secularism; the lessening of the older religious, tribal, clannish, or feudal loyalties; and, the spread of urbanization, industrialization and improved communications".[4]

A Dictionary of Political Thought defines nationalism as "The sentiment and ideology of attachment to a nation and to its interests".[5] *Dictionary of Contemporary English* defines nationalism as "desire by a group of people of the same race, origin, language etc. to form an independent country."[6] In other words, love for your own country and the belief that it is better than any other country.

Nationalism is defined as "a political creed that underlies the cohesion of modern societies and legitimizes their claim to authority. Nationalism centres the supreme loyalty of the overwhelming majority of the people upon the nation-state, either existing or desired. The nation-state is regarded not only as the ideal, 'natural', or 'normal' form of political organization, but also as the indispensable framework for all social cultural and economic activities.[7] 'Nationalism' means the sentiment of belonging to a community whose members identify with a set of symbols, beliefs and ways of life, and have the will to decide upon their common political destiny.

In fact, nationalism is a political ideology that involves a strong identification of a group of individuals with a political entity defined in national terms, i.e. a nation. In the 'modernist' image of the nation, it is nationalism that creates national identity. There are various definitions for what constitutes a nation, however, which leads to several different strands of nationalism. Nationalism is sometimes reactionary, calling for a return to a national past, and sometimes for the expulsion of foreigners. Other forms of nationalism are revolutionary, calling for the establishment of an independent state as a homeland for an ethnic underclass. Nationalism emphasizes collective identity—a 'people' must be autonomous, united, and express a single national culture. Integral nationalism is a belief that a nation is an organic unit, with a social hierarchy, co-operation between the different social classes and common political goals. However, liberal nationalists stress individualism as an important part of their own national identity.

In the context of European nationalism it is generally considered that it encompasses certain specific characteristics such as organic unity in terms of population, distinct territory, a single economy, common language, common psychological orientation and a common culture. E.H. Carr[8] has described the major traits of nationalism as under:

(a) The idea of a common government whether as a reality in the present or past, or as an as aspiration of the future;
(b) A certain size and closeness of contact between all its individual members;
(c) A more or less defined territory;
(d) Certain characteristics (of which most frequent is language) clearly distinguishing the nation from the other nations and non-national groups;
(e) Certain interests common to the individual members; and
(f) A certain degree of common feeling or will associated with a picture of the nation in the mind of the individual members.

When we analyse in deep about nationalism, these traits are not available in later kind of nationalism that spread in the Third World countries. Moreover, nationalism is sometimes associated with states whose identity as a political unit is already established. But simultaneously it can also spring up in ethnic, social or cultural communities that do not exist as independent political units but are under the domination of other states. Gandhi wrote in *Young India*, June 18, 1925 that "It is no nationalism that is evil; it is the narrowness, selfishness, exclusiveness which is the bane of modern nations which is evil". Again explaining in detail in *Young India* of September 10, 1925, Gandhi wrote that "Illustrations are taken from recent wars and administration of law in civilized societies to prove that hatred seems to be of the essence of nationalism. Nevertheless, it is the grossest of delusions." Nationalism is the dominant feature of the political thinking of Aurobindo, Gandhi, Pal, Tagore and Savarkar.

According to Wikipedia, *Indian nationalism* refers to the many underlying forces that moulded the Indian independence movement, and strongly continue to influence the politics of India, as well as being the heart of many contrasting ideologies that have caused ethnic and religious conflict in Indian society. Indian nationalism often imbibes the consciousness of Indians that prior to 1947, India embodied the broader Indian subcontinent and influenced a part of Asia, known as Greater India.

Nationalism in India can, thus, be described as the consciousness and the recognition of the socio-cultural unity in the past. But, it was more than a spiritual imperative because it has to operate as a device to letting out the aspiration and the hopes of the educated middle class.

The development of Indian nationalism was not always coherent and consistent. The liberal nationalism was primarily secular. The confluence of religion and politics in extremist nationalism succeeded in broadening the base of the nationalist movement. Religion and nationalism became almost convertible terms in the speeches and the writings of the extremists. This is true of both Hindu extremism and Muslim extremism. Gandhi was impressed by the extremists but was influenced by the liberals. Gandhi's nationalism can be described as quasi-liberal and quasi-extremist.

Gandhi's attempt to formulate the theory of nationalism on the basis of certain liberal and extremist principles was deliberate. He was half-liberal, half-extremist. He surely succeeded in striking a new track. It is interesting to note that Gandhi described himself as the true disciple of Tilak, but at the same time declared Gokhale as his political *guru*. What Gandhi borrowed from Tilak was "the love of country and the steady pursuit of *Swaraj*."

Indian nationalism has its own features. Firstly, it must be admitted that Indian nationalism has not developed in the format and stages of nationalism as that has been developed in Europe. The nature and context of Indian nationalism has been quite different from that of the European nationalism. In the European context generally a nation is considered to be composed of certain specific characteristics such as organic unity in population, district territory, a single economy, common languages, common psychological orientation and a common culture. Whereas Indian nationalism has grown and developed in a peculiar complex socio-economic and political background, hence it is different from that of the classical tradition of European nationalism.

Secondly, Indian nationalism is the by-product of struggle for freedom. The changing contours in the way of achieving the goal to free the country from colonial yoke, has also changed the very nature and scope of Indian nationalism. In other words, Indian nationalism is also not the by-product of certain revolutionary ideology or product of certain social transformation due to different stages of growth in the economic system. Rather, it has been based on certain unorthodox experiences linked to the growth of anti-imperialistic thrust of the movement. The challenges of colonial period, along with the sufferings caused to its people due to colonial rules, made its leaders to devise strategies to handle that crisis. Moreover, as a result of the prevailing foreign rule the main objective of this struggle has been towards the independence of India.

Western sociologist G. Aloysius[9] argues that Indian nationalism is "nationalism without a nation". Whereas Cambridge historians' (Percival Spear, Duncan Forbes, John Gallagher, C.A. Bayly, Judith Brown, Francis Robinson, Anil Seal, Richard Gordon, David Wash Brook, C.J. Baker, Sir Valentine Chirol etc.) view that Indian nationalism emerged more as the by-product of skilful game to be played for fame, status, survival, self-interest and advancement of personal interests, rather giving importance to certain ideals, ideas and ideological thinking. John Breuilly pointed out that, like other Third World countries, Indian nationalism is considered "primarily a form of politics" manifested in the form of anti-colonial struggle.[10] Gandhi wrote in *Young India*, "Indian nationalism is not exclusive, nor aggressive, nor destructive. It is health-giving, religious and, therefore, humanitarian".[11] Further, he wrote in *Young India*, "My nationalism is as broad as my *Swadeshi*. I want India's rise so that the whole world may benefit. I do not want India to rise on the ruin of other nations".[12]

India's concept of nationhood is based not merely on territorial extent of its sovereignty. Nationalistic sentiments and expression encompass that India's ancient history, as the birthplace of the Indus Valley Civilization and Vedic Civilization, as well as four major world religions—Hinduism, Buddhism, Jainism and Sikhism. Indian nationalists see India stretching along these lines across the Indian Subcontinent.

Indian nationalism is as much a diverse blend of nationalistic sentiments as its people are ethnically and religiously diverse. Thus, the most influential undercurrents are more than just *Indian* in nature. The most controversial and emotionally charged fibre in the fabric of Indian nationalism is *dharma*. *Dharma* forms a major, and in many cases, the central element of Indian life. Ethnic communities are diverse in terms of linguistics, social traditions and history across India.

From the study of Aurobindo, Pal, Gandhi, Tagore and Savarkar's *Thought and Action* and available literature following features of nationalism emerge: Firstly, nationalism was "incorporative" forging a nationalist harmony between different kinds of groups in India. Secondly, nationalism was pursuit of emancipation from the colonial yoke. Thirdly, nationalism has been the collective assertion of all communities, including the deprived strata of the society. Fourthly, nationalism has secular outlook, despite his being attached to *dharma*/religion. Fifthly, nationalism had internationalistic overtones. "*Vasudhaiva Kutumbakam*, Global village etc. Indian nationalism has struck a different path. It wants to organize itself or to find full self-expression for the benefit and service of humanity at large." Sixthly, Indian nationalism was not in favour of communitarian approach rather used civilizational context in terms of plurality and synthesis. Seventhly, nationalistic thrust was based on the total mobilization of the masses.

Our nationalism is beyond sectarian and narrow outlook coordinating all castes and classes together. The nationalistic thought of all thinker under this book have even pleaded for the upliftment of downtrodden, women and backward classes so that an egalitarian and harmonious social system could be evolved. Nationalism is woven in the all embracing concerns for humanity. We did not approve of "communitarian" nationalistic frame, but in favour of "civic humanism". In India nationalism is closely linked with its struggle against colonial yoke. "Therefore, nationalism could be well understood by understanding the philosophy and broad ideological moorings of these thinkers which not only worked towards the independence of India, but also integrated it in the form of a nation." Nationalism takes a different form in India from the rest of the world, although there are general features in common. The peculiarly vicious character of nationalism in India is difficult to explain in terms of any theories which we generally discuss in political science. Nationalism in India took the form of anti-imperialist movements. The Indian National Congress founded in 1885 by A.O. Hume, became a mass party and succeeded in ending foreign rule in India on 15 August, 1947.

However, the religious divide between Hindus and Moslems led to two states—India and Pakistan—being established. In fact this was a defeat of Indian nationalism. Anti-British nationalism was soon to be succeeded by rival nationalism in India. India is a 'caste societies' in which nearly all members of a society belong to caste group. Nationalism is still a issue. It is a major threat to peace and integration of pluralistic culture of India. Islamic and other fundamentalism is really a clear indication of the revival of nationalism.

Notes and References

1. See James G. Killas, 1998, *The Politics of Nationalism and Ethiicity, London*: MacMillan Press Ltd., p. 1.
2. *Ibid.*
3. Guibernau, Montserrant, 1996, *Nationalisms: The Nation-State and Nationalism in the Twentieth Century*, Cambridge: Polity Press, p. 46.
4. Hans Kohn, 1976, "Nationalism", *International Encyclopaedia of Social Sciences*, Chicago, Vol. 11, p. 64.
5. Scruton, Roger, 1982, *A Dictionary of Political Thought*, London: Pan Books, p. 315.
6. Longman, 2009, *Dictionary of Contemporary English*, Harlow: Pearson, p. 1159.
7. *The New Encyclopaedia Britannica*, 1987, Chicago, Vol. 8, p. 552.
8. E.H. Carr, 1939, *Nationalism*, p. xx.
9. G. Aloysius, 1997. *Nationalism without a Nation in India*, New Delhi: Oxford.
10. Breuilly, John, 1982, *Nationalism and the State*, Manchester, p. 1.
11. *Young India*, September 10, 1925.
12. *Harijan*, September 7, 1947.

A Note on the Study

The 'debate' has always been the part and parcel of Indian intellectual tradition. There is a Classic maxim in Sanskrit; *Vade Vade Jayete Tattvabodhah,* i.e. Truth is discovered or realized by debate and discussion. In our day to day life also, we often find people saying; *Munde Munde Matirbhinna,* i.e. different heads mean different opinions. This points out to a fact that the significance of debate has always been accepted both in the intellectual and public life of India. At the same time, it also recognizes the fact that Indian people views 'difference of opinion' as 'normal' and 'legitimate' part of life. In a sense, it also indicates that one should *not* be rigid in their attitude and develop a mentality of accepting 'others' and other's views. It is in this spirit of debate, this book *Debating Nationalism* examines the different and contesting forms of Indian nationalism that developed in the early decades of the twentieth century.

Nationalism has always been one of the debated themes in India. At present, it has taken a form of contesting discourse among the Indian scholars and common Indian people. Discussions on Indian Television channels, news paper's articles and popular speeches by leaders of different political parties amply demonstrate how 'nationalism' has become again an intense popular discourse of our time. Intellectuals, spokesperson of political parties, and common people all are trying to 're-define' and 're-formulate' Indian nationalism on the basis of their respective ideologies. Who is the patriot and who is not is also being defined and re-defined. Behind all these exercises, one of the significant questions is often overlooked and undermined as to what sort of India we want.

This study *Debating Nationalism* attempts to intervene in today's highly charged political and social milieu. This is mainly an academic work that attempts to go to the root of the evolution of Indian nationalism and shows its multidimensional nature. It analyzes the view of five different nationalists that made the significant contribution during the Indian freedom movement in the early decades of the last century of India. Their visions were not only limited to make India free from the British yoke but they also attempted to reconstruct India. We need to underline that the early decades of the last century was crucial from the Indian point of view as they provided contesting and contrasting milieu on the question of future of India. Most of the questions that we raise today have root in this time period.

Nationalism is not a 'mega event' but a 'discursive process' that produces and promotes certain kind of national values and culture in a nation. Thus, it is not only limited to generate a 'national identity', but it builds a 'national culture' also. It is a complex phenomenon that encompasses the essentials of past, present, and future of a nation. It is first a psychological picture before the people of a nation than physical. It is also related to the solidarity of a group of people living on a compact land. Further, it gives legitimacy to the state and inspires its citizen to feel an emotional attachment towards it.

In the discussion of nationalism, we must recall the fact that nationalism is primarily a European concept. It emerged in Europe, in the nineteenth century, as a vital force that transformed the whole path of European history by changing its society and culture. By the idea of nation and nationalism, European nations focused their dynamism and rational power to rebuild their history and culture as well as to determine their identity. Further, nationalism in Europe was essentially 'political' in nature which emerged against the feudalism and developed under industrialism and democracy. Nationalism in Europe also brought a great shift in its ideology as the loyalty of people changed from 'religious faith' to 'nation'. Yet, it must be recalled here that the idea of nation and nationalism in Europe was not homogeneous. There were several forms of nationalism in Europe and they were conflicting and contesting also.

When we discuss on Indian nationalism, two important dimensions need to be clearly marked. First, in the Indian context, nationalism and colonialism were interlinked. Indian nationalism emerged and evolved in a response to the colonial discourse which presented itself in the form of the meta-narrative. Ideologically, nationalism in India developed as an antithesis to colonial modernization. This development was not direct or straightforward but discursive in nature. Indian nationalism did not remain restricted to its anti-colonial position but it also tried to assert itself in the process of nation-in-making and in the formation of modern Indian nation-state.

The second significant aspect of Indian nationalism is that unlike European nationalism, which was predominantly 'political' in nature, it had 'cultural' colour also. The cultural colour evolved because of reviving and reinterpreting India's past culture and traditions by Indian nationalists. Nevertheless, the interpretation of past culture and traditions of India by nationalists thinkers and authors were not same. They had different readings of the same Indian past and culture. Thus, what we notice is that there was not 'only one' standard form of nationalism existed in India among the nationalists' thinkers. This book mainly deals with this second aspect.

Although, there are several studies and theories on Indian nationalism, yet, this book is *not* intended to take any side of the theory of nationalism developed in academic circle of nationalism. Nor it wishes to present the pros and cons of different schools of Indian nationalism based on their ideological underpinning. It, in fact, intends to examine that how Indian nationalism was conceptualized and scripted in the texts of Indian nationalist thinkers. Yet, this study is not limited to simply understand and explore the subjective intentions that lay behind these specific texts of nationalist writers. It also explores the meaning of nationalists' texts in terms of their implicit and explicit references. Thus, the study also focuses on the materiality of nationalist and colonial politics as the conceptualization and scripting of nationalism would remain incomplete without them. Consequently, the study conducted here is not limited to the level of language and analysis, but it also deals with the discourse that nationalist texts generate.

This book focuses on the texts written by Indian nationalists during the period of 1905-1923. It is important to note that in the early decades of the last century Indian nationalists were not only politically engaged performers against the colonialism but they were also the good author who produced Classics on the theme of nationalism. The texts written during this period reflect the discursive thinking of Indian nationalists. The close reading of these texts shows that their perspectives on nationalism were sometimes complementary but more often competitive. These texts also show the nationalists divergent reading of Indian past, present, and their vision to shape India. We have chosen five texts of five nationalists written during the period of 1905-1923. These are Aurobindo's *Bhawani Mandir* (1905), Gandhi's *Hind Swaraj* (1909), Bipin Chandra Pal's *The Spirit of Indian Nationalism* (1910), Rabindranath Tagore's *Nationalism* (1917) and Vinayak Damodar Savarkar's *Essentials of Hindutva* (1923).

These texts are complex and it might be read from different angles. This book employs a special kind of reading strategy to unpack the texts. We have chosen four questions, on the basis of that, the texts have been read. These are: (a) How do these texts claim Indians rights to make their own self-definition, rather than being defined by the British? In other words, how do these texts construct *a difference* between India and colonial Britain? (b) How do these texts *define civilization* in general and Indian civilization in particular? (c) How do these texts *define the nation* and offer the idea of India? (d) How do these texts *offer* the means through which divergent people within India can construct *solidarity* across cultural and class differences?

Employing this reading strategy, this book shows that Indian nationalism that was propagated previously, i.e. before 1905, took a mature form in the period of 1905-1923 and most significantly it was conceptualized and written properly. Examining these texts on nationalism, this study also points out that Indian nationalism of the early decades of the twentieth century, which had a long background of more than one hundred years, got hardened both by the materiality and ideology of nationalist and colonial politics. Most importantly, analysing these five texts, this book reveals certain commonalities that emerge in them. First, authors of all these five texts explicitly emphasize on the 'essential' and 'glorious' nature of India based on its 'antiquity'. Second, all these nationalists texts unanimously and consistently claim that Indian civilization is 'spiritual civilization', while colonial Britain represents 'materialistic civilization'. Third, all these texts unequivocally claim that India existed as a nation much before the British came to India.

Fourth, all these texts unambiguously maintain that Indian nationalists need to take some measures for the 'solidarity' of Indian people and India have a 'special mission' in this world.

However, the close reading of these texts shows that these commonalities exist only on the surface level. In fact, all the authors have their own version of 'essential' and 'glorious' India and they interpret 'antiquity' of India in a very different way. 'Spiritual civilization' of India has also been understood and defined by these authors differently. 'India as a nation' and 'idea of India' have also been viewed in a divergent manner. All the five authors find India's 'special mission' in this world in their own fashion. In short, there exist serious differences of thought among these five nationalist authors, although, they use similar and parallel vocabulary. These differences constructed contesting discourses within the Indian nationalism. In other words, Indian nationalism was not homogeneous, it had many conflicting streams and contesting shades. This is revealing and the eye-opener for our present time when 'one particular version' of nationalism is being placed before us as one and only 'standard version' of nationalism. What we learn from the history of Indian nationalism is that there was not a 'one' version of nationalism even when India was in turmoil and in the process of nation-in-making. If there could not be 'one' nationalism before the Indian interdependence, it is logical to think that there cannot and will never be 'one' nationalism when India is a free country and has developed as a modern nation-state.

This book, we humbly hope, will be useful to the scholars and students of nationalism.

Anil Dutta Mishra
Prem Anand Mishra

Contents

1
Introduction

Nationalism is a complex phenomenon that involves the elements of past, present, and future of a nation. It is first a mental picture before the people of a nation then physical. It is concerned with the solidarity to a group of people living on a compact territory. As Hans Kohn (1944) observed, "Nationalism is a state of mind permeating the large majority of a people and claiming to permeate all its members; it recognizes the nation state as the ideal form of political organization and the nationality as the source of all creative cultural energy and economic well-being. The supreme loyalty of man is, therefore, to his own nationality, as his own life is supposedly rooted in and made possible by its welfare".[1]

In fact, nationalism refers to the right of self-determination of ethnic, linguistic, territorial or religious communities sharing common history and culture and bound together by close economic ties. It is also an ideology with an alternative conception of sovereignty, authority and individual rights. Furthermore, it is also related to the larger question of a just political order. It means individuals are linked to the nation with a common orientation to, and a shared understanding of what that just political order is to be. In other words, the concept of nationalism is indicative of a psychological feeling which stresses the loyalty of the individual to the nation-state. Therefore, nationalism is basically a feeling or sentiment of belonging to and the loyalty for a politically independent group, living in a common territory. Yet the question arises: how does this feeling or sentiment of belonging and loyalty come up? It is this question the present study intends to deal with, particularly, in the context of Indian nationalism.

At the outset, it needs to be pointed out that nationalism is primarily a European concept. It emerged in Europe, in the nineteenth century, as an essential force that changed the whole path of European history by altering its society and culture. It had two important consequences. First of all, it brought to end the universalism of the Christianity and the idea of nation-state emerged. Second, it pushed religion, which was dominant in the medieval period, to the private sphere of an individual's life. This was the great shift as the loyalty of people changed from *religious faith* to *nation*. Logically this made European nations concentrate their energies and intellectual power to reconstruct their history and culture as well as to determine their identity. This led to cultural revivalism by which the fragmented groups were integrated and shaped themselves into one nation. However, in the Indian context, nationalism did not develop like Europe. As G. Aloysius (1997) points out there is a difference between European and Indian nationalism. The European nationalism was basically 'political' nationalism which emerged against feudalism and developed under industrialism and democracy, while Indian nationalism, on the contrary, had also 'cultural' colour evolved by reviving the past culture and traditions.[2]

The second important thing about the Indian nationalism is that in India, nationalism and colonialism were interlinked. However, it was not direct or straightforward. Indian nationalism was not only anti-colonial in nature, but it also tried to assert itself in the formation of nation and nation-in-making. In fact, ideologically nationalism in India developed in response to colonial modernization in a very discursive way. It was also in the response to the colonial discourse that presented itself in the form of the monologue. Historically, it arose in India when a section of the people began to challenge the colonial authority of the British in the late nineteenth and early twentieth century. In the late nineteenth century, during a period known as the Bengali Renaissance, many nationalist authors began to use nationalistic language, which then set the stage for the political mobilization and ideological and political struggle that occurred during the twentieth century.

In the late nineteenth and early twentieth century, a significant question in regard to qualification of India as a nation emerged in the context of colonialism that was addressed by many Indian nationalists. It is important to note that these nationalists were not only politically engaged actors against the colonialism and colonial authority but they were also the good reader and author. In fact, the country's leading politicians were its leading political thinkers. As Guha (2010) points out the striking thing about modern India is that the men and women who made its history also wrote most authoritatively about it.[3] Their writings were not merely of academic interest rather they had a defining power and impact on the formation and evolution of the nation—India. Further, as Chatterjee (1986) points out "nationalist texts were addressed both to 'the people' who were said to constitute the nation and to the colonial masters whose claim to rule nationalism questioned".[4] In other words, these texts sought to demonstrate the falsity of the colonial claim that the backward people were culturally incapable of ruling themselves in the conditions of the modern world. These texts denied the alleged inferiority of the Indian people and asserted that a backward nation could 'modernize'/progress itself while retaining its cultural identity.

It is also significant to note that these thinkers-activists-authors of nationalism did not speak in one voice. Their perspectives were sometimes complementary and more often competitive. But, they were always instructive. The sameness and difference of ideas by different Indian nationalists produced many discourses that might be seen still today in India.

One of the central ideas that we notice among the nationalist thinkers-activists-authors was the idea of India in contrast to the idea of Europe. This issue took representational form in the texts written by Indian Nationalists. Through this representational structure, they *asserted* the rights of Indians to make their own self-definition, rather than being defined by the British. This means they projected the difference between India and Britain in terms of histories, cultural traditions and knowledge. They also employed a *particular means* to identify these differences. By this, they were able to make the idea of India that radically differed from the British. In this connection, they also offered the *treasure* of the cultural inheritance of the Indians to challenge colonial discourse. On the other hand, they also offered the means through which divergent people within India can construct *solidarity* across cultural and class differences. This study deals primarily with these issues.

Although there are several studies and theories on Indian nationalism, yet, this book is not intended to take any side of the theory of nationalism developed in academic circle of nationalism. Nor it wishes to present the pros and cons of different schools of Indian nationalism on the line of their ideological underpinning. It, in fact, intends to present the view that how nationalism was conceptualized and scripted in the texts of nationalist thinkers. Yet, this study is not simply in understanding the subjective intentions that lie behind these specific texts of nationalist writers. It also explores the meaning of nationalists' texts in terms of their implicit and explicit reference to their logical and theoretical implications. Thus, the study begins with the materiality of nationalist and colonial politics as the conceptualization and scripting of nationalism would remain incomplete without the materiality of nationalist and colonial politics. Thus, the study conducted here is not limited to the level of language and analysis, but it also reaches to the level of discourse.

In other words, this scripting was not in the vacuum but had the background. During the late nineteenth and the early twentieth century, many Indian thinkers engaged themselves in articulating the collective self-identity of India as a nation in a response to colonialism and colonial modernity. They protested against the Western mode of thinking, and against the colonial representation of India as an inferior civilization that was divided into the lines of religion, region, language and caste. It well reflected in the literary and non-literary texts. The significant part of non-literary texts was journalistic writings. Conspicuously, in an attempt to articulate an alternative collective self-definition, they interrogated not only the Indian past and tradition, but also the categories of modernity.

What is significant to note at the outset is that the history of Indian nationalism has not been homogeneous. In fact, in the period of almost two hundred years of colonial subjugation, one may find many contradictories, competing and complementary nationalists' vision in the history of Indian nationalism. It is neither possible nor reasonable to cover all of them in this study. Moreover, in the period of two hundred years of colonial subjugation, the intensity of national feeling was also not the same. Moreover, such feeling was localized and based on very petty issues. In response to colonial subjugation, only in 1857, all India movement came up. This was suppressed and new colonial policies were introduced. Around this period there were many local institutions emerged on the line of 'reform' or 'revival'. For example, in the line of 'reform', East India Association in 1866 by Dadabhai Naoroji in London, Poona Sarvajanik Sabha in 1870 by Justice Mahadev Govind Rande, Ganesh Vasudev Joshi, S.H. Chiplunkar, Indian Association in July 1876 by Anand Mohan Bose and Surendranath Banerjee were established. In the same way, in 1884, M. Viraraghavachari, G. Subramania Iyer, Ananda Charlu and other formed the Madras Mahajan Sabha. In Bombay, Pherozeshah Mehta, K.T. Telang, Badruddin Tyabjii and others formed the Bombay Presidency Association in 1885. These small organizations were preparing ground for an all India organization that finally came into existence in 1885 in the form of Indian National Congress.

At the same time, on the other hand, 'revival' tendency was at work. One may cite here work of Dayanand Saraswati who was a renowned religious and social reformer and the founder of Arya Samaj. In 1875, he also wrote a book in Hindi *Satyarth Prakash*. He wrote *Satyarth Prakash* in order to spread the knowledge of the *Vedas* and to educate people on the true qualities of God. The *Satyarth Prakash* contains exposition and clarifications of Vedic principles. The book advocates Vedic monism based on *Advaita Vedanta*. Some of the important topics in the *Satyarth Prakash* include worship of one God, explanation of the main principles of the Vedas, the relationship between religion and science and between devotion and intellect, elimination of the Caste system and of different religious beliefs for the strengthening of society, eradication of superstitions, false notions and meaningless customs, shunning narrow-mindedness and promoting the brotherhood of man. These were attempts to regenerate India from the spiritual point of view. Similarly, the Ramakrishna Mission, founded in 1892 by Swami Vivekananda called for the building of an Indian nation on the basis of the Hindu religion/spirituality. Vivekananda argued that liberty required freedom from all bondage—physical, mental, as well as political—and he thus incorporated the Western idea of political and social liberty into the Classical Indian conception of freedom as spiritual salvation. His writings also influenced many other future nationalists to think nationalism in the term of an ancient spiritual height of India.

At the level of materiality of colonial and nationalist politics, after the establishment of Indian National Congress in 1885, a new wave of nationalism we see in India led by English speaking elite class of Indian people. They had the different notion of nationalism as these liberal and pro-British elite people had the different reading of India and its relation to British Empire. On the other hand, at the cultural level, India was facing a crucial question of 'social reform' and 'revivalism' and sometimes both to arm itself against the Colonial subjugation. These reform and revivalism were influenced by the very *different* reading of historical actuality posed by colonials. Thus, they were also not same and sometimes they also conflicted with each other. It is this material and ideological context that prepared the bedrock for the coming nationalists. In fact, it is only during the partition of Bengal (1905) and *Swadeshi* Movement (1905-07), Indian nationalism showed its power in new formulations that challenged the colonial power and its discourses. The partition of Bengal was the "moment of crisis" that produced exemplary nationalists' thinkers-activists-authors who produced several writings on the issue of conceptualization of the nation India and its features. Behind this conceptualization, there was a long intellectual and institutional materiality of nationalist and colonial politics. This study begins from that.

The study is located in the time period of the year 1905 to 1923. Materially, this phase in Indian freedom struggle and in nationalist discourse represents a period of transition and uncertainty. One can also find indecisiveness towards the future of India during this time period. It was only after this phase Indian nationalism took a unilinear politics under Gandhi's non-violent politics under the flag of Indian National Congress. In other words, the method, philosophy, and ideology of Indian nationalism were, if not entirely than substantially, determined only after this phase. In terms of an event, if the year 1905 began with *Swadeshi* Movement, 1924 has represented the beginning of *Swaraj* Party. Between these two points of time, we notice many competing and conflicting attitudes of Indian nationalists and colonial response towards them. This resulted in series of events as the split of Congress in moderates and extremists in Surat Congress, Morley-Minto Reforms offered by colonials, Home Rule Movement, the establishment of Muslim League, World War, Champaran Movement, *Jalianwalla Bagh* massacre, Non-cooperation Movement and *Khilafat* Movement. These challenging events were challenging and it was quite natural for Indian nationalists to respond them in their own way. Thus, these 18 years were more significant than other years of freedom struggle as they were more conflicting, competing and contrasting period of discursive nationalist and colonial politics. As mentioned above, these 18 years also shaped the future of India in their way.

The texts written by Indian nationalists during this period of 1905-1923 reflect the discursive thinking of Indian nationalists. It shows nationalists reading of Indian past, present and their vision to shape India. We have chosen five texts of five nationalists written during this period. Chronologically, these are: (a) Aurobindo's *Bhawani Mandir* (1905), (b) Gandhi's *Hind Swaraj* (1909), (c) Bipin Chandra Pal's *The Spirit of Indian Nationalism* (1910), (d) Rabindranath Tagore's *Nationalism* (1917), and (e) Vinayak Damodar Savarkar's *Essentials of Hindutva* (1923).

These texts are non-fictions except Aurobindo's *Bhawani Mandir*. Even to some extent the *Bhawani Mandir* can be called non-fiction as it is in form of essay that summarizes Aurobindo's view on the Indian Nationalism. The texts are representative of mood and tone of conflicting and competing Indian nationalist politics. The texts are embedded in past (what was the feature of Indian civilization?), present (contemporary nationalistic politics and reflection on colonial response to them), and future (How India could be shaped? or which course of action Indians should take?). On the other hand, they are also interpretations of Indian historical actuality of their time.

At this point it is important to mention two things; first of all the conceptual terms like humanism, universalism, cosmopolitanism, nationalism or internationalism are not universal terms. These terms are the product of a specific culture, thus its merits must ultimately be assessed by measures arising out of that culture. Second which is a corollary of the first is that the views presented on nationalism by the authors of Indian nationalism were formulated from the point of view of Indian civilizational values.

Organization and Methodology of the Study

As mentioned, the texts under consideration of this study are non-fictions. They show the political discourses of their time in their own way. These discourses were not produced in the vacuum, but in the political and public sphere of 1905-1923. This period had, no doubt, the legacy of past and materiality of the present. Thus, to unpack the texts it is desirable to present the overall milieu of the political arena in which these nationalist thinkers-activists-authors fought with colonials at the level of discourse. It is striking to note that although these nationalists' thinkers-activists-authors had same political materiality, they reflected sometimes in the same way and sometimes in a very different and opposite way on the problem of nationalism in India. The reason for sameness and differences seems to depend upon the nationalist's own life experience of colonial encounter, their own lineage and affiliation of the Indian past and intellectual development. Thus, the study also brings in the brief view of author's life and his intellectual formation. This, we assume, will help to understand the text properly. The reason of sameness of the ideas of these nationalist thinkers-activists-authors, to some extent, was that they all had to face the similar discourses of colonialism, which was based on colonials superiority and natives inferiority. Thus at face value, they all responded these colonial discourse by rejecting it. Nevertheless, in the closer analysis, these nationalists-thinkers-activists-authors in reading the colonial discourses focused on the particular aspects of colonial discourse and individually reflected more than others on that aspect. This resulted in the differences among the nationalist thinkers-activists-authors. However, the major project before these nationalists was to present an idea of India to deal with the past, present and future of the nation-in-making. This idea of India was an essential qualification for rising nationalism among the Indian people. And it is this project on which these five texts seem more focused.

Like the authors, all five texts being considered here have their history. Before reading the texts, the journey of the formation of text has been explored to make sense of the arguments presented in the texts. This is followed by the close reading of texts.

Reading Strategy

These texts are complex and it might be read from different angles.

We have chosen four questions, on the basis of that, the texts have been read. These are:

1. How do these texts claim Indians, rights to make their own self-definition, rather than being defined by the British? In other words, how do these texts construct *a difference* between India and Britain?
2. How do these texts *define civilization* in general and Indian civilization in particular?
3. How do these texts *define nation* and *offer the idea of India*?
4. How do these texts offer the means through which divergent people within the India can construct *solidarity* across cultural and class differences?

As we note these readings are not only for intellectual understanding. They make discourses. The main objective of this reading is to demonstrate that how these discourses were competing to each other and how they collectively challenged or subverted the Colonial discourses. Yet it must be pointed out that these discourses are not only the matter of past that shaped the vision of India, thus, useful to understand Indian present, but they also give the lessons as to what course of discourse and action could lead to what kind of society and future. This has been examined in the last Chapter of the study.

In brief, this study has three interrelated parts: *context, texts,* and *discourse.* It is imperative here to define what we mean by these terms and how they have been used in the study.

Context: In the study, context refers to something more dynamic and less unified than "historical background". It suggests the many dominant issues, debates and knowledge in circulation at the time of the texts have been written. It also suggests the various and competing ways in which people conceived of the reality of the past. This is general material and non-material background of the milieu in which the text has been scripted.

Text: The text does not passively reflect the world but actively interrogates it, take up various positions in relation to prevailing views, resist or critique dominant ways of seeing. Reading a text in relation to its context involves doing two things simultaneously. First identifying how such contexts are made present or absent in a text, and second, exploring how the text itself may intervene in debates of its day and applaud or resist dominant views of the world.

Discourse: In this study, the term discourse has been used to show that how different ideas were put on the same issue. This shows similarity and difference of authors' views on a particular issue.

Structure of the Study

The study comprises nine chapters. The chapter one is as usual *Introduction*. Chapter second *"Materiality of Nationalist and Colonial Politics in India in the early decades of the Twentieth century"* demonstrates the colonial policies and their nationalist responses from 1905 to 1923. It presents the brief review of early nationalist phase, Partition of Bengal, *Swadeshi* movement, Morley-Minto Reforms, Surat Split, Home Rule Movement Non-cooperation Movement and *Khilafat* Movement. This provides the material background in which the texts, under this study, have been written. The chapter third is *"Writings on Indian Nationalism in India in late nineteenth century: A thematic Analysis"*. The texts under consideration in this study cannot be separated from the intellectual environment of the latter half of the nineteenth century. This chapter provides the review of early nationalists' writings. It is divided into fiction, non-fiction, and journalistic writings. This chapter mainly focuses on textual analysis. The chapter provides thematic analysis of writings on Indian nationalism in the aforementioned time period.

Chapters, four, five, six, seven and eight includes close reading of the texts taken in this study. In this section, as mentioned earlier, the chapters have been organized in a particular structure. First, all the chapters begin with the brief introduction and significance of the text. Then, they look into author's life, his intellectual formation and his engagement in the political activities to sense the undercurrent of the text. This serves as author's specific ideological, political as well as intellectual formation and position in which the author produced his text. Finally, the chapters focus on the close reading of the texts. All five texts have been put in chronological manner.

The chapter four Sri Aurobindo's *Bhawani Mandir* (1905) begins with the brief introduction of Aurobindo's life, his political career, intellectual formation, and analysis of his other writings. The chapter presents the close reading of his text *Bhavani Mandir* written in 1905. There is a reason to select this text under this study. The *Bhawani Mandir* gets the significance place in the literature of Indian nationalism. In spite of the fact that it is a small booklet that contains only twelve pages, in 1918, Sedition Committee set-up by British Government adjudged it as "seditious matter" in its report. The report further read that the booklet shows "a remarkable instance of perversion of religious ideals to political purposes". The booklet was confiscated by the British police and was considered as spiritual dynamite to blow off the colonial rule over India. In its effect, it caused endless nightmares to British administration; but it proved to be a mighty inspiration and supreme driving force to countless revolutionaries.

The chapter five presents an analysis of Gandhi's *Hind Swaraj* (1909). *Hind Swaraj,* or *Indian Home Rule* is a small tract written by Mahatma Gandhi (1869-1948) in his native language Gujarati in 1909. It is considered as Gandhi's Classic and his foundational text. *Hind Swaraj,* which is known as "a severe critique of modern civilization" is also an intervention in nationalist and colonial discourses. The reason to select this text in this study is that the text tells us about a new form of nationalism based on non-violence. Moreover, the form of nationalism that *Hind Swaraj* suggests is not limited to political in the real sense of the term. It encompasses chiefly a moral/spiritual dimension of nationalism that is all inclusive. Through close reading of the text, the chapter also traces that how Gandhi looks into the question of nation and nationalism in his text and how he criticizes the existing forms of nationalism and proposes his own non-violent nationalism against colonials.

The chapter six Bipin Chandra Pal's *The Spirit of Indian Nationalism* (1910) presents the brief out line of Bipin Chandra Pal's life, his political career and intellectual formation as well as his views on Indian nationalism. This chapter focuses on the close reading of his original text. *The Spirit of Indian Nationalism.* It is a long essay containing 58 pages written in 1910. The central project that the text seems to accomplish is to provide the philosophical and cultural justification to the emerging extremist nationalism in India and put a vehement criticism of moderate politics carried out by Indian National Congress since 1885. The chapter demonstrates that how the text presents a new reading of *Swadeshi*

Movement and claims that after *Swadeshi* movement nationalism in India became at once the name of a "common ideal, a common purpose, one general spirit, and impulse that moved the classes and the masses alike in more than one Indian province". The chapter also shows how Pal was close to a kind of nationalism that favoured, in unintended way, Hindu nationalism.

The chapter seven Rabindranath Tagore's *Nationalism (1917)* focuses on Tagore's views on nation and nationalism as depicted in his book *Nationalism* published in 1917. Tagore's *Nationalism* is also considered a very significant text in Indian nationalist literature as it informs us about a different vision of nation-state, and moreover how the East should adjust to modernization. In fact, Tagore's voice on nationalism was not confined to one particular country or tradition. It was cosmopolitan in nature based on human love. Through his text Nationalism, he reinforced his faith in the eternal and everlasting reason and goodness of human being which is universal qualities. The chapter shows that how his views on nation and nationalism emerge in the context of his overall reading of Indian history, development of the modern nation and development of nationalism in Europe and its corresponding relation to the materialism.

Chapter eight is about Savarkar's *Essentials of Hindutva* (1923). This text is becoming more 'popular' and 'significant' in contemporary India. The text *Essentials of Hindutva,* written in 1923, by Vinayak Damodar Savarkar (1883-1966) has taken a place of Classic in the literature of *Hindutva* and Hindu nationalism. To find the undercurrent of Savarkar's *Hindutva,* the chapter first examines Savarkar's life, work and intellectual formation in brief and then offers the reading of his seminal text. This chapter shows how the text attempts to construct and define the idea of Hindu, Hinduism, and *Hindutva* through a new interpretation of Indian history. Through close reading of the text, the chapter also demonstrates that how Savarkar tried to give a new shape to Indian nationalism on the basis of the idea of *Hindutva*. The text also shows the lofty idea of Hindu nation and nationalism and justify it with the example of ancient Indian past that was, in Savarkar's view, essentially Hindu in its form and content.

The chapter nine is *Epilogue*. There are some important common themes that emerge in texts considered in this study. The themes that most prominently come-up in these texts are; a particular essential nature of India in comparison to colonial Britain, notion of civilization, idea of nation as well as idea of India, and methods taken for solidarity among Indians. Yet, as noticed, underneath the treatment of these common themes there exists serious variations. They form discourses. This last section/chapter deals with the commonalities and variations emerging out of aforementioned themes and discourses surrounded them. It also briefly illustrates the inherent problems of nationalist discourses and how they are still affecting India.

References

1. Hans Kohn. 1944, *The Idea of Nationalism.* Bombaly: MacMillan Publications, p. 4.
2. Aloysius, G., 1997, *Nationalism Without A Nation in India.* New Delhi: Oxford, p. 51.
3. Guha, Ramachandra. 2010, *Makers of Modern India.* New Delhi: Penguin, p. 1.
4. Chatterjee, Parth. 1986, *Nationalist Thought and the Colonial World: A Derivative.* Discourse. London: Zed Books, p. 30.

2

Materiality of Nationalist and Colonial Politics in India in the Early Decades of the Twentieth Century

The nationalist texts under consideration in this study are from 1905 to 1923. As any text cannot be separated from the context, it seems reasonable to present the context of the texts. We would like to call the context here as the materiality of nationalist and colonial politics which acted and reacted upon each other in a very discursive way. The materiality of nationalist and colonial politics took a significant shape in the early decade of the twentieth century especially in 1905 when Bengal was divided into two administrative units. This was followed by *Swadeshi* movement. The *Swadeshi* movement symbolizes both continuation and break of Indian nationalists temper. It was the continuation of the Indian nationalist agenda that focused on Indian culture and tradition as an alternative to British colonial civilization, at the same time it also indicated a break from the liberal moderate nationalist politics that was going on since the establishment of Indian National Congress (1885). It needs to be pointed out that the texts under consideration here (except Savarkar's *Essentials of Hindutva* written in 1923) mentions *Swadeshi* movement in a very substantial way, although the reading of *Swadeshi* is different in these texts.

As mentioned, *Swadeshi* movement in some respect shows the continuity of nationalist feeling which was increasing since long. It had the background of the previous phase of Indian nationalism, thus, a brief review of the previous phase of nationalism is essential to get the clear view of *Swadeshi* movement, its related politics, and texts engagement with it.

Indian nationalism, besides the indirect consequences of modern English education, was also the result of the new social material conditions and the new social forces which had appeared within the Indian society because of the colonial presence. In other words, Indian nationalism emerged as the conflict of interests between the British colonial power and Indian people. On the one hand, British colonials wanted to keep India politically and economically subjected to it for their own interest while Indian people had their own political, economic and cultural interests that were gradually becoming difficult to realize within the British colonial rule. It is because of this *tension* Indian nationalism crystallized as a national movement in the latter half of the nineteenth century. Yet Indian nationalism was not an abrupt growth, but it passed through various phases of development. As it advanced from one phase to another its social basis broadened, its objective became more clearly defined and bold, and its forms of expression more varied.

Geographically, the first phase of Indian nationalism that developed in the early nineteenth century was dominated by people from Calcutta and Bombay. The reason was that it is these two places where Indians first came in contact with the British and their education system. In the first phase, Indian nationalism had a very narrow social base and was dominated by social-religious reforms. Nationalists of this phase also stood-up for democratic rights, such as the freedom of the press, and put forth demands like the right of the nation to have a voice in the administration of the country.

In this regard, Raja Ram Mohun Roy and his group of enlightened Indians might be cited who were pioneers of the Indian nationalism. The first phase extended till 1885 and culminated in the rise of the Indian National Congress in that year.

The second phase roughly begins from 1885 and extends up to 1905. In this phase, the leaders of the Congress were the leaders of the Indian nationalist movement. Their ideology and methods determined the programmes and forms of the movement. These programmes, in fact, reflected the interests of the newly emerging middle class of India. Yet, the social base of the nationalist movement expanded in this phase as the educated middle class had considerably grown by the end of the nineteenth century because of the expansion of modern education. A section of merchant class also joined in this phase that had developed by this phase as a result of the growth of Indian and international trade. It should also be pointed out that modern industries had also grown steadily by this phase, thus, the class of industrialists emerged and began to gain strength. Thus, it was not surprising that they inclined towards the Congress and Congress also adopted the programme of industrialization of the country.

This phase was dominated by the Liberals. The Indian National Congress under the leadership of the Liberals naturally echoed the demands of the educated classes and the mercantile middle class. These demands included: Indianization of British services, the association of the Indians with the administrative machinery of the state and the halt of the economic drain. The Indian National Congress also set forth democratic demands as those of representative institutions and civil liberties. Although the role of liberals, that were called 'moderate' by historians, later on, were criticized, but their contribution cannot be undermined. In fact, the moderates made an ample number of people awaken of the evils of British subjugation and of the need for fostering nationalism.

Liberals believed in purely Constitutional methods to fight against British colonialism and they agitated for "step-by-step reforms" in the Indian administrative system. As a result, they imparted the necessary political training to Indian people and to some extent they also succeeded to create democratic temper among the Indian people.

As mentioned, the Liberal Congress method was mainly Constitutional agitation. When the British colonial government did not accomplish essential demands of the Indian nationalist movement, disenchantment prevailed among a section of the nationalists regarding the political orientation and methods of the Liberals. Thus, a political group with a new political ideology as well as a new conception of the methods of struggle developed within the Congress. This group within the Congress was called 'extremists'. There were some material conditions that also helped to create this group. First, it was the problem of increasing unemployment among the educated middle-class youth because of the inability of the social and state set-up to incorporate them in British colonial system. Second, it was the economic misery among the people owing to devastating epidemic and famines that occurred in the last decade of the nineteenth century. These two significant conditions created appropriate conditions for the growth of the extremists.

Besides, during 1885-1905, certain developments in India and abroad also generated a new kind of nationalism called "militant nationalism". In the Indian context, especially during the viceroyship of Lord Curzon, various unpopular measures such as the Indian Universities Act and the partition of Bengal alienated Indian people from the government and made the politically conscious middle class attracted to the extremists' ideology. Moreover, the personality and vision of extremists' leaders like as B.G. Tilak (1856-1920), Aurobindo Ghose (1872-1950), Bipin Chandra Pal (1858-1932) and Lala Lajpat Rai (1865-1928) also influenced the mindset of Indian middle-class people. It is also important to note here that by 1905; even some of the Liberals also began to lose faith in the British government. However, they did not give-up their political philosophy and methodology of struggle.

The year 1905 is the most significant year in the history of Indian freedom struggle. The Indian national movement, with the start of the *Swadeshi* movement in 1905, took a major turn. Although, every movement owes to some ideological context or other and also become the context of another ideological context for future but in the case of the *Swadeshi* Movement of 1905-07 it is more than this. It constitutes a great footstep in the annals of modern history so much so that it was the cumulative effect of an indigenous Indian nationalist thought-structure or what is sometimes called, the genuine Indian variant of nationalism.

In the *Swadeshi* movement, for the first time women, students and the large section of the urban and rural people of Bengal and other parts of India actively participated in politics. Yet, the richness of the movement was not confined to the politics alone. The period also saw a new dimension in the development of Indian art, literature, music, science, and industry. Furthermore, on the one hand, *Swadeshi* movement was an experiment within the India society; on the other, it also showed the creative tension of the Indian society.

Politically, the *Swadeshi* movement had its genesis in the anti-partition movement which started to oppose the British decision to partition of Bengal. Bengal with a population of 78 million had become administratively unmanageable, thus, British colonials argued that it should be divided, but the real motive for partitioning Bengal was different. In July 1905, Lord Curzon issued an order dividing the province of Bengal into two parts: Eastern Bengal and Assam with a population of 31 million and rest of Bengal with a population of 54 million. It was said that the existing province of Bengal was too big to be efficiently administered by a single provincial Government. However, as mentioned the official who worked out the plan had different ends in their mind. They hoped to curb the rising tide of nationalism in Bengal. The partition of the state intended to curb Bengali influence by not only placing Bengalis under two administrations but by reducing them to a minority in Bengal itself. It can be well illustrated from one of the official note written by Herbert Risley. Risely, the Home Secretary to the Government of India, wrote in an official note on 6th December, 1904 that Bengal united is a power; "Bengal divided will pull several different ways"[1]. Curzon himself wrote in a similar vein in February, 1905,

> "The Bengalis, who like to think themselves a nation and who dream of a future when the English will have been turned out, and a Bengali Babu will be installed in the Government House, Calcutta, of course bitterly resent any disruption that will be likely to interfere with the realization of this dream. If we are weak enough to yield to their clamour now, we shall not be able to dismember or reduce Bengal again, and you will be cementing and solidifying on the eastern flank of India, a force already formidable, and certain to be a source of increasing trouble in future".[2]

The Indian National Congress and the Nationalists of Bengal strongly opposed the partition. Within the Bengal different sections of the population—*Zamindar*, Merchant, Lawyer, Student, and even Women—rose up in spontaneous opposition to the partition of their province. The nationalists viewed the act of partition as a challenge to Indian nationalism and not merely an administrative measure. They clearly saw that it was an intentional attempt to divide Bengali and to interrupt and weaken nationalism in Bengal. They also found that it would also be a big blow to the growth of Bengali language and culture. They pointed out that administrative efficiency could have been better secured by separating the Hindi-speaking Bihar and the Oriya speaking Orissa from Bengali speaking part of the province. Moreover, the official step had been taken completely neglecting the public opinion.

The Swadeshi Movement

One of the most significant features of the Anti-Partition movement, followed by *Swadeshi* movement, was that it was the work of the entire national leadership of Bengal. At the initial stage, its most prominent leaders were mostly moderate leaders like Surendranath Banerjee (1848-1925) and Krishna Kumar Mitra (1852-1936). Militant and revolutionary nationalist took over this movement in the later stages. Thus, both the moderate and militant nationalists cooperated with one another during the course of the movement. History informs us that the Anti-Partition movement was initiated on 7 August, 1905. On that day a massive demonstration against the partition was organized in the Town Hall in Calcutta. From this meeting, representative dispersed to spread the movement to the rest of the province.

However, the partition took effect on 16 October, 1905. This day was declared by the leadership of the protest movement as a day of national mourning throughout Bengal. It was also observed as a day of fasting. There was a *hartal* in Calcutta. It also got the religious colour as people walked bare footed and bathed in the River Ganga in the early morning hours. On this occasion, Rabindranath Tagore composed a national song which was sung by huge crowds parading the streets. The streets of Calcutta were full of the cries of *Bande Mataram* which overnight became the national song of Bengal and which soon became the theme song of the national movement. The ceremony of *Raksha Bandhan* was utilized in a new way. On that day people of Bengal tied the *Rakhi* on one another's wrists as a symbol of the unbreakable unity of the Bengalis and of the two halves of Bengal.

In the afternoon, there was a great demonstration when the veteran leader Ananda Mohan Bose (1847-1906) laid the foundation of a Federation Hall to mark the unshaken unity of Bengal. He addressed a crowd of over 50,000 and the meeting passed a resolution pledging to do their utmost to maintain the unity of Bengal.

The Bengal leaders felt that mere demonstrations, public meetings, and resolutions were not promising to have much effect on the colonials. More positive actions were needed to reveal the intensity of popular feelings. The answer was *Swadeshi* movement and Boycott. Mass meeting was held all over Bengal where *Swadeshi* or use of Indian goods and boycott of British goods were declared and pledged. In many places, the public burning of foreign cloth was organized and shops selling foreign cloth were picketed. The *Swadeshi* movement was an immense success. On the other hand, the *Swadeshi* movement gave a great deal of encouragement to Indian industries. Thus, many textile mills, soap and match factories, handloom weaving concerns, National Banks, and Insurance companies were opened. Acharya P.C. Ray (1861-1944) organized his famous Bengal Chemical *Swadeshi* stores. Even the great poet Rabindranath Tagore (1861-1941) helped to open a *Swadeshi* store.

Besides, the *Swadeshi* movement made several effects in the realm of Culture. Nationalist poetry, prose, and journalism came into existence. Another constructive activity undertaken at the time was that of National Education. National education institutions where literary, technical, or physical education was imparted were opened by nationalists who regarded the existing system of education as 'denationalizing' and in any case, incompetent. On 15 August, 1906, a National Council of Education was set-up. A National College, with Aurobindo Ghose as Principal, was started in Calcutta.

It is noteworthy that in the *Swadeshi* movement, students of Bengal played the prominent role. They practiced and propagated *Swadeshi* and took the lead in organizing picketing of shops selling foreign cloth. They were perhaps the main makers of the *Swadeshi* spirit in Bengal. The Government made every attempt to curb the student. Orders were issued to penalize those schools and colleges whose students took an active part in the *Swadeshi* movement. Grants of such colleges were to be withdrawn and even they were to be disaffiliated. Students of those colleges were not to be permitted to compete for scholarships and were to be barred from all services under the government. Disciplinary action was taken against students who were found guilty of participating in the nationalist agitation. Many of them were fined, expelled from schools and colleges, arrested and sometimes beaten by the police with *lathis*. The students, however, refused to be cowed down. Further, a noteworthy aspect of the *Swadeshi* agitation was the active participation of women in the movement. The traditionally home-centred women of the urban middle classes joined processions and picketing during the movement. Further, it also showed, to some extent, the composite culture of India as many prominent Muslims also joined the *Swadeshi* movement including Abdul Rasul, the famous barrister, Liaquat Husain, the popular agitator, and Gaznavi, the Businessman. The major role in spreading the *Swadeshi* movement to the rest of the country was played by Bal Gangadhar Tilak who saw that this movement in Bengal would open a new chapter in the history of Indian nationalism. In short, the movement made a major contribution in taking the idea of nationalism in a truly creative fashion, to many sections of people, hitherto untouched by it. By showing the courage to say no, it further eroded the hegemony of colonial idea and institution. The *Swadeshi* influence in the realm of culture and idea was crucial in this regard and has remained unparalleled in Indian history.

The Extremist and Moderate Conflict

The extremist and moderate conflict within the Congress was another major event during 1905 to 1923 that changed the direction of Indian Nationalism. There was an ideological rivalry between the moderates and the extremists since the beginning. Though their goal was same their method was different. Finally, there was a split in the Surat Congress Session held in 1907 between moderates and extremists.

There were reasons for rising of extremism in India during that time. Extremists alleged that moderates policy of prayer, petition and protest type of politics could not turn to be effective. Thus, they were to offer new tactics and ideology. Second, political awareness had been on rising in people. Third, Bengal was divided against the will and wishes of people thus people understood the British policy of divide and rule. People also found that Boycott movement, irrespective of its intensity turned to be deaf ears. Further, people like Savarkar brothers and Chapekar brothers started advocating extremism. Fourth, moderates remained distant from masses hence their mass appeal remained ineffective. Fifth, an emergence of leaders like Tilak and Ras Bihari Ghosh in Congress led to new kind of environment that was more favourable to the extremists. Youth element in Boycott and *Swadeshi* movement also paved way for extremism.

In fact, the fundamental differences between the moderates and the extremists lied on the questions of the loyalty to the English crown and the continuation of British rule in India. The moderates believed in loyalty to the English crown and they also considered that the continuation of the British colonial rule was in the interests of the people of India, while the view of the extremists was totally different. Extremists believed that the British colonial rule in India was a curse. Bipin Chandra Pal wrote that the time has come when all lies must be conscientiously eschewed from above political platform. The second major difference between the moderates and the extremists was on the issue of emphasis on the ultimate goal. As seen, the moderates believed in a policy of appeasement and accommodation. They were satisfied with the small concessions given by the British Government from time-to-time, while the extremists did not believe in the petty concessions given by the British Government. Nor, they considered the petty reforms significant. For the extremists, *Swaraj* alone was the final solution. Moreover, they did not have faith in Englishmen and their proclamation of justice. They were convinced that the Englishmen would not treat the Indians in the same way as they were treating the people of Canada or Australia.

Further, the moderates and the extremists also differed in their approach and strategy. Moderates depended for their success on the goodwill and sympathy of the Englishmen, while the extremists rejected such an approach. They believed that the people of India were the masters of their own destiny and not of any foreign power. For example, Tilak pointed out that although Dadabhai Naoroji had spent 25 years in England to convince the people of England that injustice was being done to India, nothing had come out of it.[3]

In the same way, after a visit to England, Lala Lajpat Rai observed in 1905 that the British democracy was too busy in their affairs to do anything for them, that the British press was not willing to champion Indian aspirations. On his return to India the message he brought to his people was that if they really cared for their country, they would have to strike the blow for freedom themselves.

Further, the moderates and the extremists also differed on the issue of whether Indians are capable of ruling themselves in the absence of British Government. The moderates believed that the people of India were still not capable of self-government while extremists believed that the people of India were fit to rule themselves and self-government. Further extremists argued that Indians could not be denied their self-government on the ground of their capability. Most significantly, the moderate believed that they can achieve their target without any suffering, while the extremists held the view that the salvation of India was not possible without sufferings and self-sacrifice. For example, Lala Lajpat Rai pointed out that tyranny was like hell and could not be easily conquered. This needs the sacrifice.

Because of these reasons, the moderates and the extremists were in conflict even during the nineteenth century; however, events during the Viceroyship of Lord Curzon provoked the matters. In fact, the rift between these two sections became apparent at the Banaras Session (1905) when some nationalists-led by Tilak denounced the method of the moderates and suggested passive resistance. They also advocated the boycott of British goods and government institutions. At the end of this session, Lokmanya Bal Gangadhar Tilak, and his followers held a separate conference and announced the formation of the Extremist Party. However, they decided to work as a part of the Indian National Congress. In 1906, at Calcutta Session, the rift between moderates and extremists further widened. Both the groups put their candidates for presidentship, but Dadabhai Naoroji (1825-1917) was accepted as a compromise candidate by both the groups. The extremists also succeeded in getting a resolution which emphasized the principle of *Swadeshi*, boycott, and national education.

But moderates did not accept what had happened at the Calcutta session in 1906 and were determined to undo the same at the Surat split 1907. Extremists were also equally determined to see that the moderates were not able to have their way. In Surat session, extremists tried to push the candidature of Lala Lajpat Rai for Presidentship of Congress and Moderates Dr. Ras Behari Ghosh to be the President. The situation was saved by Lala Lajpat Rai and stepping down and Dr. Ras Behari Ghosh became the President. The real trouble started when the moderates tried to repudiate the resolution on the boycott, *Swadeshi*, and national education which has been adopted in 1906. This was not acceptable to the extremists. As a result, open clashes took place and session was suspended. Thereafter, moderates held a separate convention from which the extremists were excluded. This marked a complete split in the Congress.

The division was further cemented in 1908 when the Indian National Congress at the Madras session made a change in its Constitution. It provided that the Congress delegates were not to be elected only by the Congress committee and associations affiliated to the Congress. The net result of this change was that the Extremists were excluded from the Congress. Tilak and his followers remained outside the Indian National Congress till 1915 when a compromise was arrived at.

The Surat Split 1907 was a turning point in the history of the Nationalist movement in India. It meant a victory of the extremists over the moderates. It also marked a change in the policy and attitude of the government towards the nationalist moderates to the government side. Yet, the split also greatly weakened both the parties. The extremists were hounded by official repression and moderates were abandoned by their own people. It cannot be denied that the Surat split not only weakened the Indian National Congress, but it virtually destroyed its effectiveness till the Lucknow session in 1916. For the next 8 years, India's Nationalist Movement remained a house divided against itself, half constitutional and half revolutionary in aspirations.

Minto-Morley Reforms: Colonial Politics

Minto-Morley Reforms of 1909 was one of the significant events that occurred during 1905 – 1923. This reform can be said to be the direct outcome of the Surat Split 1907. As a result of the strong popular reaction after the Partition of Bengal, Lord Curzon was replaced by Lord Minto as the Viceroy in November 1905; he was assisted by Lord Morley as the Secretary of State. Though the British intensified their policy of repressing the extremists, they simultaneously also tried to pacify the moderates through certain reforms. In 1909, they announced the Indian Councils Act, popularly known as the Minto-Morley Reforms. The main features of this Act were:

(a) The membership of the Central Legislative Council and the Provincial Legislative Councils was enlarged.

However, less than half of the members were elected members. Also, the elected members were not to be elected by the people but by the influential sections of the society such as landlords, *zamindars,* and businessmen.

(b) The system of separate electorates was introduced. The Muslims were grouped into separate constituencies from where only Muslim candidates could contest elections. This provision was made to cut-off the Muslims from the National movement by treating them as separate from the rest of the nation and to prevent Hindu-Muslim unity.

(c) No significant improvement was introduced by these reforms. The British refused the Indian demand for '*Swaraj*'. The Congress opposed the creation of separate electorates for the Muslims. This system of separate electorates for the Muslims sowed the seeds of the policy of communalism.

The reforms of 1909 could yield no answer to the Indian political problem. The real political solution was lying in complete self-rule and responsible governance, but the 1909 Act was only a face-saving device. The position of the Governor-General remained unchanged and his veto power remained undiluted and the Act successfully maintained relentless Constitutional autocracy. Under such circumstances, narrow franchises, indirect elections, limited powers of the Legislative Councils ushered a complete irresponsible government. The Act rather added new political problem with the introduction of the separate electorate system. While the parliamentary forms were introduced, no responsibility was conceded. At the same time, there was no connection between the supposed primary voter and a man who sits as his representative on the Legislative Council. In such a situation, the political participation, awareness, and education remained a distant dream. In nutshell, it can be said that 1909 Act was "the shadow rather than the substance".[4]

Home Rule Movement

Another significant event from 1905 to 1923 was Home Rule Movement. In 1916, two Home Rule Movements were launched in the country; one under the leadership of Bal Gangadhar Tilak and the other under Annie Besant (1847-1933).

In April, 2016, Tilak setup the Home Rule League at the Bombay Provincial Conference held at Belgaum. Tilak's League was to operate in Maharashtra, Karnataka, the Central Provinces and Berar. It was organized into six branches. Tilak popularized the demand for Home Rule mainly through his lectures. He argued that "India was like a son who had grown up and attained the majority. It wasn't right now that the trustee or the father should give him what was his due. The people of India must get this affected. They have a right to do so".[5] The objectives of the Home Rule League were: (a) Establishment of self-Government for India in British Empire; and (b) Working for national education and social and political reforms.

On the other hand, Annie Besant, who had for long closely associated with the social and political regeneration of India, established the All India Home Rule League. In September 1916, Besant announced the formation of Home Role League, with George Arundale, her Theosophical follower, as the organizing secretary. Jamnadas Dwarkadas, Shankarlal Banker, Indulal Yagnik, George Arundale, L.P. Ramaswamy Iyer were among the prominent members of Besant's League. It was a political organization which aimed at self-government, that was termed as "Home Rule". The league wanted to secure for India the status of a dominion within the British Empire, such as countries like Australia, Canada, South Africa, New Zealand and Newfoundland then. Besant's League had an All India character, but was founded on Besant's Theosophical contacts; it was set up in 1916 and reached its zenith in 1917 with 27,000 members.[6]

The Home Rule League used to organize discussions and lectures and set-up reading rooms, also distributing pamphlets educating people of what they sought to achieve through this movement. One of the important features of this movement was that the members of the League were powerful orators. On their behalf, petitions of thousands of Indians were submitted to the British authorities. The League received support from North India as well as South India; from the Tamil Brahmin community of Madras and also communities like the Kayasthas of United Provinces (now Uttar Pradesh), Kashmiri Brahmins. Some Muslims, Hindu Tamil minority, young Gujarati industrialists and traders and lawyers in Bombay and Gujarat also supported the League. The ideology of the league was a combination of theosophy, social reform, and ancient Hindu wisdom. It may be recalled that a lot of young men groomed by the Home Rule Movement went on to become future leaders in Indian politics, namely Satyamurti of Madras, Jitendralal Banerji of Calcutta, Jawaharlal Nehru of Allahabad, Jamunadas Dwarkadas, and Indulal Yagnik, among others.

The Home Rule Movement played a significant role in the history of the national struggle. The leaders of the Home Rule League placed before the Government a concrete proposal of Self-Government. It also produced a new set of the political leader, who were prepared to devote their full-time and energy to the case of national struggle. Further, it created a generation of ardent nationalist who formed the backbone of the National movement in the coming years. This leadership played important role in Gandhi era. The Home Rule League also created an organizational link between town and the countryside which proved valuable in the later years. Further, by popularizing the idea of Home Rule or Self-Government, and making it a common place thing, it generated a widespread pro-nationalist atmosphere in the country.

The Colonial Response: Montague-Chelmsford Reforms

In the First World War, Indians had participated with British colonials with over one million soldiers despite their resentments and discontentment with the British. They had hope that after the war British would be obliged to concede to self-rule in recognition of their loyal services. However, as the time passed, Indians became disillusioned as the British did not make any promises regarding Self-Government. Thus, Indians pressed for immediate reforms. It was also anticipated by the British that a civil disobedience movement might be launched jointly by Congress and Muslim League against them.

In view of these circumstances, the British recognized to pacify Indians. At that time, Edwin Montague was the Secretary of State for India. In his famous August Declaration presented before the House of Commons on 20 August, 1917, Montague said that in order to satisfy the local demands, his government was interested in giving more representation to the natives in India. Lord

Chelmsford was sent to India as the new Governor General. He stayed for six months and held numerous meetings with different government and non-governmental people. Edwin Montague in collaboration with Lord Chelmsford collected data and made a report about Constitutional reforms in 1918. The report was discussed in the House of Common and later on it was approved by the parliament. The Bill was introduced in India in 1919 and became Act of 1919. This Act, commonly known as Montague-Chelmsford Reforms, introduced the following reforms:

(a) The Council of the Secretary of State was to comprise eight to twelve people. Three of them should be Indian, and at least half of them should have spent at least ten years in India.
(b) The Central Legislature was to consist of two houses, Upper House (Council of the State), and the Lower House (Legislative Assembly). Council of the State was to consist of 60 members, out of them 35 members would be elected and rest of them would be nominated by the Governor General. The Legislative Assembly was to consist of 144 members, out of them 103 were to be elected and 41 to be nominated by the Governor General. The duration of the Upper House was five and of the Lower House was three years.
(c) Powers were divided between the centre and the provinces. The important subjects were vested with the centre and unimportant remained with provinces. The important central subjects were defence, foreign affairs, customs, and relations with Indian states, currency, and railway. On the contrary, unworthy provincial subjects were local self-government, public health, education etc.
(d) The salary of the Secretary of State for Indian Affairs should be paid from British exchequer; previously, his salary was paid by Indian treasury.
(e) The system of 'Diarchy' or a kind of double government in the Provinces was introduced. Provincial subjects were divided into two categories: "Transferred and Reserved." Transferred subjects which were public health, education, local self-government, and agriculture were under the control of Minister; likewise, all transferred subjects were

unimportant. Reserved subjects included administration, police, land revenue etc. which were under the control of Governor with the help of his secretaries. It was indirect control over transferred department by reserved department. Hence, Governor was the head of transferred and reserved subjects.

Indian Constitutional Act of 1919 was passed to satisfy Indian people. Yet, Indian people opposed it because the Act went against Congress-League Pact, thus, resulting in the Hindu opposition. Muslims partly accepted the Montague-Chelmsford reforms with certain reservations and demands regarding the safety of Muslim states. Gandhi categorically rejected this scheme and Congress denounced it as inadequate, unsatisfactory and disappointing. Besides these problems, the events like Rowlatt Act, the *Jallianwala Bagh* tragedy, and *Khilafat* movement further aggravated the situation and doomed the reforms to failure. Thus, there erupted violent communal riots and anti-British agitations creating a disdain for British rule. Montague-Chelmsford also failed as the two vanguard parties had rejected its reforms and considered them to be unsatisfactory. The only point of the reforms appreciated by the Indian was that after ten years, a commission was to assess the reforms and to bring further improvement in them.

Gandhi and Non-cooperation Movement

We noted that the reception by Indians of the Reforms of 1919 was a mixed one. It is notable that the reforms also caused a split in the Congress ranks. The moderate element in the Congress had already formed the National Liberal Federation in November 1918 at Bombay under the leadership of Surendra Nath Banerjee. These Liberals, in their Annual Conference held in 1919, whole heartedly accepted the Reforms. However, the Indian National Congress, in its annual session held at Amritsar in December 1919, declared the reforms as "inadequate, unsatisfactory and disappointing". At the same time, it also decided to work the Reforms, so as to secure the earliest establishment of responsible government. The attitude of cooperation with the Reforms was exhibited by the Congress even after the tragedy of *Jalianwala Bagh*. All this became possible because of the efforts of Mahatma Gandhi, who till then believed in the wisdom of cooperation, with the Government. The offer of cooperation was made even when Mrs. Besant had pronounced the Reforms as being unworthy of England to offer and India to accept. As noted Tilak had characterized the Reforms as unsatisfactory and disappointing a sunless dawn. But during the course of the following nine months, certain events happened, which changed the whole attitude of Mahatma Gandhi towards the British Government. When a special session of the Congress was held in Calcutta in September 1920, the entire outlook of the Congress had transformed and it adopted the non-cooperation programme and decided to boycott the reformed councils. Mahatma Gandhi who had taken the lead in December 1919 at Amritsar in offering cooperation was now mainly instrumental to adopt the policy of direct action, i.e. non-cooperation and civil disobedience against the Government.

The Non-Cooperation Movement opened a new chapter in the history of the Freedom Movement in India. It was the beginning of the Gandhian Movement against the British.

It needs to be recalled that India had helped the British people in the worst moments of their history during the war period, in men, money, and materials with an expectation of better reforms by the government. But instead, India was paid back through repressive measures by the use of Rowlett Laws. In order to show India's disapproval to the Act, Gandhi asked his countrymen for a nationwide *Satyagraha* and *hartal* on 6th April, 1919. This resulted in infamous *Jalianwala Bagh* Massacre. As a result of the repressive measures, the *Jalianwala Bagh* Massacre came as a crowning act of the British Government. Gandhi and the Congress demanded justice but justice was denied. Gandhi, therefore, came to his conclusion that "the only effective means to vindicate national honour and to prevent a repetition of the wrongs in future is the establishment of *Swaraj*". This was the background of Non-Cooperation Movement.

On 1 August, 1920, Non-Cooperation Movement was announced formally. This was a mourning day when early in the morning, the news of the death of Bal Gangadhar Tilak arrived. Gandhi and a crowd of around 2 lakh people paid its respect to this "Maker of Modern India". The Movement started with strikes and processions all over India. On 4 September, 1920, Congress met in Calcutta in a special session presided by Lala Lajpat Rai. In this session, Gandhi projected that if the Non-cooperation movement gets successful, *Swaraj* could be attained in one year. In December 1920, Congress met once again in the Nagpur Session. A programme of the surrender of titles, the boycott of schools, courts and councils, the boycott of foreign goods, the promotion maintenance of a Hindu-Muslim unity and strict non-violence was adopted.[7]

In Indian history, the Non-cooperation Movement was the first nationwide mass movement. The year 1921-22 witnessed an unprecedented movement in the nation's history when there was a widespread unrest among students. A nationwide tour was taken up by Mahatma Gandhi and Ali Brothers of *Khilafat* movement. C.R. Das, Moti Lal Nehru, M.R. Jayakar, Saifuddin Kitchlew (Punjab), Vallabhbhai Patel, C. Rajagopalachari, T. Prakasam and Asaf Ali left their legal practice and jumped into the full-fledged politics of Congress. Thousands of students left Government schools and colleges and joined the movement. Maulana Mehmud Hasan laid the foundation stone of Jamia Millia Islamia at Aligarh on Friday, October 29, 1920. Gujarat Vidyapith, Ahmedabad and Bihar Vidyapeeth came into existence. The leaders of Indian movement started teaching in the pure Indian educational institutions. In some provinces, such as Bengal and Punjab, there was a complete boycott of education by the *Firangi*. The shops which sold foreign clothes were picketed. *Khadi* and *Charkha* became the symbol of the national movement. In Bengal, Someshwar Prasad Chaudhary led the peasants in an anti-indigo cultivation. The Tana-Bhagat sect of Bihar boycotted the liquor. In Punjab, Akali Movement, that was originally for reforms in the *Gurdwaras* got linked with the non-cooperation movement. Yet, the movement was weak in the Presidency of Bombay, where, the people were mourning on the demise of Tilak. The Gandhi magic did not work there. In Andhra Pradesh, Alluri Sitarama Raju organized the tribal and linked with the Non-cooperation movement. In March, 1921, there was a Congress session at Vijayawada, in which the Congress rookies were directed to collect funds, enroll more-and-more members and distribute *charkhas*. On July 21, 1921, All India *Khilafat* Conference was called in Karachi. Here, Maulana Mohammad Ali initiated a resolution that no Muslim should serve in the British Indian Army. So, the Ali brothers were arrested for sedition. But, later Congress also passed a similar resolution and the Government had to ignore the whole episode.

In Midnapore of Bengal, a movement was led by Birendranath Sasmal against the Union Board of Taxes. People in various parts of the country happily joined the No-tax to Government Movement. It was successful in the Andhra region.[8]

However, on 5th February, 1922, at Chauri Chaura, in Gorakhpur District of U.P. 21 policemen and a sub-inspector were burnt alive in a police station by an infuriated mob. Mahatma Gandhi felt so horrified at this fact of brutal violence that he gave order for suspending the movement at once.

The most significant impact of the Non-cooperation Movement was that it brought Gandhi in the front line of National Politics in India. He was also regarded as a logical heir of Bal Gangadhar Tilak. During movement, there was a mass imprisonment and the sense of terror of the jails was removed and "going to jail" became a badge of honour. Yet, the movement had also some negative impact. Gandhi's decision to withdraw movement after Chauri Chaura incident had given a sudden jolt to the Congress. The reasons for which it was started were the *Jalianwalla Bagh* tragedy, *Swaraj*, problems of *Khilafat* volunteers etc. could not be solved. Gandhi's idea of *Swaraj* in one year proved to be a bubble. The boycott of the educational institutions was not accepted by many of the leaders such as Lala Lajpat Rai. Some leaders did not like the way it was started, many other did not like the way it was conducted and most of them could not digest the sudden withdrawal. Some new outfits were born parallel to Congress, because Congress was left without any political programme.

On the other hand, in spite of that the Congress became the party of the common man. Now, it had the widespread support of the average peasants, workers, and the intellectuals. *Charkha* and *Khadi* became the symbol of Indian Nationalism. Gandhi was able to see the real picture of India. He realized that the real power of India lies in the rural areas and not in the urban area. There was a need for general awakening of the masses to their political rights and privileges, and further, there was a total loss of faith in the system of government. People could realize that it was only through their own efforts that India could hope to be free. It revealed that the Congress was the only organization while could properly direct national effort to gain freedom. The movement also revealed that communal problem is going to be a big problem and this problem of communalism is absolutely state sponsored.[9]

Issue of *Khilafat* Movement

Khilafat movement was another significant event that occurred during the initial decade of the twentieth century. This was a problem that occurred outside India but it took an important role in Indian and colonial politics. The *Khilafat* issue gave the way for the consolidation of the emergence of a radical nationalist trend among the younger generation of Muslims and the section of traditional Muslim scholars also who were becoming increasingly critical of the British rule. The reason of this movement was the treatment given to Turkey by the British after the First World War. The Muslims in India, as the Muslims all over the world, regarded the Sultan of Turkey as their spiritual leader, called *Khalifa*, thus, naturally their sympathies were with Turkey. During the War, Turkey had allied with Germany and Austria against the British. When the War ended, the British took a stern action towards Turkey—Turkey was dismembered and the *Khalifa* was removed from the power. This outraged Muslims all over the world.

In India, too, the Muslims demanded from the British that (i) the *Khalifa*'s control over Muslim sacred places should be retained; and (ii) the *Khalifa* should be left with sufficient territories after territorial arrangements. As noted above, in early 1919, a *Khilafat* Committee was formed under the leadership of the Ali brothers, Shaukat Ali and Muhammad Ali, Maulana Azad, Ajmal Khan and Hasrat Mohani, to force the British Government to change its attitude towards Turkey. Thus, the grounds for a country-wide agitation were prepared. Initially, the *Khilafat* leaders limited their actions to meetings, petitions, deputations in favour of the *Khilafat*. Later on, a militant trend emerged, demanding an active agitation such as stopping all cooperation with the British.

Thus, at the "All India *Khilafat* Conference" was held in Delhi in November 1919 and a call was made for the boycott of British goods. Gandhi, who was the president of the All India *Khilafat* Committee, saw in the issue a platform from which mass and united Non-cooperation could be declared against the British Government.

Although Gandhi was in favour of launching *Satyagraha* and non-cooperation against the Government on the *Khilafat* issue, the Congress was not united on this form of political action. Tilak was opposed to having an alliance with Muslim leaders over a religious issue and he was also skeptical of *Satyagraha* as an instrument of politics.

There was opposition to some of the other provisions of the Gandhi's non-cooperation programme also, such as the boycott of councils. Later on, however, Gandhi was able to get the approval of the Congress for his programme of political action and the Congress felt inclined to support a non-cooperation programme on the *Khilafat* question because it was recognized that this was a golden opportunity to cement Hindu-Muslim unity.

The reason was that it could also bring Muslim masses into the National movement, thus, different sections of society—Hindus, Muslims, Sikhs, Christians, peasants, artisans, capitalists, tribal, women, and students—could come into the National movement by fighting for their own rights and realizing that the colonial rule was opposed to them.

On the other hand, the Muslim League also decided to give full support to the Congress and its agitation on these political questions. Thus, in early 1920, a joint Hindu-Muslim deputation was sent to the viceroy to seek redress of grievances on the issue of *Khilafat*, but the mission proved abortive. In February, 1920, Gandhi announced that the issues of the Punjab wrongs and Constitutional advance had been overshadowed by the *Khilafat* question and that he would soon lead a movement of non-cooperation if the terms of the peace treaty failed to satisfy the Indian Muslims. In May, 1920, The Treaty of Sevres with Turkey, signed in May, 1920, completely dismembered Turkey. In June 1920, an all-party conference at Allahabad approved a programme of the boycott of schools, colleges and law courts, and asked Gandhi to lead it. On 31 August, 1920, the *Khilafat* Committee started a campaign of non-cooperation and the movement was formally launched.

History informs us that the movement witnessed the spread of nationalism to the remotest corner of the country. It transformed the Indian National Congress from a deliberative assembly into an organization for action as evidenced from the various programmes of the movement. It marked the height of Hindu unity which could be seen in the merger of the *Khilafa*t movement with this movement. Thus, though the movement failed to achieve any one of its main demands, it was, nevertheless, a great step forward in the courses of the Indian Nationalist movement.

Notes

1. Quoted in Penderal Moon. 1999, *The British Conquest and Domination of India,* New Delhi: India Research Press, 1999, p. 935.
2. Ibid.
3. Quoted in Stephen Hey. *Source of Indian Tradition,* Vol. 2, New Delhi: Penguin Books, 1992, p. 144.
4. *http://www.indian-councils-act-1909-morley-minto-reforms-communal-representation/*
5. *wwwfacts-about-india.com/home-rule-movement.php.*
6. *https://cultural.maharashtra.gov.in/english/.../VOL.../HOME_RULE_MOVEMENT.pdf*
7. *http://www. non-cooperation-movement-1920/.*
8. *Ibid.*
9. *Ibid.*

3

Writings on Nationalism in India in the Late Nineteenth Century: A Thematic Analysis

In the previous chapter, we saw that how colonial policies and strategies had shaped the colonial politics in India and how it was responded by the Indian nationalists. The colonial politics and its response by the Indian nationalists in the early decade of the twentieth century constituted the materiality of Indian politics of that era. Yet, it needs to be pointed out that the colonial politics, its strategies, and policies were part of the larger colonial discourse that was ideological in nature. This ideology was chiefly centred on the view that why India needs British presence (read subjugation). In response to this colonial discourse, Indian nationalists constituted their own response in the form of discourses to provide the philosophical justification of Indians demand of self-rule. These discourses can be found in the texts written by the Indian nationalists. These written texts include both fictions and non-fictions. A close reading of these texts not only reflects the prevailing competing and conflictual situation, but also the nationalist inspirations. They also seriously engage themselves with the materiality of their time and based on it, they also propose a future for India. These texts are mainly in the vernacular language, Sanskrit, and English.

But, how did Indian nationalists get the idea to respond colonials at the level of discourse? The answer lies in the impact of English thought on Indians. Through the introduction of English system of education, the British colonials indirectly transmitted the culture and temper of the European Renaissance and reformation to the Indians. Ideas of Jeremy Bentham (1748-1832), James Mill (1773-1836), Carlyle (1795-1881) and Coleridge (1772-1834) got available to Indians and they began to re-examine their own life, society, and culture in the light of aforementioned thinkers. In this regard, as noted by Iyer (1983) the vision of Benthamism dominated the Western thought in Indian context.[1] This led to a new awareness of the value of liberty, democracy and rule of law among Indians. Thus, in the second half of the nineteenth century, Indian nationalists who were the product of the British English education introspected themselves and recognized the difference between Indian people and British. On the other hand, Indian nationalists also compared their plight with the affluence in the West. Further, Indians also began to realize that while the British policy alternated between repression and liberalism, it had become a support for the continuation of despotic rule and feudal lifestyle in India. It made Indians, in due course, feel that the British colonization in India ought to end. This feeling generated a spirit of nationalism in Indians both at political or material and intellectual level.

At political level several associations were formed either for 'conformity' with British or in the line of 'reform', or to 'revive' the Indian society. For example, in the line of reform, in 1866, East India Association was established by Dadabhai Naoroji (1825-1917) in London. Similarly, in 1870, Poona Sarvajanik Sabha was established by Justice Mahadev Govind Rande, Ganesh Vasudev Joshi, and S.H. Chiplunkar. Further, Indian Association was established in July 1876, by Anand Mohan Bose (1847-1906) and Surendra Nath Banerjee (1848-1925). On the other hand, Sisir Kumar Ghosh (1840-1911) founded Indian League in 1875. The Indian League was the first body in India which set up links with political groups outside Bengal. In the same way, in 1884, M. Viraraghavachari, G. Subramania Iyer, Ananda Charlu and other formed the Madras Mahajan Sabha. In Bombay, Pherozeshah Mehta (1845-1915), K.T. Telang (1850-1893), Badruddin Tyabji (1844-1906) and others formed the Bombay presidency association in 1885. It must be mentioned that these associations were advancing the idea of reforms in colonial policies which were merely political in nature. The Indian National Congress, established in 1885 was the result of a large number of forces operating in the latter half of the nineteenth century such as English education, the press, quicker means of transport and communication, a strong and uniform system of administration, internal security and freedom from external danger. To these may be added a growing national consciousness in the country which in itself was fostered by a number of pioneers in the field of education, journalism, and social system.

Although the impact of Western thought in India is well accepted by scholars, but it was not only the British influence which worked on Indian intellectuals. There were many who were impressed with the German idealism especially by the ideas of Schelling (1775-1854), Fichte (1762-1814), Kant (1724-1804) and Herder (1744-1803). In this connection Mehta (1992) argues, "When Indian reaction started against the British Raj, people also reacted against some of the ideas of the rulers, particularly against individualism, materialism, and *laissez faire*. In order to find a philosophical justification for some of their own ideas, they turned to German philosophy. The idea of *volk*, community, duty, and nation appealed to them".[2]

Mehta's arguments have point as it might be recalled here that by the middle of the nineteenth century there had been the almost half of the century of interaction between German and Indian thought. People like Goethe (1749-1832) and Schelling (1775-1854) were deeply influenced by the idealism depicted in Upanishadic thought. Some of the Indian intellectuals also thought that the only way to expose the weakness of utilitarianism and British liberalism, which lay in the roots of English administration in India, is to counter them by interpreting German notion of community, volk, and obligations in the Indian context. They too desired democratic norms and various freedoms but, according to them these must always remain secondary to the need for preservation of Indian identity, upholding the traditional values, protection of people against economic and political domination by others. Thus, some Indian intellectual rejected the social advantage or economic advantages which came in the track of the British Raj. They further thought that it would lead to an unwarranted English interference in the social life of India. These ideas were taken over by people like Bankim Chandra Chattopadhyay (1838-1894) and Swami Vivekananda (1863-1902). They influenced the entire philosophy of nationalism that was later on developed by Bipin Chandra Pal and Aurobindo. They all pleded that India had a unique mission;

it alone could be the spiritual leader of mankind. To some extent, this might be referred to the impact of "affirmative orientalism" on Indian nationalists. Here, it is not our focus to go into the detail of the German idealism's influence on Indian nationalists. But the radical departure from the so-called liberal politics of colonials certainly demands fresh theoretical analysis of Indian nationalism.

Thus, the spirit of Indian nationalism reflected in the texts—both fiction and non-fiction—written by these new Indian intellectuals in the second half of the nineteenth century. These nationalist texts were written in the forms of novels, poems, plays and essays. Let us briefly examine some of the representative texts and their features in regard to nationalism.

An overview of these texts shows two important characteristics in regard to nationalist consciousness in India. First, whether written in the provincial language or in English; these texts carry strong nationalist consciousness both in the form of 'resistance to colonials' policies and 'reform' of Indian society. As Rainee and Kumar inform (2013) us, "the instinct of anti-coloniality can be traced right from the beginning of Indian literature in English but the first text which has the spirit of anti-colonial nationalism is *A Journey of Forty-Eight Hours of the Year 1945* (1835) by Kylas Chunder Dutt".[3] It is about the imaginary revolt against the British army by the Indians and was published in *Calcutta Literary Gazette* and *Saturday Evening Hurkaru*. It is one of the outstanding documents available in history that is prior to the formation of Indian National Congress. From the early nineteenth century, Indian middle class has already been dreaming of coming out from the British clutches but they were not sure about the form of struggle. Therefore, the writers in that era started creating their own heroes to lead the people against British rule.[4] Another earlier Indian writer, Shoshee Chunder Dutt (1824-1886) was also a radical anti-colonialist in his writings. He was an essayist, poet, historian and novelist. His *Selections from Bengalinama* contains some of his most significant essays and short stories. His work *Shunkur* is the fictional representation of the resistance of 1857 against the colonial power. It depicts the exploitative nature of some of the British officers like Bernard and Mackenzie who rape the women who have given them shelter. One may also note the notion of resistance in, as early as 1859, Dinbandhu Mitra's (1830-1876) play *Neel Darpan*. This play was translated by Rev. James Long in 1861. It exhibits the strong protest against the exploitation of the indigo workers in Bengal. The play was banned and James Long was prosecuted for having aided in the translation of the play.

On the other hand, 'revival' tendency may be seen in the work of Swami Dayanand Saraswati (1824-1883) who was a renowned religious and social reformer and the founder of *Arya Samaj*. In 1875, he wrote a book in Hindi titled as *Satyarth Prakash*. The central aim of the book was to spread the knowledge of the *Vedas* among the Hindus and to educate people on the true qualities of God. The *Satyarth Prakash* contains exposition and clarifications of Vedic principles and advocates Vedic monism based on *Advaita Vedanta*. Some of the important topics in the *Satyarth Prakash* include worship of one God, explanation of the main principles of the *Vedas*, the relationship between religion and science and between devotion and intellect, elimination of the Caste system and of different religious beliefs for the strengthening of society, eradication of superstitions, false notions and meaningless customs, shunning narrow-mindedness and promoting the brotherhood of man. Thus, the texts written during the nineteenth century were proposing a revival of Indian culture or resistance to colonials.

The second feature of these Indian nationalist texts was that they were *divergent in nature* on the issue of the role of tradition in confronting colonials. For example, like Harishchandra Mukherjee (1824-1861) in his article *The Hindu Patriot* asserted that the time has come when problems of India must be solved by themselves valuing the Indian civilization. He was confident that indigenous thought had the necessary vitality to meet the new situation. On the other hand, there were people like Jogendranath Vidyabhusan (1845-1904) who highlighted the corrupt nature of the ancient Indian Brahmanism and argued that the liberalism and positivism which we had learned from our contact with British were the coming religion of the future. Further, there were people like Surendra Mohan Tagore (1840-1914), who was greatly influenced by Comte (1798-1857) and James Mill (1773-1836) and held the idea that instead of rejecting the tradition, we should combine it with modernity. Moreover, according to him, some of the modern ideas were already present in the ancient Indian text.

Looking from a different angle, the nationalist texts written during the latter half of the nineteenth century in response to colonialism were of *three kinds*. The first kind of text was in the form of the *appreciation of the role of the British* in India. This kind of texts may be seen fully developed in the writings and ideas of M.G. Ranade (1842-1901), Gopal Krishna Gokhale (1866-1915) and entire liberal school in the country. Although they challenged the British colonialism in due course of time, but it may be noted, in that process they *never* referred to the glory of the Ancient Indian Civilization and Culture. In other words, they were propagating political nationalism. On the other hand, the second kind of writings included the work of Bankim Chandra Chattopadhyay, Swami Vivekananda, Swami Dayananda Saraswati (1824-1883), and Bipin Chandra Pal (1858-1932) who tried to challenge British on the ground of glory of ancient Indian civilization and propagated nationalism through their writings. These nationalists were representing cultural nationalism based on the cultural heritage of India. Nevertheless, it is worth mentioning here that there were significant differences in the analysis of these cultural nationalists and their response to British civilization.

There also existed a third kind of writing that tried *to assimilate Indian culture with Western Culture.* The key figure of such writing is Raja Ram Mohan Roy (1772-1833). Roy's appreciation of Western value is evident from one of his letters to Lord Amherst written on 11 December, 1823:

> "...Sangscrit system of education would be the best calculated to keep this country in darkness if such had been the policy of the British Legislature. But as the improvement of the native population is the object of the Government, it will consequently promote a more liberal and enlightened system of instruction, embracing mathematics, natural philosophy, chemistry and anatomy, with other useful sciences which may be accomplished with the sum proposed by employing a few gentlemen of talents and learning educated in Europe, and providing a college furnished with the necessary books, instruments and other apparatus...".[5]

In spite of his appreciation of Western value, Roy by his multidimensional creativity inaugurated the modern age in India. He has also been regarded as the father of Indian Renaissance and the maker of Indian nationalism who represented a synthesis of the thought of East and West. In fact, he stood for the reform of Hinduism by employing the basic Western ideas of rationalism, scientific temper, and humanism. Roy wanted India to learn from the West, but this learning was to be intellectual and creative process through which Indian culture and thought were to be renovated, it was not to be an imposition of the Western culture on India. Thus his nationalism was selective and assimilative.

If Raja Ram Mohan Roy's texts represented the assimilation of Indian and Western thought and a liberal form of nationalism, Bankim Chandra Chattopadhyay (1838-1894) and his texts represented a different form of nationalism. Bankim Chandra Chattopadhyay known as the "Literary King of Bengal" and one of the prominent authors of the Bengali Renaissance contributed in the nationalist literature by writing *Durgesh Nandini, Kapal Kundala, Visha Briksha, Shikar,* and *Chandhrani*. One of the significant features of his writings is that he drew inspiration from Indian spiritual heritage. He argued that the people of the region constituted a distinct nation based on their shared spirituality in contrast to the rational materialism of Europe. Bankim questioned the history of Bengal also that had been written by outsiders and noted that "[a]nyone who uncritically accepts as history the testimony of these lying, Hindu-hating Musalman zealots is not a Bengali" and famously observed in 1880 that "[w]e have no history, we must have a history!"[6] He argued that the history of the Hindu nation of Bengal needed to be written. Further, concerned about the absence or loss of history and historical consciousness, Bankim sought an alternative in imagination. His novels and essays echo the disavowal of native Bengali/Indian history claimed in colonialist historiography. They point to the ideological imperatives and mythification involved in the writing of colonial history.

His latter writings particularity his novel *Anand Math* (1882) known as the Bible of Indian nationalism presented a different view of nationalism. This novel *Anand Math* needs to be discussed in detail as it provides a basis for the new form of nationalism in India. *Anand Math* skilfully attempts to "invent a tradition" and an "imagined political community of India". For this purpose, he invents a usable past to suit the anti-colonial agenda of the time and shows how the creation of "national identification must essentially proceed through the imaginary, not through 'natural' affiliations". Thus, the text narrates a very powerful discourse on nationalism. One of the important features of *Anand Math* is that it also attempts to make Indian nationalism masculine.[7] The novel demonstrates the causes and consequences of the loss of masculinity and the possibilities of reparation. This is primarily made possible through a drive for physical regeneration, militancy for the nation, celibacy, and devotion to a mother nation. In the novel, Bankim also puts forward the notion of ascetic nationalism. This ascetic nationalism is an ideology that promises citizenship and the nation-state to the colonized, the emphasis on *brahmacharya*—celibate dedication—facilitates a relational construction of masculinity.

It is important to note that how *brahmacharya* becomes a crucial marker of difference within the society, and by extension the nation and empire. In other words, only those with certain behavioural characteristics, who have made certain kinds of sacrifices for the nation, can claim legitimate authority to be its leaders. *Brahmacharya,* as we know, has been the part of Indian spiritual tradition and it got prominence even in Gandhi's non-violent nationalism.

Anand Math also shows how 'national' culture is often invented in relation to a number of internal colonialism. For instance, Bankim's iconography of the mother-as-land is based on a search for origins that legitimizes certain class, gender, and religious groups.

Later on, as well known, one of Bankim's poems, *Bande Mataram,* which means 'Hail Mother' referring to the motherland, became the main slogan of the *Swadeshi* movement. Shouting *Bande Mataram* at rallies against the partition of Bengal was common and eventually was banned in the streets because the meaning was deemed illegal. The poem begins by evoking images of the bucolic beauty of Bengal by describing the land as a mother that nurtures the population as her children. However, towards the end of the poem the mother is revealed to be a Hindu goddess and the children become the Hindu population of Bengal.

The discussion on nationalism developed in the late nineteenth century will remain incomplete without mentioning the lectures and writings of Swami Vivekananda. Swami Vivekananda believed that there is one all dominating principle manifesting itself in the life of each nation. In an interview in 1897 he told, "in each nation, as in music, there is the main note, a central theme, upon which all others turn. Each nation has a theme, everything else is secondary India's theme is religion. Social reform and everything else is secondary"[8].

Swami Vivekananda felt that Indian nationalism had to be built on the stable foundation of the post-historical heritage. Hence, he declared that the national life should be organized on the basis of the religious idea. As a supporter of this idea, he revived the eternal things of the *Vedas* and *Upanishads* to strengthen nation's growth and faith in its individuality. As Verma (1980) notes, Vivekananda's soul, like that of Bankim was lit with the luminous vision of mother India as a deity.[9]

Thus, Swami Vivekananda advocated for the religious basis of nationalism. This line of thinking was later on developed by nationalists like Sri Aurobindo and Bipin Chandra Pal. Here spirituality or religion was not to be confused with rituals, social dogmas, ecclesiastical formulations and obsolete costumes. By religion, Vivekananda understood the eternal principles of moral and spiritual advancement. He believed in universal toleration and not in social and religious imposition.

Vivekananda also mentioned that India has own destiny, it must accomplish that. He mentioned, "Each nation has the destiny to fulfil, each nation has a message to deliver, each nation has a mission to accomplish. Therefore, we must have to understand the mission of our own race, the destiny it has to fulfil, the place it has to occupy in the March, of nations, the role which it has to contribute to the harmony of races".[10]

It needs to be pointed out that for Vivekananda India didn't just mean either a geographical entity or a heaven of opportunity for the elite. Hence, he worked for awakening the masses, the development of their physical and moral strength and creating in them a consciousness of the pride in the ancient glory and greatness of India. It is, therefore, he was hailed as one of the great architects of modern nationalism in India.

In fact, through his writings, he imparted among the nationalists a sense of pride in the past and gave a cultural confidence to people who had lost their self-esteem. At a time when the Indian intelligentsia was busy imitating the Westerners, Vivekananda boldly proclaimed that the West had to learn much from India.

These illustrations tell us two major themes on nationalism in India that emerged in the late nineteenth century; revival based on Indian spiritual past and reform based on modern western political thought. These two different themes represented two different paradigms that also inform us about the two ideas of India they projected in response to the British colonials. It is these two major conflicting paradigms that were followed by other nationalists with some variations in the early twentieth century.

Besides these literary works by Indian nationalists, one of the important textual sources that focused on Indian nationalism by highlighting the evil of colonial rule was newspapers. Some of the newspapers may be discussed here that played an important role in shaping the mind of Indian elite class and middle class. These newspapers were in fact 'views paper' of nationalists who tried to awaken the consciousness of Indian people in general. It will not be out of context to say that the texts under consideration of this study were also the culmination of the thought pattern shaped by these news/views papers.

In this regard, Hindi *Patriot* established in 1853 by the author and playwright Girish Chandra Ghosh is worth mentioning. The paper became popular under the editorship of Harish Chandra Mukherjee. In 1861, the paper published a play *Neel Darpan* as mentioned above, and launched a movement against the British. It urged the people to stop cultivating the crop for the white traders. This resulted in the formation of a Neel Commission. Later on, the paper was taken over by Ishwar Chandra Vidyasagar (1820-1891). Showing a nationalist temper, the paper strongly opposed the British Government's excesses and demanded that Indians must be appointed to top government posts. There was another contemporary paper *The Indian Mirror* that was popular among the Indian readers. Similarly, weekly *Amrita Bazar Patrika* published from Jessore also presented nationalist temper. It was so critical of the then government, that its proprietors had to face trial and conviction. In 1871, the *Patrika* moved to Calcutta and another Act was passed to suppress it and other native journals.

Other important journals were *Gyan Prakash* as well as the *Indu Prakash.* Veteran liberal leader Mahadev Govind Rande (1842-1901) used to write in both these journals. It helped awaken the conscience of the downtrodden masses. Another Marathi weekly, *Kesari* was started by Bal Gangadhar Tilak from 1st January, 1881.

He along with Agarkar and Chiplunkar started another weekly journal *Maratha* in English. The Editor of the *Deccan Star* Nam Joshi also joined them and his paper was incorporated with *Maratha*. These weeklies were sc powerful in spreading nationalist feeling that Tilak and Agarkar were convicted for their writings against the British and the Diwan of Kolhapur. In fact, Tilak's *Kesari* became one of the leading instruments to propagate the message of the freedom movement. It also made the anti-partition movement of Bengal a national issue. In 1908, Tilak opposed the Sedition ordinance. He was later exiled from the country for six years. Hindi edition of *Kesari* was started from Nagpur and Banaras also.

In respect to rising nationalist spirit, the power and reputation of these newspapers might be gauged from the fact that at the time of the birth of the Indian National Congress those who occupied the front line seats in the first ever Congress session held in Bombay in December 1885 were some of the editors of Indian newspapers. The influence of these editors was such that many resolutions were proposed or seconded by them. For example, the first ever resolution at this Session was proposed by the editor of *The Hindu*, G. Subramaniya Iyer. In this resolution, it was demanded that the government should appoint a committee to inquire into the functioning of Indian administration. The second resolution was also moved by a journalist from Poona, Chiplunkar in which the Congress was urged to demand the abolition of India Council which ruled the country from Britain. The third resolution was supported by Dadabhai Naoroji who was a noted journalist of his time. The fourth resolution was proposed by Dadabhai Naoroji. There were many Congress Presidents who had either been the editors or had started the publication of one or the other newspapers. In this context, particular mention may be made of Pherozeshah Mehta who had started the *Bombay Chronicle* and Pandit Madan Mohan Malviya who edited daily, *Hindustan*. Lala Lajpat Rai inspired the publication of three journals, *The Punjabi, Bande Mataram* and *The People* from Lahore.

The significance of newspaper in arousing national unconsciousness becomes also evident when we consider the fact that during his stay in South Africa, Gandhiji had also brought out *Indian Opinion*. After settling in India, he started the new journals; *Young India, Navjeevan, Harijan, Harijan Sevak* and *Harijan Bandhu*.

Subhas Chandra Bose (1897-1945) and C.R. Das (1869-1925) were not journalists, but they acquired the papers Forward and Advance which later attained national status. Jawaharlal Nehru founded the *National Herald*. So far as the revolutionary movement is concerned, it did not begin only with guns and bombs but also started with the publication of newspapers. First, to be mentioned in this context is *The Yugantar*, publication of which was started by Barindra Kumar Ghosh who edited it also.

The nationalist newspapers were not confined only to the Indian Territory. When the Ghadar party was organized in America, Lala Hardayal started publication of the journal '*Ghadar*'. Within one year, millions of copies of this journal were published in Hindi, Urdu, Punjabi, Gujarati, Marathi and English and sent to India and to all parts of the world where Indians were residing. In 1905, Shyamji Krishna Verma (1857-1930) started publication of a journal *Indian Sociologist* from London. It used to publish reports of political activities taking place at the India House in London. In 1909, two printers of this journal were convicted. Shyamji Krishna Verma left England for Paris from where he started the publication of the journal. Later on, he had to leave for Geneva. He continued to bring out the journal from there for two or three years more. In Paris, Lala Hardayal (1884-1939), in collaboration with Madam Cama (1861-1936) and Sardar Singhraoji Rana brought our *Vandematram* and *Talwar*. After *The Yugantar*, it was *Vandematram* that played a significant role in the awakening of Indian people. This journal was established by Subodh Chandra Malik, C.R. Das, and Bipin Chandra Pal on August 6, 1906. The significance of these newspapers can be understood when the editor, Aurobindo Ghosh, the editor of *Sandhya* B. Upadhyay and editor of *TheYugantar* B.N. Dutt had to a face a trial for espousing the cause of freedom. So far as the Hindi papers were concerned, they looked to government for support for some time. Bhartendu Harish Chandra was the first to start a journal *Kavi Vachan Sudha* in 1868. Its policy was to give vent to the miseries of the people of India. When the Prince of Wales visited India, a poem was published in his honour. The British authorities were given to understand that the poem could also mean that the Prince of Wales should get a shoe-beating. The government aid to journals like *Kavi Vachan Sudha* was stopped for publishing what was objectionable from the government point of view. Bhartendu

Harish Chandra resigned from his post of an honourary Magistrate. His two friends, Pratap Narain Mishra and Bal Krishna started publication of two important political journals *Pradeep* from Allahabad, and *Brahman* from Kanpur. The *Pradeep* was ordered to be closed down in 1910 for espousing the cause of freedom. The *Bharat-Mitra* was a famous Hindi journal of Calcutta which started its publication on May 17, 1878, as a fortnightly. It contributed a lot in propagating the cause of nationalism. The journal exposed the British conspiracy to usurp Kashmir. Several other papers published from Calcutta which played an important role in awakening nationalism included Ambika Prasad Vajpayee's *Swantantra,* Ramanand Chatterjee's *Modern Review* in English, *Pravasi Patra* in Bengali and *Vishal Bharat* in Hindi. One of the foremost Hindi journalists who have earned a name for his patriotism was Ganesh Shanker Vidyarthi. In 1913, he brought out weekly *Pratap* from Kanpur. As we know, later on, he made the supreme sacrifice in 1931 in the cause of Hindu-Muslim unity. Krishna Dutt Paliwal brought out *Sainik* from Agra which became a staunch propagator of nationalism in western U.P. The noted Congress leader, Swami Shraddhanand, started the publication of Hindi journal *Vir Arjun* and Urdu journal *Tej*. After the assassination of Swami Shraddhanand (1856-1926), Vidyavachaspathi and Lala Deshbandhu Gupta continued the publication of these journals. They were themselves prominent Congress leaders. In Lahore, Mahashaya Khushal Chand brought out *Milap* and Mahashaya Krishna started publishing Urdu journals which helped a lot in promoting the national cause. In 1881, Sardar Dayal Singh Majitha on the advice of Surendra Nath Banerjee brought out *Tribune* under the editorship of Sheetala Kant Chatterjee. Bipin Chandra Pal also edited this paper for some time. Later in 1917, Kalinath Rai joined the paper as its editor.

It needs to be pointed out that Bipin Chandra Pal was among the first to vigorously articulate the new philosophy of organized resistance to British rule. On the first anniversary of the '*Swadeshi* Movement' and 'Boycott Movement' in 1906, Bipin Chandra Pal with a modest capital of Rs. 500 took the bold decision to launch an English Daily, '*Bande Mataram*' which was to create a special niche for itself in the history of our freedom movement. Bipin Chandra Pal invited Aurobindo Ghosh (1872-1950) to join the Editorial team of *Bande Mataram*. Aurobindo Ghosh readily accepted. *'Bande Mataram'* now could boast of a highly talented editorial team with Bipin Chandra Pal as Editor, Aurobindo Gosh as Assistant Editor and Hemendra Prasad Ghosh, Shyam Sundar Chakravarthy and Bijoy Chatterjee as Assistants. Thus, there started the unique political partnership of Bipin Chandra Pal and Aurobindo Ghosh. Aurobindo Ghosh was a powerful writer and master of the written word. He preferred to work behind the scene. Bipin Chandra Pal, on the other hand, was a powerful orator and loved to be on stage amidst the people. Both these outstanding leaders understood and complemented each other.

It is important to note that there was not a single province in India which did not produce a journal or newspaper to uphold the cause of nationalism. A.G. Horniman (1873-1948) made the *Bombay Chronicle* a powerful instrument to promote militant nationalism. He himself took part in the meetings where *Satyagraha* used to be planned. He published vivid accounts of *Jalianwala Bagh* carnage for which one correspondent of his paper, Goverdhan Das, was sentenced to three years' imprisonment by a military court. Horniman too was arrested and deported to London even though he was ill at that time. Amritlal Shet brought out the Gujarati Journal *Janmabhumi* which was an organ of the people of the princely states of Kathiawar, but it became a mouthpiece of national struggle.

Thus, the press was a weapon in the hands of the nationalist groups, to popularize among the people their respective political programmes; policies and methods of struggle and to form organizations with a broad popular basis.

Note and References

1. Iyer, Raghavan, N., 1983, *Utilitarianism and All That*, Santa Barbara, CA, U.S.A: Concord Grove Press, p. 70.
2. Mehta, V.R., 1992, *Foundation of Indian Political Thought*, New Delhi: Manohar, p. 152.
3. Rainee and Kumar, *International Journal of English and Literature* (IJEL)ISSN(P): 2249-6912; ISSN(E): 2249-8028, Vol. 3, Issue 5, Dec. 2013, 21- 26. p. 21.
4. In this regard, Pamela Lothspeich draws our attention to the fact that more than eighty novels, besides a number of poems, plays, and children's stories, were published between the 1860s and the

First World War and that the "height of 'Mutiny fiction' was in the 1890s...when nineteen novels were published" (*see* Lothspeich, Pamela. "Unspeakable outrages and Unbearable Defilements: Rape Narratives in the literature of colonial India". *International Journal of Postcolonial Studies. Postcolonial Text,* Vol. 3. No. 1 (2007).

To some extent, it can be said that the Indian nationalist movement began not as an anti-colonial violent insurgency. In its early phases, it was an ideology of the indigenous bureaucracy of the *Raj*. Macaulay's education system started creating a class of interpreters between British and the millions whom they govern. The colonizers want to create a class of persons Indian in blood and colour, but English in tastes, in opinions, in morals and in intellect in the later part of the nineteenth century. It was this class of interpreters who initiated and supported a nationalist movement which attempted to control the state bureaucracy.

5. Bruce Robertson (ed.) 1999. The *Essential Writings of Raja Rammohan Ray,* New Delhi: Oxford University Press, p. 262.
6. Chatterjee, Partha. *The Nation and its Fragments: Colonial and Postcolonial Histories,* Princeton, NJ: Princeton University Press, 1993.
7. Chattopadhyay, Bankimchandra. 1992, *Anandamath.* Trans. and adapt. Basanta Koomar Ray. Bombay and Delhi: Vision, p. 76.
8. *The Complete Works of Swami Vivekananda,* (CW), Vol. V, Calcutta: Advaita Ashrama, 1962, p. 36.
9. Verma, V.P., 1980, *Modern Indian Political Thought,* New Delhi: Sterling, p. 117.
10. *Op.cit., The Complete Works of Swami Vivekananda,* Vol. III, 1962, p. 336.

4
Sri Aurobindo's Bhawani Mandir (1905)

The *Bhawani Mandir* written by Sri Aurobindo in 1905 during the *Swadeshi* movement gets the significance place in the literature of Indian nationalism. In spite of the fact that the *Bhawani Mandir* is a small booklet that contains only twelve pages, in 1918, Sedition Committee set up by British Government adjudged it as "seditious matter" in its report. The report further reads that the booklet shows "a remarkable instance of perversion of religious ideals to political purposes".[1] The Committee also mentioned that the text "set out the aims and objectives of revolutionaries" and it "cleverly associated the religious and political aspects of the question from the point of the view of so-called Indian nationalism".[2] The significance of this text can also be found out in the fact that a copy of this pamphlet was also put in as evidence when Sri Aurobindo was arrested in Alipore bomb case in 1908-09. It has been rightly pointed out that the text served as a "handbook for the revolutionary group of Bengal" during the early decades of the twentieth century.

It is quite interesting to note that the booklet *Bhawani Mandir* covers total 16 pages in *The Complete Works of Sri Aurobindo* (pages 76-93) including the cover photo of the pamphlet and Appendix. Appendix also includes three pages thus the text is limited to only 12 pages[3]. There are approximately 4200 words in the pamphlet. In spite of this, the booklet was confiscated by the British police and was considered as spiritual dynamite to blow off the colonial rule over India. In its effect, it caused endless nightmares to British administration; but it proved to be a mighty inspiration and supreme driving force to countless revolutionaries. Of course, the scheme remained at the level of ideas and was never carried out in reality. Yet, the booklet maps out India's all-round development to stand as an independent nation; and to wrest sovereign power from the colonial master.

I

Before we deal with the text *Bhawani Mandir* it seems reasonable to have a look into author's life, his intellectual formation and his engagement in the political activities to sense the undercurrent of the text. Born in Bengali Hindu family in Calcutta on August 15, 1872, Sri Aurobindo (1872-1950) grew up in a European atmosphere. His father Dr. K.D. Ghosh had adopted the English way of life and wanted to keep all his children ignorant of Indian languages, religion, and way of life. Before his education in England, Sri Aurobindo received education through the medium of English in India at different schools. In England, he acquired proficiency in the Classics and the English language. He also mastered languages like French and Latin. His extraordinary brilliance in studies led him to obtain distinction in the first part of the Tripos at King's College. His fourteen years of stay in England (1879-1893) was the formative period of his life, both as a period of his intellectual growth and preparation for the life to come in India. It was in England that his desire to serve his motherland became explicit. His association with the *Indian Majlis*, a student's association, and a secret group of revolutionary Indians known as the "lotus and Dagger" gave him ample opportunity to foster his patriotism. This revolutionary fervour of Aurobindo came out openly when he returned to India in 1893. As a professor of English and French in Baroda State Service and as the principal of the National College at Calcutta, Aurobindo always felt an urge to do something more effective and lasting for the good of mankind. In 1904, he started the practice of *yoga* as he felt that it could be the only cure for his own deep-rooted sorrow and for the manifold ills of humanity. Taking part in political movements from 1905 to 1910, finally, in 1910 he withdrew from active politics and went to Chandra Nagar and later on moved to Pondicherry for spiritual practice until his death (1950).

Aurobindo's political career began in India in 1893 when he took a lively interest in it by writing columns for *Indu Prakash*, a

Marathi daily published from Bombay. Aurobindo through his writings expressed dissatisfaction over the policy of "prayer and petition" pursued by the moderate leaders of the Indian National Congress. However, the event of the partition of Bengal (1905) proved milestone in the political career of Aurobindo. He resigned from his job in Baroda in 1906 and plunged into active politics which marked the beginning of the important phase of his life. This phase of political activism was very brief (1906-1910). During this period, he participated actively in politics and supported the radical group led by Tilak. He participated in the Surat session of the Congress. He also wrote extensively on various topics of national importance in this period. In 1908, he was implicated and arrested in the Maniktola Bomb Case. He was honourably acquitted in 1909. After his release, he remained involved in politics for a shortwhile. As mentioned, in 1910, he withdrew from active politics and went to Chandra Nagar and later on moved to Pondicherry and established *Ashram* and lived there until his death. His sudden withdrawal from active politics was a result of his desire for spiritual development. In this regard, it would not be incorrect to say that Aurobindo's political theory was firmly grounded in and grew out of his deep spiritual convictions. Politics for him was the extension of his theory of personal, national and universal development. The period of 1893-1905 can be called a preparatory phase of his short but impressive career of active politics which culminated in this equally dramatic withdrawal in 1910. As it appears, if Aurobindo's life was very dramatic, his active political career (1905-1910) was very short. In spite of that Aurobindo wrote extensively on political issues during his active but short political life and later on the subject of spiritualism.[4]

As far as his intellectual development is concerned, even a cursory look at his writings suggests he was deeply influenced by his profound study of Indian philosophy as well as the focused and comparative study of different world civilizations. Of these, the Indian tradition of idealism in philosophy seems to have impressed him the most. The study of *Gita, Upanishads* and *Vedanta* had a deep impact on his political thinking. Further, Vedantic philosophy as propounded by Ramakrishna (1836-1886) and Vivekananda (1863-1902) also influenced Aurobindo's thinking. He was also inspired by the remarkable vitality and diversity of the Indian intellectual tradition. He believed that the writings of the Vedantic sages and the Buddha reflect the genius of the Indian mind.

Besides these Indian intellectuals' influences, the great European philosophers from Homer (850 B.C.) to Goethe (1749-1832) influenced him the maximum during his formative London period (1879-1893). However, in given historical context and necessity, Aurobindo developed a whole new lexis for his political thought that suited both Indian political situation and Indian mind. Thus, it is unsurprising to see what Romaine Rolland said that Sri Aurobindo was "the highest synthesis of the genius of Asia and the genius of Europe".[5] Aurobindo also accepted in one of his letter dated 13 August, 1907, "I have adopted the principles of the political philosophy of the West and I have assimilated that to the immortal teaching of Vedantism".[6] In fact, it is this political Vedantism by which he tried to understand the Indian political reality and attempted to interpret some of the spiritual concepts of Vedantic philosophy in the given Indian political context.

The text considered here is his pamphlet *Bhawani Mandir.* It was written in 1905 and distributed during *Swadeshi* movement. But before we deal with *Bhawani Mandir* it would not be out of context to assess Aurobindo's political writings before the publication and distribution of *Bhawani Mandir.* At contextual level, Aurobindo's first political writings—the nine articles comprising New Lamps for Old published in the *Indu Prakash* of Bombay from 7 August, 1893 to 6 March, 1894—describes Aurobindo's views on the political situation of India. Deeply imbued with the ancient Indian heritage; in the first two articles, he bitterly attacked the moderate policies of Indian liberals, not only their policy of mendicancy but also their emphasis on individualism, materialism and liberal democracy. Criticizing Congress which was then mouthpiece of liberals, he wrote, "I say of the Congress, then, this-that its aim are mistaken, that the spirit in which it proceeds towards their accomplishment is not spirit of sincerity and whole-heartedness and that the methods it has chosen are not right methods, and the leaders in whom it trust not the right sort of men to be leaders – in brief, that we are at present the blind led, if not by blind, at any rate by the one-eyed".[7] Furthermore, he felt that the Congress leadership had not perceived the British rule correctly and therefore, instead of boldly asserting their goal, the leaders relied on the sense of justice and benevolence of the British rulers. As they resorted to futile petitions and requests in the annual sessions of the Congress, therefore, Aurobindo stressed the need for a broad-based organization that could channelize the entire power of the country to free it from foreign rule. Thus, his insistence on enthusing the masses with the spirit of independence was one of the first efforts to give a mass character to the freedom movement.

Aurobindo's earlier writings (1893-1910) also show the vehement criticism of British rule. Unlike his contemporary national movement leaders, his criticism of British rule was direct and severe. Through such criticism, he wanted to strengthen the anti-British sentiments in the country as well as to break the myth of British superiority. On the other hand, he also expressed the view that the British administrative system in India was thoroughly unsuitable to the Indian people, their socio-economic system, their mind, and genius. Thus, he believed that copying the British model was not in the interest of our country. He, however, did not object to learning from the experience of the British, though he was against the thoughtless imitation of European ideas and ideals. He objected to the growing tendency among Indians to ignore the past and of having no clear vision for the future. Regarding the nature of the British rule in India, he expressed the view that it is mercantile in the foundation and exploitative in character. It must be, therefore, weakened from its base itself, in order to achieve freedom and independence of the country.

II

It is this ideological, political and intellectual context, Aurobindo wrote his small, but significant booklet *Bhawani Mandir.* This pamphlet was unsigned but it was the open secret that it was written by Sri Aurobindo and issued in 1905. This pamphlet has also been hailed as the "handbook for the revolutionary group of Bengal".[8] In Gordon's views, "the pamphlet syncretizes religious elements and national messianism".[9] At face value, the text seems to advance the idea of *Anand Math* of Bankim to celibate muscular Hindus against the British colonials. This was to occur through an armed struggle for the liberation of the motherland. Yet, *Bhawani Mandir* contains no direct reference to Bankim's novel and it indicates that Aurobindo perhaps presupposed the reader's familiarity with the novel *Anand Math.* It must be noted that Bankim was the first thinker to collude – in the Bengali/Indian context – the concepts of mother-goddess and native land into "motherland," and Aurobindo had hailed him as the seer and the "first prophet of nationalism". Aurobindo adopts Bankim's metaphor of the mother-goddess-land, in the text and then seeks to redefine and expand on the relationship between the mother-goddess and the motherland using classical Hindu motifs. As Urban (2007) points out "Aurobindo reinterpreted Bankim's story, transforming it into a radically anti-colonial call to revolution."[10]

As discussed above, the text covers total 16 pages in *The Complete Works of Sri Aurobindo* (pp. 77-92) including the cover photo of the pamphlet (p. 77) and Appendix. Appendix also includes three pages, thus, the text is limited to 12 pages only. There are approximately 4200 words in the pamphlet. However, the pamphlet has special significance in the literature of Indian nationalism. It should be noted that a copy of this pamphlet was also put in as evidence when Sri Aurobindo was arrested in Alipore bomb case in 1908-09. Later on the text, *Bhawani Mandir* was adjudged "seditious matter" by the British Government of India. On 10 December, 1917, the British Government set-up a Sedition Committee with Mr. Justice Rowlatt as President and the Committee submitted its report on 15 April, 1918.[11] Among the materials it studied, three books, in particular, drew its attention. *Bhawani Mandir* was the first. According to this report, "The *Bhawani Mandir* (temple to Bhawani, one of the manifestations of Goddess Kali) exalts Bhawani as the manifestation of *Shakti.* Indians must acquire mental, physical, moral and spiritual strength.... They must draw strength from religion. How this is to be done is described in moving and powerful terms. The book is a remarkable instance of perversion of religious ideals to political purposes".[12] A little further the Sedition Committee's Report again refers to *Bhawani Mandir.* It notes, that the pamphlet 'set out the aims and objectives of revolutionaries'. "It was remarkable in more ways than one and cleverly associated the religious and political aspects of the question from the point of the view of so called Indian nationalism".[13] It further mentions, "The central idea as to a given religious order is taken from the well-known novel *Anand Math* of Bankim Chandra. We find the glorification of Kali, under the names of *Shakti* and Bhawani (two of her numerous names) and the preaching of the gospel of Force and Strength as the necessary condition for political freedom. The necessity for Indians to worship *Shakti* (or Bhawani manifested as the Mother of Strength) is insisted upon if success is desired. A new order of political devotee was to be instituted. A new organization of political *Sannyasins* was to be started, who were to prepare the way for revolutionary work. It was the liberation of India from foreign yoke".[14] The Committee admitted though that "at this stage, there is no reference to violence or crime". The Committee also drew the following conclusion from this book. The Report states that, "The samitis and associations formed later than 1908, gradually dropped the religious ideas underlying the *Bhawani Mandir* pamphlet and developed the terroristic side with its necessary accompaniments of dacoity and murder". But, in spite of all these, Justice Rowlatt had to praise *Bhawani Mandir:* "It was remarkable in more ways than one".[15]

Lord Ronaldsey in his book *The Heart of Aryavarta,* writes about *Bhawani Mandir.* "Couched in sparkling English, the booklet is a piece of inspired writing. These ideas seem indeed to have been the main spring behind Sri Aurobindo's activities in support of the revolutionary movement."

Bhawani Mandir is a "spiritual treatise" with political undertones, that announces the formation of a company of nationally-minded revolutionary ascetics, clearly based on the prototype of the Children in *Anand Math,* and dedicated, like them, to the liberation of the motherland from the invader. However, one may also argue that, as Barin pointed out, the appeal that *Bhawani Mandir* made was "more in the nature of a spiritual than a political one". In his words, "the failure of the first attempt (1902-1904) at the formation of a secret society clearly proved that without spiritual background, the movement was not likely to have the moral stamina required for the facing of death ungrudgingly, nor for giving moral tone to terrorist activities."[16]

The cover of the *Bhawani Mandir,* it seems, had a drawing of a falchion on it. It came to official notice only in August 1905. Interestingly, there was nothing on the pamphlet to show who the author or the publisher was. However, it was the open secret that the author was Aurobindo Ghosh. During the searches in Calcutta in May, 1908, the police found three copies of *Bhawani Mandir:* one in the *Bande Mataram* office, a second in the bomb store at 134

Harrison Road, and a third in the house of Debabrata Bose, one of the chief writers with Barin for the revolutionary Bengali journal, the *Yugantar.* Whether *Bhawani Mandir* exists or not is not of so much significance but of the more importance is the language of righteousness in which the manifesto is worded. The pamphlet opens with an invocation of Bhawani, and in most stirring and appealing language, it calls for initiatives to develop a new cult and spirit for Nationalism.

The text begins with a Sanskrit sentence that reads as "*Om Namah Chandikayai*". It emphasizes on the erection of a temple dedicated to Bhawani. "A temple is to be erected and consecrated to Bhawani, the mother, among the hills. To all the children of the mother, the call is sent forth to help in the sacred work".[17]

Thus, the text is in the form of a proposal that is intended to its countrymen and makes an emotional appeal to children of the nation to "help in the sacred work" of erecting a temple. The term sacred is the religious one, thus, the religious sentiment is aroused to the children of the country for erecting the temple. Here, the "erecting temple" has the symbolic meaning; it means to build the nation by the children of the nation. Not only is the making of a nation but also for the consecration that is devotion to the nation asked by the author. The temple that is to be erected is, at face value, of Bhawani, the mother. Two significant points may be noted here first the "personification of the nation" and "nation as a mother".

Soon after the call, the text attempts to clarify that who is Bhawani and what is the purpose of erecting her temple. Posing it in the question form it reads, "who is Bhawani the mother, and why should we erect a temple to Her?" Then it responds, "Bhawani is infinite energy". In the last part of the pamphlet, the author writes "if you ask who is Bhawani, the mother, She herself answers you, "I am the Infinite Energy which streams forth from the Eternal in the world and Eternal in yourselves. I am the Mother of the Universe, the Mother of the Worlds, and for you who are children of the Sacred land, *aryabhumi,* made of her clay and reared by her son and winds, I am Bhawani Bharati, Mother of India".[18]

Yet in the beginning of the text, in an attempt to throw the light on the nature of Bhawani as an "infinite energy", the text invokes the Indian philosophical insight of 'eternity' and wheel of time and notes that "Sometimes She is Love, sometimes She is

Knowledge, sometimes She is Renunciation, sometimes She is Pity. This Infinite Energy is Bhawani. She also is Durga, She is Kali, She is Radha the Beloved, She is Lakshmi. She is our Mother and the Creatress of us all."

We may note that these Goddesses are different Hindu Goddesses still worshipped by different Hindu sects. Stating that they seem to men in "various aspects and infinite forms, but are really one", Aurobindo tries to unify different Hindu sections under one umbrella Goddess mother Bhawani. Further, he does not negate the significance of other forms or aspects of Goddess as he argues that each aspect of her creates and marks an age of 'love', 'knowledge', 'renunciation', and 'pity'; and in this present, she is manifested as *Shakti*. Thus, he reinforces religious pluralism in a society divided on the ground of religious sects.

Thus, the text claims that Bhawani is *Shakti*, and "In the present age, the Mother is manifested as the mother of Strength. She is pure *Shakti*". Giving a metaphysical status to Bhawani and characterizing it as a mother who is pure *Shakti*, Aurobindo claims through some illustrations both from the west and Asia that the whole world is growing full of the mother *shakti*.

The text interprets the world and its major phenomenon in terms of the Mother, the *Shakti*. It claims that wherever we see, we find "huge masses of strength rise before us". It also claims that "all is growing large and strong". We come across "tremendous, swift and inexorable forces, gigantic figures of energy, terrible columns of force" in the world that are manifestations of the mother the shakti. The author of the text invites us to see this *Shakti* in the war, science, and wealth which is more "mighty and colossal", "fierce", "rapid and busy" and "more prolific" in the "recorded history". Thus, it asserts that "everywhere the Mother is at work". And "from Her mighty and shaping hands enormous forms of *Rakshasas, Asuras, Devas* are leaping forth into the arena of the world".

It also mentions that there are two major appearances of this *Shakti*—*Mlecchashaktis* and *Arya shaktis*, but "all are the Mother in her new phase, remoulding and creating". While *Mlecchashaktis* are "clouded in their strength, black or blood-crimson with *tamas* or *rajas*, other are *aryashaktis*; bathed in a pure flame of renunciation and utter self-sacrifice". So far the text seems philosophical in nature discussing the question of *shakti* and its forms but soon it gives a political turn to the question of *shakti*. It attempts to define the rise of empire and the nation in the term of *shakti*. Because of this *shakti*, the text asserts "we have seen slow but mighty rise of great empires in the West". Thus, the mother, the *Shakti* is everywhere showing Her mighty strength, but Aurobindo laments that in India she is "striving to be re-born, striving with agony and tears". Introspecting the causes of why the Mother, the *Shakti* is not manifested as it should be, the author argues, "We have all things else, but we are empty of strength, void of energy. We have abandoned *Shakti* and therefore abandoned by *Shakti*".[19]

How have Indians abandoned *Shakti*? He gives the reason, "The mother is not in our hearts, in our brains, in our arms". Thus, in the author's view, Indians are not worshipping physically, emotionally and intellectually to strength. It is not that Indians do not wish to be powerful, but, as he mentions, because of *tamas* and inertness the power does not become enduring in our social sphere. Writing in a self-reflective manner, Aurobindo mentions,

> "How many attempts have been made, how many movements have been begun, in religion, in society, in politics! But the same fate has overtaken or is preparing to overtake them all. They flourish for a moment, then the impulse wanes, the fire dies out, and if they endure, it is only as empty shells, forms from which the *Brahma* has gone or in which it lies overpowered with *tamas* and inert. Our beginnings are mighty, but they have neither sequel nor fruit".[20]

Thus, in Aurobindo's description strength is the central quality that Indians lack and they must possess it. All other developments, he points out including then existing industrial development has no meaning "unless we first seek the one essential thing, unless we acquire strength".

It needs to be pointed out that when Aurobindo talks about the strength he is not mentioning only physical strength. His idea of strength includes intellectual, moral and spiritual strength also that are evident in latter part of the text. Once making it clear that India has failed in all things because of lack of *Shakti*, the text considers three important issues *Jñāna*, *bhakti* and *karma* and Indians' response to them. It is worth mentioning that all three things; *Jñāna, bhakti* and *karma* are purely Hindu philosophical categories. They are not also in separation but unity that Aurobindo brings in the picture.

Posing a question the text invites us to think; "is it the knowledge that is wanting?" Aurobindo argues that since the beginning of 'race', '*Jñāna*' (Knowledge) has been 'stored' and 'accumulated' by Indians and what we have today is 'inherited gains of many thousands of years'. He also accepts that "great giant of knowledge" still arises among Indians and "add knowledge to the store". "Our capacity has not shrunk, the edge of our intellect has not been dulled or blunted, its receptivity and flexibility are as varied as of old".[21] But in the very next sentence he claims, "But it is a dead knowledge, a burden under which we are bowed, a poison which is corroding us rather than as it should be a staff to support our feet, and a weapon in our hands; for this is the nature of all great things that when they are not used or are ill used, they turn upon the bearer and destroy him".[22]

This is significant in the sense that here Aurobindo does not blindly glorify the greatness of Indian knowledge or its abstractness like his other counterparts but evaluates knowledge in its utility and in terms of action. Devoid of action our knowledge has, in his words, become 'dead', 'a poison' and "self-destroying". Why has such situation raised? His answer is that "Our knowledge then, weighed down with a heavy load of *tamas*, lies under the curse of impotence and inertia". Thus, again Aurobindo comes to his central point of acquiring strength and in his view this is the lack of strength due to "heavy load of *tamas*" and inertia that we are in such a condition. On the other hand, he also criticizes the 'imitative' attitude of Indians and argues that imitation of the Western science or copy of methods of any nation will not solve our problem. Challenging the notions of limitations of the West that were prevalent in his time, he asks, "Imitative and incapable of initiative, we have striven to copy the methods of England, and we had not the strength: we would now copy the methods of the Japanese, a still more energetic people; are we likely to succeed any better?"[23]

In a very direct way, Aurobindo also criticizes the power of knowledge of Western science. It is important to note that many Indians believed that India was subjugated by the British because of their superiority in science. It is on this basis many nationalists had argued that India also should adopt the British model. But as Aurobindo argues such imitation is not only of any help to Indians but also the might of knowledge of western science is in itself self-destructive as the "mace of *Bhimsen*". In his words, "The mighty force of knowledge which European Science bestows is a weapon for the hands of a giant, it is the mace of Bhimsen: what can a weakling do with it but crush himself in the attempt to wield it?"[24]

After showing that how Indians lack *Shakti* in the field of knowledge had made them imitative and incapable of taking initiative, Aurobindo turns to the issue of *Bhakti*. He writes that "*Bhakti* is ingrained in the Indian nature, but in the absence of *Shakti*, we cannot concentrate, we cannot direct, we cannot preserve it." Making an analogy of "fuel and flame" in the context of *Bhakti* and *shakti*, he writes, "*Bhakti* is the leaping flame, *Shakti* is the fuel". And, "if the fuel is scanty how long can the fire endure?"[25]

But what is *Bhakti*? Although there are many definitions and criterion of *Bhakti* in Indian religious traditions, from total surrender to God (*Vaishnava* tradition) to understanding the real nature of *Maya* and *Brahma* (*Advaita* tradition), Aurobindo defines *Bhakti* in a very eclectic way. He writes, "When the strong nature, enlightened by knowledge, disciplined and given a giant's strength by *Karma*, lifts itself up in love and adoration to God that is the *Bhakti* which endures and keeps the soul for ever united with the Divine". On the other hand, the weak person cannot bear the might of perfect *Bhakti*. Because *Bhakti* is such a thing, that cannot be sustained without *Shakti*.

With this analysis, Aurobindo reaches to the conclusion that India needs only one thing that is *Shakti*; and another thing else will be added to it easily and naturally. Thus he observes, "we must strive to acquire before all others, is strength—strength physical, strength mental, strength moral, but above all spiritual strength which is the one inexhaustible and imperishable source of all the others".[26]

Here, it may be viewed that when Aurobindo calls for *Shakti*, it is not physical strength alone. It is intellectual, moral and as he points out "above all spiritual strength". Like many nationalists, we find here that Aurobindo also sees the real source of strength in spiritualism. As noted above, he also finds this spiritual strength "inexhaustible and imperishable" source of all the other strengths.

Then, what should India do? It is another significant concern that is revealed in the middle part of the text. Aurobindo puts a homology between an "old person" and a 'nation' to make his point clear. Like an "old person", he writes, India has grown 'old'. His argument is that the excess of knowledge and experiences freeze the power and will of action to old persons, thus, they hesitate, ponder, discuss, make tentative efforts or wait for the safest and easiest way instead of taking the most direct action. In the same way, he asserts, India is behaving. In his words, "Our race has grown just such an old man with stores of knowledge, with ability to feel and desire, but paralysed by simple sluggishness, senile timidity, senile feebleness".[27] His answer is that "If India is to survive, she must be made young again". He convinces us that India must 'reborn' as "it was in the old times, like the surges, vast, puissant, calm or turbulent at will, an ocean of action or of force."

He writes that because of *tamas* or heavy inertia our condition has become such that many people have begun to believe that "India is decayed, bloodless and lifeless, too weak ever to recover; that our race is doomed to extinction'. It cannot be reborn. Aurobindo counters such arguments by asserting that such beliefs are 'foolish' and "idle saying" as "No man or nation need be weak unless *he* chooses, no man or nation need perish unless *he* deliberately chooses extinction".[28]

The power of this sentence is quite impressive. It is here Aurobindo gives all responsibility to the person and his choices. It is individual who can decide his fate, no other factors are so important than his choices.

It should also be pointed out that it is the first time in the text Aurobindo come to the issue of the nation. Thus, from the proposal of the erection of Bhawani temple to the analysis of Indians weakness that is a lack of strength among Indians, Aurobindo attempts to define the nation. It is through this definition of nation Aurobindo brings spirituality and politics together. In his words, "For what is a nation? What is our mother-country? It is not a piece of earth, nor a figure of speech, nor a fiction of the mind. It is a mighty *Shakti*, composed of the *Shaktis* of all the millions of units that make up the nation, just as *Bhawani Mahisha-Mardini* sprang into being from the *Shaktis* of all the millions of gods assembled in one mass of force and welded into unity. The *Shakti* we call India,

Bhawani Bharati, is the living unity of the *Shaktis* of three hundred millions of people; but she is inactive, imprisoned in the magic circle of *tamas*, the self-indulgent inertia and ignorance of her sons. To get rid of *tamas* we have but to wake the *Brahma* within".[29]

This paragraph is the crux of the whole text. In this piece of writing, Aurobindo claims that nation is not a territory, nor "an imagined community". Invoking the homology of *Bhawani Mahisha-Mardini*, a mythical and powerful goddess who was created by assembling the powers of many gods—with the nation, Aurobindo claims that nation is united *Shakti*, the *Shakti* what he calls India or Bhawani Bharati in his text. It is the first time in the text Aurobindo makes it clear that Bhawani is India and it symbolizes the nation. For him, the nation is *Shakti* of its millions, it is "living unity of the *Shaktis* of three hundred millions of people of India". But he laments that she is inactive because of *tamas* or gross inertia. This *Shakti* can be revived by overcoming this *tamas* or waking-up *Brahma* within.

What is this *Brahma*? In the latter part of the text, the author reveals that, "the *Brahma* within, the one and the indivisible ocean of spiritual force is that from which all life material and mental is drawn". He further mentions that spiritual energy is the source of all other strength. Invoking the Adavaitic philosophical category of *Brahma*, Aurobindo seems following the Shankar in his political description and awakening of India. In fact, the text employs both term *'Brahma'* and *'Maya'* which are the foundation of *Advaita* philosophy of Shankara. Through example the text also tells us that everyone in India from 'King' to 'coolie' and *'Brahman'* to *'Pariah'*, there is the same essence or *Brahma* or God is within us. Aurobindo also informs us that for thousands of years this has been taught by *Sadhus* and *Sannyasis* through their living. In this regard, he also points out two recent figures in his text Ramakrishna Paramahansa and Vivekananda. We may recall that these two figures were not only celebrated figures in India but their influence also reached abroad and they were accepted as the authority on Hindu religion and more especially *Advaita* philosophy of *Hindu Dharma*. Interpreting *Advaita* philosophy in his own way, he categorically writes,

> "We are all gods and creators because the energy of God is within us and all life is creation; not only the making of

> new forms is creation, but preservation is creation, destruction itself is creation. It rests with us what we shall create; for we are not, unless we choose, puppets dominated by Fate and *Maya*: we are facets and manifestations of Almighty Power".[30]

In spite of the dark cloud of *tamas* that Aurobindo repeatedly mentions in his text that has kept Indians to this pathetic condition, Aurobindo is hopeful. And it is in this hope Aurobindo's philosophy transcends the national boundary. He argues that India's regeneration is not only important for India but also for the whole humanity. "India cannot perish, our race cannot become extinct because among all the divisions of mankind it is to *India that is reserved the highest and the most splendid destiny, the most essential to the future of the human race.* It is *she* who must send forth from herself the future religion of the entire world, the Eternal religion which is to harmonise all religions, sciences, and philosophies and make mankind one soul".[31]

One may find here that Aurobindo is convinced that India has a special mission in the world. Also, India is contrasted with "other divisions of mankind" or civilization and in Aurobindo's view India is 'reserved', 'highest', and "most splendid". Not only this, India cannot perish because it is "the most essential to the future of the human race". In Aurobindo's views, India has the special task to send forth a future religion of the entire world what he terms the "Eternal religion" that will harmonize all religion, philosophy, and science. One may note here that India's superiority is proclaimed here in the field of spirituality and by this, the author constructs a difference between India and others.

This becomes quite evident when the text constructs a binary opposition of mlecchahood / aryanisation and argues that India's mission is "to purge barbarism (mlecchahood) out of humanity and to aryanise the world". Here again, we may note how others are assumed as '*mleccha*' or barbaric and how India is assumed as civilized. Thus, what we note is that India is velorized and 'other' needs spiritual guidance from India. Yet, this is not to happen automatic what Aurobindo feels is that for such a great project India "must first re-aryanise herself".

Aurobindo also feels that this is "the greatest and most wonderful work ever given to a race". Thus, glorification of India and its inherent spiritual power serves as a powerful tool to counter British colonials' civilization mission arguments.

How can India be Re-aryanised? Aurobindo gives the example of Ramakrishna Paramahansa and Vivekananda again. Clearly here Aurobindo is referring to Vivekananda's speech at Chicago given in 1893 that set the spiritual tone of India in the Western world.

Aurobindo's project of the spiritual regeneration of the world and larger humanity begins from India. Again Aurobindo argues that for the above purpose Indians have to first come out of the "terrible cloud of *tamas*".

Thus, in a very emphatic way Aurobindo announces "Strength then and again the strength and yet more strength is the need of our race". He then provides the rationale of worshipping *Bhawani* to get strength as "if it is strength we desire, how shall we gain it if we do not adore the Mother of strength?". But why should one worship Bhawani and how it will help to get strength? Aurobindo states, "She demands worship not for Her own sake, but in order that She may help us and give Herself to us. This is no fantastic idea, no superstition but the ordinary law of the universe. The gods cannot, if they would give themselves unasked. Even the Eternal comes not unaware upon man. Every devotee knows by experience that we must turn to Him and desire and adore Him before the Divine Spirit pours in its ineffable beauty and ecstasy upon the soul. What is true of the Eternal is true also of Her who goes forth from Him".[32]

Aurobindo knew that to a rational mind this could be taken as superstition. Thus, he invites those Indians who were "possessed with Western ideas" to consider some of the facts. First, he gives the example of "marvellous and sudden upsurging nation" Japan. He argues that the reason of the strength of Japan was religion. In his words, "It was the Vedantic teachings of Oyomei and the recovery of *Shintoism* with its worship of the national *Shakti* of Japan in the image and person of the Mikado that enabled the little island empire to wield the stupendous weapons of Western knowledge and science as lightly and invincible as Arjun wielded the *Gandiva*".[33]

The personification of ideal is key here and it is possible that Aurobindo's personification of *Shakti*/strength as Bhawani might be taken from this Japan example. However, he argues that revival of strength in the case of India is more difficult than Japan. Because "the Japanese had only to revitalize and perfect a strength that already existed", but in the case of India we have to "create strength where it did not exist before".[34] Aurobindo wishes a radical change in Indians that is not reformative or cosmetic. He wants the total change in the perspective of Indians and their lifestyle. Thus, Indians "have to change our natures, and become new men with new hearts, to be born again". What does it mean by "to be born again"? He replies in the text, "To be born again means nothing but to revive the *Brahma* within us, and that is a spiritual process,—no effort of the body or the intellect can compass it".[35] He asserts that *Shakti* cannot be gained through the mechanical or artificial or scientific process. It can be drawn only "from the internal and inexhaustible reservoirs of the Spirit, from that *Adya-Shakti* of the Eternal which is the fountain of all new existence".

The second point that he calls for consideration is the significance of religion in public life of India. His argument is that in India national energy has always drawn strength from religious awakening. Whenever and wherever religious awakening has been complete and grand, the national energy it has created has been gigantic and puissant. On the other hand, whenever the religious movement has been incomplete or narrow, the national movement has been broken, imperfect or temporary. On this basis, he argues that the persistence of this phenomenon is proof that religion is ingrained in the temperament of the race. Thus, he points out that religion is the natural path to Indian mind.

On the other hand, he also mentions that if Indian tries other and foreign methods, they shall either gain their end with tedious slowness, painfully and imperfectly, or they shall not attain it at all. Then, the natural question he places before us as to "why abandon the plain way which God and the Mother have marked out for you to choose faint and devious paths of your own treading"?

Finally, Aurobindo presents "three fundamental laws" before the Indians.[36] First is "We *cannot get strength unless we adore the Mother of Strength*". He also provides the full detail of personification of the Mother of Strength. In his view "We will, therefore, build a temple to the white Bhawani, the mother of strength, the *Mother* of *India*".[37] The white Bhawani is baffling here as traditionally in Bengal or in the north part of India, *Kali* or *Durga* the goddess of power is generally portrayed as black. The use of term 'white' clearly shows the new personification of the mother of strength which is Aryan in nature as Aryan were depicted white in the colour. The black *Kali* also gives the impression of *Tantra* sect of Hinduism that is still prevalent in India today that symbolizes magical and brutal power as well as the sacrifice of others. In contrast to Black *Kali*, Aurobindo's personification of the mother of strength as white Bhawani symbolizes personal sacrifice, *Sannyasi* culture, and adherence to the purity of means and ends.

The other details of the place and location of temple construction is also quite interesting that has much symbolic significance. Let us first see the plan of temple construction:

> "...we will build it in a place far from the contamination of modern cities and as yet little trodden by man, in a high and pure air steeped in calm and energy. This temple will be the centre from which Her worship is to flow over the whole country; for their worshipped among the hills, She will pass like fire into the brains and hearts of Her worshippers. This also is what the Mother has commanded".[38]

"Far from contamination of modern cities" shows that how tradition has to be revived and preserved outside the symbol of modernity—the city which is impure or contaminated. The purity of tradition and impurity of the city was a common discourse of the early twentieth century and city life was always seen as against the pristine traditional and peaceful village life of India. The reason of such discourse was that colonials saw progress or modernity in terms of the development of the city. On the other hand, many Indian nationalists viewed the city as 'unnatural' and artificial entity created by the greed of the people in contrast to villages that were considered natural, real and undisturbed by the greed of men. The other thing that is important to remind here is that city and city life were finally assumed as an extension of materialism while villages were considered the place for spiritual development. Another reason to prefer "far from modern cities" was that cities were considered crowded and noisy that was not favourable for spiritual progress.

Another part of the sentence, "a high and pure air steeped in calm and energy" may also be well considered. 'High' and 'pure', as well as "air steeped in calm and energy" are also symbolic. It shows the glory of the location in which the temple is to be constructed. Temple being a pious entity has to always be in a pure and high place like on the hill. Moreover, the location of the temple has to be in the centre of the India so that devotees could come from all sides. Aurobindo also views that worship of the mother will pass like fire into the brains and hearts of Her worshippers. "Fire into brain and heart" signify that the worship will intellectually and emotionally fire the whole personality of Her devotees. Aurobindo also mentions that this is not his plan but this is the command of the mother.

The second law, according to Aurobindo, is that *Adoration will be dead and ineffective unless it is transmuted into Karma.*[39] Aurobindo tells us that *Karma* is not the ritual or a habit but it is changed form of worship. To put this theory into practice, Aurobindo plans to have "a *math* with a new Order of *Karma-Yogins* attached to the temple". Here one may note how Aurobindo attempts to translate the idea of Bankim's *'Anand Math'* into a concrete plan. He mentions that "men who have renounced all in order to work for the Mother" will stay in *math*. Yet, he also gives some relaxation in some cases as he notes, "Some may, if they choose, be complete *Sannyasins*, most will be *Brahmacharins* who will return to the *grihasthashrama* when their allotted work is finished; but all must accept renunciation.[40]

Aurobindo gives us two reasons for such renunciation. First, following the Indian philosophical and religious tradition he argues that abandoning the material things is prerequisite to return to "the ocean of spiritual force within us". Second, material things, lust, and desire are distracting while "for the development of *Shakti*, entire concentration is necessary", thus one should avoid material things. He mentions, "We need a nucleus of men in whom the *Shakti* is developed to its uttermost extent, in whom it fills every corner of the personality and overflows to fertilise the earth. These, having the fire of Bhawani in their hearts and brains, will go forth and carry the flame to every nook and cranny of our land."

Third law what he calls "a great message" is about the *Jñāna*. It states as *Bhakti and Karma cannot be perfect and enduring unless they are based upon Jñāna.*[41] His argument is that knowledge is a base and it should be as sound as 'rock'. *Brahmacharins* of the Order, he says, should be taught to fill their souls with the knowledge.

But what shall be the basis of their knowledge? He replies emphatically, "What but the great *so-aham,* the mighty formula of the *Vedanta,* the ancient gospel which has yet to reach the heart of the nation, the knowledge which, when vivified by *Karma* and *Bhakti,* delivers man out of all fear and all weakness."

Before the Appendix that informs about the work and rules of the new Order of *Sannyasis,* the author epitomizes the message of the mother. The message is given by the mother herself. "I am the Mother of the Universe, the Mother of the Worlds, and for you who are children of the Sacred land, *aryabhumi,* made of her clay and reared by her son and winds, I am Bhawani Bharati, Mother of India".[42]

Here Sacred land, *aryabhumi* is of much significance as it gives a pride to the Indians that has been captured by the *Mleccha* power. Second, it also calls for the personification of the nation in the form of *Bhawani Bharati,* Mother of India. One of the central themes that the texts renders are "to Aryanise the world". The mother says Her children that by constructing Her temple, "You will be helping to create a nation, to consolidate an age, to aryanise the world. And that nation is your own, that age is the age of yourselves and your children, that the world are no fragment of land bounded by seas and hills, but the whole earth with her teeming millions".[43] Thus, the text shows its both contextual specific and universal meaning.

The appendix (from page number 90 to 92 in *CWSA*, Vols. 6-7) informs us about the new Order of *Sannyasis*. It provides a sketchy blueprint for the *Sannyasis* who will follow the path described in the pamphlet. First, it provides the general rule for *Sannyasis* and informs that how *sannyasi* will work for the people, pursue middle class and wealthy class for the cause of country and finally it leads down the general work for the country. The first general rule is that "All who undertake the life of *Brahmacharya* for the Mother, will have to vow themselves to Her service for four years, after which they will be free to continue the work or return to family life".[44]

Strictly observing the discipline and rules of *achar* and purity, bodily and mental, prescribed by the Heads of the Order, *Math* the general rule informs us about simple living of *sannyasi,* no ranking in *Math,* no desire for personal fame, little comfort and detachments from worldly life. The *sannyasi* will not stay all four years in *Math* but "they will be given periods for rest or for religious improvement during which they will stop at the *math*". "The greater part of the year", the rule informs, "they will spend in work outside". However, "this rule will apply to all except the few necessary for the service of the Temple and those required for the central direction of the work".

The rules chalked out for the people include mainly mass instruction and help to the poor and ignorant through lectures, public demonstrations, religious teachings and nursing the sick and finally what the *Math* approves.

To pursue middle class the *sannyasi* will undertake "various works of public utility in the big towns and elsewhere connected especially with the education and religious life and instruction of the middle classes, as well as with other public needs".[45]

The *sannyasi* will approach *zamindars*, landholders and rich men "to promote sympathy between the *zamindars* and the peasants and heal all discords" as well as "to create the link of a single and living religious spirit and a common passion for one great idea between all classes". They will also pursue the "rich men to works of public beneficence and charity to those in their neighbourhood independent of the hope of reward and official distinction".[46]

There is also provision to send some *sannyasis* to foreign countries, "who will never lose hold of their habits of purity and self-abnegation" there, and they will "study lucrative arts and manufactures" in that country and after coming back "they will establish with the aid of the Order, factories and workshops, still living the life of *Sannyasis* and devoting all their profits to the sending of more and more such students to foreign countries."

There is also a provision to send other *sannyasi* to "travel through various countries on foot, inspiring by their lives, behaviour and conversation, sympathy and love for the Indian people in the European nations and preparing the way for their acceptance of Aryan ideals".[47]

As mentioned previously, this revolutionary booklet was impounded by the British police and was considered as spiritual dynamite to blow off the colonial rule over India. It caused endless nightmares to British administration; but on the contrary, it proved to be a mighty inspiration and supreme driving force to countless revolutionaries. Of course, the scheme remained at the level of ideas and was never carried out in reality. The booklet maps out India's all-round development to stand as an independent nation, and to wrest sovereign power from the colonial master. It brought out a new phase in Indian nationalism.

Notes and References

1. Sedition Committee, 1918, Calcutta: Superintendent Government Printing India, p. 100.Visit *https://archive.org/details/sedition reportooindirich/downloaded on* 20-04-2012.
2. *Ibid.*
3. *The Complete Works of Sri Aurobindo* (*CWSA*), *Bande Mataram, Political Writings and Speeches: 1890-1908*. Vols. 06-07, Pondicherry: Sri Aurobindo Ashram Trust, 2002.
4. It is important to note that like Gandhi Aurobindo did not write systematically on political thought, yet his political outlook can be constructed on the basis of his political writings. Apart from writings in *Bande Mataram* (1893 -1908), in 1910 he founded two weekly papers, *Dharma* (Bengali) and the *Karmyogin* (English). Both papers were short-lived, however, Aurobindo published several significant series of essays on Indian history and culture in the *Karmayogin* that later appeared in the book form, including *The Ideal of the Karmayogin, A system of National Education,* and *The National Value of Art.* From 1914 to 1921 he published a monthly journal, the *Arya,* to disseminate his ideas. With the exception of *Savitri,* all of his most important works— *The Ideal of Human Unity, The Life Divine, The Human Cycle, Essays on the Gita, The Foundation of Indian Culture, The Future Poetry, On Yoga I,* and *On the Veda,* originally appeared serially in the *Arya.* The central theme of all his writings rests on the belief that God exists in all of Nature and that spiritual intuition makes it possible for every individual to become conscious of his own divinity. As he emphasizes on the unity of existence, his philosophy has been labelled "integraliam". His more celebrated book *The Life Divine* presents a systematic account of humankind's eventual ascent to a higher level of consciousness. This metaphysical idea takes practical shape in his books, *Essays on the Gita* and *On Yoga I,* in which Aurobindo explains his system of *Yoga* and its role in preparing the soul to accept the Spirit. *Savitri* is Aurobindo's poetic expression of this process of transformation. In *The Human Cycle* Aurobindo explains his evolutionary theory in historical and psychological terms and states the necessary conditions for the arrival of the next evolutionary stage the "Age of Spirit".
5. Quoted in Verma, V.P., 1960, *The Political Philosophy of Sri Aurobindo,* Delhi: Motilal Banarasidass, p. 34.
6. *See* Nahar Sujata, *Mother's Chronicles* Book 5, Pondicherry: Sri Aurobindo Ashram Trust, p. 264.
7. *The Complete Works of Sri Aurobindo (CWSA), Bande Mataram, Political Writings and Speeches: 1890-1908.*Vols. 06-07, Pondicherry: Sri Aurobindo Ashram Trust, 2002, p. 22.

8. See Hugh B. Urban. 2007. *Tantra: Sex, Secrecy, Politics, and Power in the Study of Religion*. Delhi: Motilal Banarasidass, p. 95.
9. *See ibid.*
10. *Ibid.*, p. 94.
11. Sedition Committee, 1918, Calcutta: Superintendent Government Printing India, p. 110.
12. *Ibid.*, pp. 23-24.
13. *Ibid.*, p. 101.
14. *Ibid.*, p. 101.
15. *Ibid.*, p. 102.
16. Nahar, Sujata, *Mother's Chronicles Book* 5, Pondicherry: Sri Aurobindo Ashram Trust, pp. 102, 264.
17. *CWSA*: 06-07:79
18. *Ibid.*, 6-07:89.
19. *Ibid.*, 6-07:80.
20. *Ibid.*
21. *Ibid.*, 06-07:81.
22. *Ibid.*
23. *Ibid.*
24. *Ibid.*
25. *Ibid.*, 06-07:82.
26. *Ibid.*
27. *Ibid.*, 06-07:83.
28. *Ibid.*
29. *Ibid.*
30. *Ibid.*, 06-07:84.
31. *Ibid.*
32. *Ibid.*, 06-07:85.
33. *Ibid.*, 06-07:86.
34. *Ibid.*
35. *Ibid.*
36. *Ibid.*, 06-07:87.
37. *Ibid.*
38. *Ibid.*
39. *Ibid.*
40. *Ibid.*, 06-07:88.
41. *Ibid.*
42. *Ibid.*, 06-07:89.
43. *Ibid.*
44. *Ibid.*, 06-07:90.
45. *Ibid.*, 06-07:91.
46. *Ibid.*
47. *Ibid.*, 06-07:92.

5

Gandhi's Hind Swaraj (1909)

Hind Swaraj or *Indian Home Rule* is a small tract written by Mahatma Gandhi (1869-1948) in his native language Gujarati, during 13 November to 23 November, 1909, on the return voyage from London to South Africa. It is considered as Gandhi's Classic and his foundational text. It is also a work which Gandhi himself translated from Gujarati into English: no other work of his, not even his *Autobiography* enjoys this distinction. Structurally, the text is less than 100 pages, consisting of around 30,000 words and comprises twenty short chapters. The text is cast in the form of the dialogue between "The Editor" who is Gandhi himself, and "The Reader" his interlocutor. This dialogue covers a ranges of topics including the Congress Party and its official, Partition of Bengal, the state of India, the reasons of India's colonization, the meaning of *Swaraj* and the best means to attain it, Gandhi's vision of ideal society, the definition and practice of *Satyagraha,* Hindu-Muslim unity, railways, Doctors, Lawyers and Machinery and modern education. The text in its texture seems to attempt to accomplish multiple tasks; from political to civilizational.

In *Hind Swaraj,* there is no direct discussion on the Indian nationalism. In the text, Gandhi's version of nationalism emerges out of his discourse on civilization. The central argument that Gandhi makes in the text is that India has superior civilization to the Western civilization because Indian civilization is spiritual while latter is materialistic. On this basis, he suggests that India should adopt a superior method of nationalism based on spiritual force, and overcome the other forms of nationalism which are imitative to Western nationalism that is the corollary of its materialistic civilization.

Thus, the form of nationalism that *Hind Swaraj* suggests is not limited to political in the real sense of the term. It encompasses chiefly a moral/spiritual dimension of nationalism that is all inclusive. As mentioned, *Hind Swaraj* does not have any direct reference to Indian nationalism; it emerges out of the different set pieces of dialogues between the Reader and the Editor. More concretely and specifically it can be explored in the dialogues between the reader and editor on the issues of moderate and extremists, revolutionary nationalism, the relation between nation and religion, nation and *Swaraj*, and the role of the national elite in achieving *Swaraj*. The text also offers a new method of resistance to Indian nationalists what Gandhi calls in his text passive resistance and put a vehement moral and strategic critique to revolutionary violence adopted by some of the Indian nationalists.

The text is the fine amalgam of Gandhi's reading of materiality of colonial and nationalist politics and his universal idealistic vision. Gandhi's reading of political events of India and their interpretations, future outcome of those events, their danger show that how he was serious to the political happenings of India despite the fact that he was not even present in India. It might be recalled that when Gandhi wrote this booklet he was not engaged in Indian national movement but he was advancing the causes of Indians in South Africa. While engaging in South Africa, his concern to the different versions of Indian nationalism, and their critique also shows Gandhi's nationalist aspiration that he could fulfil when he returned to India in 1915.

I

Mohandas Karamchand Gandhi was born on October 2, 1869, at Porbandar (Gujarat), located on the western coast of India. It was then one of the many tiny states in Kathiawar. His father, Karamchand Gandhi, was a *Dewan* or Prime Minister of Porbandar. He belonged to a middle-class *Bania* family. His mother, Putlibai, was a very religious lady and left a deep impression on Gandhi's mind. Gandhi's *Autobiography* informs us that he was a mediocre student and was excessively shy and timid in his childhood. He was married at the age of thirteen to Kasturbai when he was in high school at that time. Later on, as his autobiography tells he denounced the custom of child marriage and termed it as cruel.

After matriculating from the high school, he joined the Samaldas College in Bhavnagar. After the death of Gandhi's father in 1885, a family suggested that if Gandhi hoped to take his father's place in the state service he should become a barrister which he could do in England in three years. Gandhi welcomed the idea but his mother objected to the idea of going abroad. To win his mother's approval he took a solemn vow not to touch wine, women, and meat and remained true to them throughout his stay in England.

Gandhi sailed for England on September 4, 1888. Initially, he had difficulty in adjusting to English customs and weather but soon he overcame it. His stay in London was formative period of his life. In London, Gandhi encountered theosophists, vegetarians, and others who were disenchanted not only with industrialism but with the legacy of Enlightenment thought. They themselves represented the fringe elements of English society. He completed his Law degree in 1891 and returned to India. He also decided to set up a legal practice in Bombay but could not establish himself. He returned to Rajkot but here also he could not make much headway. At this time, Gandhi received an offer from Dada Abdulla & Co. to proceed to South Africa on their behalf to instruct their counsel in a lawsuit. Gandhi jumped at the idea and sailed for South Africa in April, 1893.

It was in South Africa where Gandhi's transformation from Mohandas to Mahatma took place. Gandhi landed at Durban and soon he realized the oppressive atmosphere of racial snobbishness against Indians who were settled in South Africa in large numbers. After about a week's stay in Durban Gandhi left for Pretoria, the capital of the Transvaal, in connection with a lawsuit. When the train reached Pietermaritzburg, the capital of Natal, at about 9 p.m. a white passenger who boarded the train objected to the presence of a 'coloured' man in the compartment and Gandhi was ordered by a railway official to shift to a third class. When he refused to do so, a constable pushed him out and his luggage was taken away by the railway authorities. It was winter and bitterly cold.

This incident changed Gandhi's life for ever. He decided to fight for the rights of Indians. Gandhi organized the Indian community in South Africa and asked them to forget all distinctions of religion and caste. He suggested the formation of an association to look after the Indian settlers and offered his free time and services.

During his stay in South Africa, Gandhi's life underwent a profound change and he developed most of his political ideas. Gandhi decided to dedicate himself completely to the service of humanity. He realized that absolute continence or *brahmacharya* was indispensable for the purpose as one could not live both after the flesh and the spirit. In 1906, Gandhi took a vow of absolute continence. In the course of his struggle in South Africa, Gandhi developed the concepts of *Ahimsa* (non-violence) and *Satyagraha* (holding fast to truth or firmness in a righteous cause). Gandhi's struggle bore fruit and in 1914 in an agreement between Gandhi and South African Government, the main Indian demands were conceded. Gandhi returned to India in 1915 and on the advice of his political *guru* Gopal Krishna Gokhale, spent the first year touring throughout the country to know the real India.

After a year of wandering, Gandhi settled down on the bank of the River Sabarmati, on the outskirts of Ahmedabad, where he founded an *ashram* called *Satyagraha Ashram*. Gandhi's first *Satyagraha* in India was in Champaran, in Bihar. In 1920, Gandhi gave the call for Non-cooperation movement against the ills of British rule. Gandhi's call roused the sleeping nation. Many Indians renounced their titles and honours, lawyers gave-up their practice and students left colleges and schools. After the outbreak of Second World War in 1939, Gandhi again became active in the political arena. British Government wanted India's help in the War and Congress in return wanted a clear-cut promise of independence from the British government. But British government dithered in its response and on August 8, 1942, Gandhi gave the call for Quit India Movement. Soon the British Government arrested Gandhi and other top leaders of Congress. Disorders broke out immediately all over India and many violent demonstrations took place. While Gandhi was in jail his wife Kasturba passed away. Gandhi too had a severe attack of Malaria. In view of his deteriorating health, he was released from the jail in May, 1944. Second World War ended in 1945 and Britain emerged victoriously. In the general elections held in Britain in 1945, Labour Party came to power, and Mr. Atlee became the Prime Minister. He promised an early realization of self-government in India. A Cabinet Mission arrived from England to discuss with Indian leaders the future shape of a free and united India, but failed to bring the Hindus and Muslims together. India attained independence but Jinnah's intransigence resulted in the partition of the country. Communal riots between Hindus and Muslims broke out in the country in the aftermath of partition. Tales of atrocities on Hindus in Pakistan provoked Hindus in India and they targeted Muslims. Gandhi worked ceaselessly to promote unity between Hindus and Muslims. This angered some fundamentalists and on January 30, 1948, Gandhi was shot dead by one such fundamentalist Nathu Ram Godse while he was going for his evening prayers.

As for personal as well as impersonal sources of inspiration, Gandhi notes in his *Autobiography* (1927), "Three moderns have left a deep impress on my life and captivated me. Raychandbhai by his living contact; Tolstoy by his book, *The Kingdom of God is within You*; and Ruskin by his *Unto This Last*."[1] Besides these three personalities, Gopal Krishna Gokhale and the *Gita* and the *Bible* were lifelong sources of inspiration for Gandhi.

Gandhi met Raychandbhai (or Shri Rajchandra) immediately on his return from London to India at Bombay. Gandhi was at once convinced that Raychandbhai was a man of great character and learning. He was a real seeker after truth. Gandhi very often found him absorbed in Godly pursuits in the midst of weighty business transactions. Gandhi never saw him lose his state of equipoise. Gandhi enjoyed the closest association with him. Above all Raychandbhai's impression as a spiritual guide on Gandhi's mind was unrivaled and Gandhi implicitly believed that Raychandbhai would never willingly lead him astray and in turn, Raychandbhai would always disclose in Gandhi his innermost thoughts. In Gandhi's moments of spiritual crisis, as in South Africa, Raychandbhai was Gandhi's refuge.

Another figure that impressed Gandhi was Gopal Krishna Gokhale. He was the rare gem among contemporary moderate political leaders. Gandhi writes in his autobiography that Gokhale seemed to him like the Ganga where one could have a refreshing bath in the holy river. In the sphere of politics, the place that Gokhale occupied in Gandhi's heart was absolutely unique. Gokhale embodied the goal of spiritualizing (i.e., values of life) in politics and Gandhi steadfastly adhered to it by enriching it. It is significant to remember that Gandhi has devoted seven chapters exclusively to Gokhale in his *Autobiography*.

There are also several books that made a lasting effect on Gandhi's mind. Among them, one was John Ruskin's seminal work

Unto This Last. Soon after reading *Unto This Last,* Gandhi set about establishing the Phoenix community which was based on the values that Ruskin had promoted. Gandhi also published a Gujarati translation of the work so that it could receive wider readership. Another deep influence on Gandhi's thinking was the writings of Leo Tolstoy, especially the essay *The Kingdom of God is Within You* which mapped out Tolstoy's individualistic interpretation of Christian living. Gandhi was so inspired by Tolstoy's teachings that he started writing to him in 1909. In 1910, along with his friend Kallenbach, Gandhi started a community settlement where he lived with his family and other community residents. The settlement was named Tolstoy Farm and became an experimentation community living that was to build on the Phoenix experience. Gandhi was also influenced by Thoreau. He later on notes, "I read Thoreau ... I read Walden first ... and his ideas influenced me greatly. I adopted some of them and recommended the study of Thoreau to all my friends who were helping me in the cause of Indian Independence ... There is no doubt that Thoreau's ideas greatly influenced my movement in India".[2]

Hind Swaraj has an interesting history. It is the first definitive writing of Mahatma Gandhi that continues to evoke critical interest even today. This small book was written in Gujarati in November 1909 on the board of the ship Kildonan Castle during Gandhi's return trip from England to South Africa after an unproductive mission. It was written within 10 days, from November 13 to 22. The original manuscript was prepared by using the ship's stationary using both right and left hand. Forty pages out of the 275 pages were written with the left hand.

It was first published in the *Indian Opinion* in Natal and was soon banned by Government in India because it contained "matter declared to be seditious". Responding this ban, Gandhi published the English translation from Natal to show the innocuous nature of its contents. The ban was finally lifted on 21 December, 1938. A number of editions have been published thereafter. Interestingly, in 1924, an American edition, called "*Sermon on the Sea*", (Intro. by John Haynes Holmes) was published from Chicago. As stated by Gandhi himself: "I wrote the entire *Hind Swaraj* for my dear friend Dr. Pranjivan Mehta. All the arguments in the book are reproduced almost as it took place with him".[3]

In the *Foreword* of Gujarati edition of *Hind Swaraj* (22 November, 1909), Gandhi wrote about the motive to write this small text. In his words, "The only motive is to serve my country, to find out the truth and to follow it." In the English translation of the text further, he wrote, "My countrymen, therefore, believe that they should adopt modern civilization and modern method of violence to drive out English. *Hind Swaraj* has been written in order to show that they are following a suicidal policy, and that, if they would but revert to their glorious civilization, either English would adopt the latter and become Indianised or find their occupation in India is gone".[4]

Later on, writing in *Young India* on 7 May, 1925, Gandhi further stated the aims of the Pamphlet, "Let my friend [referring to V.D. Savarkar and colleagues] remember that Indian Home rule as the booklet itself states, was written in answer to the revolutionary's arguments and methods. It was an attempt to offer the revolutionary something infinitely superior to what he had, retaining the whole of the spirit of self-sacrifices and bravery that was to be found in the revolutionary".[5]

It is also interesting to note that *Hind Swaraj* was to become an iconic work of Indian nationalism, in fact, few in India noticed it when it was first published and it took a decade for it to become well known. In fact, Indian edition with a new foreword and a 'Note' by C. Rajagopalachari was first published in 1919. Later on, in 1921, Gandhi published the English edition under a modified new title: *Hind Swaraj* or Indian Home Rule. The decision to incorporate the Gujarati title into the English edition is noteworthy, suggesting as it does a desire to impress Gandhi's own terminology on the English language.

II

Gandhi's *Hind Swaraj* begins with the analysis of "home rule wave" and the role of Indian National Congress to advance it. In the first chapter of the book the Congress and its officials, Gandhi examines the debate on moderate and extremist views on nationalism. The chapter praises the role of moderates, mention the name of Gokhale as "pillar of home rule", Naoroji as "author of nationalism", Justice Budruddin Tyabji who "sowed the seed of home rule" in detail but does not mention 'extremists' like Tilak or Aurobindo or 'revolutionaries' like Savarkar. One may well argue; why did

Gandhi not mention the names of 'extremists' and 'revolutionaries', though he claimed his book was in response to the misguided youth? In fact, Gandhi's silence has strategic meaning; it is an indication of Gandhi's distance from them.

Positioning *Hind Swaraj* among Indian nationalist discourses was not an easy task. As we have noted in earlier chapters, Indian nationalist discourses had many shades; it was a reform, a renaissance, and a nationalist movement. It was also a movement for religious revivalism under the name of cultural/Hindu nationalism. Thus, against the colonialism in India, Gandhi realized that, on the one hand, there were 'modern' forward-looking movements, on the other; there were revivalist nostalgia and national re-purification programmes which were defining Indian nationalism. Moreover, he also realized that the privileged intelligentsia was tending to confuse culture with religion. Consequently, the dream of cultural revival was paving the way to religious revivalism; cultural nationalism was turning to religious purification. In short, Gandhi realized that in Indian nationalism the traditionalizing and the modernizing impulses existed simultaneously. Inside the Congress politics, such an incompatible discourse, reflected in the political break between moderates and extremists in December 1907 at Surat Congress mentioned earlier. This break had the cultural perspective; extremists were representing the nationalism grounded in Indian/ Hindu culture while moderates nationalism was based on the European model of civilizational progress.

Gandhi as a journalist as well as a well-informed politician was aware of this break and in his view, it was "not a good thing" for the country. He observes in the second chapter of *Hind Swaraj* titled as Partition of Bengal, "Our leaders are divided into two parties: the Moderates and the Extremists. These may be considered as the slow party and the impatient party. Some call the Moderates the timid party and the Extremists the bold party. All interpret the two words according to their preconceptions. This much is certain that there has arisen an enmity between the two. The one distrusts the other and imputes motives. At the time of the Surat Congress, there was almost a fight. I think that this division is not a good thing for the country, but I think also that such divisions will not last long. It all depends upon the leaders how long they will last".[6]

Even the cursory look of the text reveals that Gandhi defends moderates. Thus, the moderate leader Gokhale gets the important place in the text because of his "service to the nation". Comparing the role of moderates and the extremists Gandhi provides a hint to readers that the moderates are as "ancestor who has played out their roles", while the extremists are 'impatient' whose "rash action" may result in "self-destruction". The service and role of the moderates are well described through the example of Gokhale. Gandhi writes, "Professor Gokhale in order to prepare the nation embraced poverty and gave twenty years of his life. Even now, he is living in poverty." When the 'reader' challenges Gandhi, in regard to the service of Gokhale, Gandhi replied, "Moreover, how many Indians were there like Professor Gokhale, when he gave himself to Indian education? I believe that whatever Professor Gokhale does, he does with pure motives and with a view of serving India. His devotion to the Motherland is so great that he would give his life for it, if necessary".[7]

One of the major tasks that the text seems to accomplish is to reconcile the extremist and moderate factions of Indian nationalists. The 'reader' of the text, who represents extremist's views, shows the severe difference with the 'editor' [Gandhi] who is the defender of the moderates. When the 'reader' asks as to whether one should follow Gokhale in every aspect, Gandhi replies : "If we conscientiously differed from him, the learned Professor himself would advise us to follow the dictates of our conscience rather than him. Our chief purpose is not to decry his work, but to believe that he is infinitely greater than we are, and to feel assured that compared, with his work for India, ours is infinitesimal".[8]

For Gandhi, Gokhale occupies the place of a 'parent'. Thus, "What does it matter if he cannot run with us? A nation that is desirous of securing Home Rule cannot afford to despise its ancestors. We shall become useless if we lack respect for our elders. Only men with mature thoughts are capable of ruling themselves and not the hasty-tempered".[9]

One might note here how the Indian idioms as "place of a parent", "respect to elders", 'ancestors', "embracing poverty", "grand old man of India" are being used in the favour of moderates to exemplify their significance in historical context. On the other hand, he warns the 'reader' that not the "hasty-tempered" extremists but "only men with mature thought" like the moderate leaders are fit to rule themselves. In regard to the growing criticism against the moderates that they are pro-British, Gandhi replies, "It is a bad habit to say that another man's thoughts are bad and ours only are good, and that those holding different views from ours are the enemies of the country."

Gandhi's defence of the moderates and his efforts to convince the extremists in regard to moderates' role in spreading nationalism might be seen as his strategy to reconcile the differences between the moderates and extremists. Through an example, Gandhi attempts to illustrate that how the moderate and the extremist factions of nationalists are really interrelated. Indirectly the example also suggests that how extremist politics has reached its present stage because of the moderates' efforts. Gandhi argues, "Is Dadabhai less to be honoured because, in the exuberance of youth, we are prepared to go a step further? Are we, on that account, wiser than he? It is a mark of wisdom not to kick against the very step from which we have risen higher. The removal of a step from a staircase brings down the whole of it. When, out of infancy, we grow into youth, we do not despise infancy, but, on the contrary, we recall with affection the days of our childhood." As noted above, Gandhi was pained to see the division of moderates and extremists or the fall out of 1907 Surat Congress. Moreover, he recognized the division as a serious blow to growing nationalist movement; thus, reconciliation was inevitable, if India had to fight against the colonials.

Hind Swaraj also highlights the role of Congress in spreading nationalism in India. Gandhi points out, "The Congress brought together Indians from different parts of India, and enthused us with the idea of nationality".[10] Further, responding to the reader's critique of Congress as "Young India seems to ignore the Congress", he praises Congress for giving the "foretaste of Home Rule" that led the foundation of Home Rule in India. Gandhi again used reconciliatory strategy, as he knew that Congress was the only institution that was 'established' and had the capacity to 'forge' a national movement. Hence, he said "to deprive it of the honour is not proper, and for us to do so would not only be ungrateful, but retard the fulfilment of our object".[11]

Although Gandhi defends the moderates and gives credit to them to 'serve' India selflessly but he criticizes their methodology/ strategy in then existing context. Examining the importance of moderate's strategy of 'petitioning', he writes that although it serves as useful purpose as a means to educate the people, yet without the backing of force it is useless. In his words, "It is a fact beyond dispute that a petition, without the backing of force, is useless. However, the late Justice Ranade used to say that petitions served a useful purpose because they were a means of educating people. They give the latter an idea of their condition and warn the rulers. From this point of view, they are not altogether useless".[12] But Gandhi admits its limitation as a strategy in specific conditions, "A petition of an equal is a sign of courtesy; a petition from a slave is a symbol of his slavery. A petition backed by force is a petition from an equal and, when he transmits his demand in the form of a petition, it testifies to his nobility".[13]

In short, what Gandhi seems suggesting is that moderates had begun well, with good intention, but it was the time that they re-thought their goals, methods, and priorities. He showed possibilities in *Hind Swaraj* where there was an alternative to both "un-creative constitutionalism" of moderates and "cultural revivalism of extremists".

One of the important tasks that *Hind Swaraj* accomplishes is that it shows the limit of revolutionary nationalism. In Gandhi's views, this limit is both ethical and strategic. Particularly in chapter XV of *Hind Swaraj,* we may sense that Gandhi was well informed about the activities of secret societies and revolutionaries activities in India and abroad. For example, the chapter mentions "Dhingra's act" and "such other acts" in India. In fact, Gandhi wrote this whole text in response to the questions raised by Indian school of violence. He recalled in 1921, how on his 1909 visit to London he had come into contact with "every known anarchist" there and he wanted to write a book in answer to Indian school of violence. On the use of violence, he, later on, declares his position in his book, "I felt that violence was no remedy for India's ills and that her civilization required the use of a different and higher weapon for self-protection".[14]

Gandhi asserts that India's civilization is *different,* not only *different but higher,* thus it needs a higher weapon for self-protection. One might argue; on what basis did Gandhi consider Indian civilization was *different* and *higher*? What does Gandhi propose as an alternative for self-protection if not violence?

Gandhi is convinced that India's civilization is spiritual and superior, thus, it is different and higher than the Western civilization which is body centric and materialistic. It is on this basis he argues that India does not need European form of violent nationalism that European civilization offers. Instead, India needs its own form of nationalism that will reflect the true spiritual essence of Indian civilization. This is highlighted by a set of dialogue between the 'reader' and the 'editor' that confirms Gandhi's views on the relation between civilization and nationalism.

Inspired by Italy's nationalist Mazzini, the 'reader' summarizes the revolutionary's strategies to make India free from British, "At first, we shall assassinate a few Englishmen and strike terror; then, a few men who will have been armed will fight openly. We may have to lose a quarter of a million men, more or less, but we shall regain our land. We shall undertake guerrilla warfare, and defeat the English".[15] Gandhi responds it by saying, "that is to say, you want to make the holy land of India unholy". And "to arm India on a large scale is to Europeanize it. Then her condition will be just as pitiable as that of Europe". Moreover, "This means, in short, that India must accept European civilization, and if that is what we want, the best thing is that we have among us those who are so well trained in that civilization. We will then fight for a few rights, will get what we can and so pass our days. But the fact is that the Indian nation will not adopt arms, and it is well that it does not".[16] For Gandhi, such a thought to make India free by using violence was the impact of modern civilization. He said, "Do you not tremble to think of freeing India by assassinations… those who are intoxicated by the wretched modern civilization think these things"[17].

Gandhi also found that employing the violent method to overcome British rule is also strategically wrong. He writes, "Many people exult at the explosion of bombs. This only shows ignorance and lack of understanding. If all the British were to be killed, those who kill them would become the master of India, and as a result, India would continue in a state of slavery. The bombs with which the British will have been killed will fall on India after the British leave".[18]

One of the themes that emerge in *Hind Swaraj* in reference to Indian nationalism is the tone of reconciliation with the English people. Gandhi asserts the common perception. "That the English people are somewhat more selfish than others is true", however, "that does not prove that every Englishman is bad." For example, about Allen Octavian Hume who helped Indians to establish Indian National Congress, he tells the 'reader', "How can we forget what Mr. Hume has written, how he has lashed us into action, and with what effort he has awakened us, in order to achieve the objects of the Congress." His reconciliatory tone reachs to the optimum height when he says, "Sir William does not wish ill to India—that should be enough for us." His view behind this reconciliation is that "if we shun every Englishman as an enemy, Home Rule will be delayed. But if we are just to them, we shall receive their support in our progress towards the goal".[19]

The theme of nationalism also emerges in *Hind Swaraj* when the reader and the editor engage themselves over the question of the relation between nation and religion. We have seen in the earlier chapter that relation between nation and religion had become a crucial issue because of the extremists' politics. The extremists' politics had confused the culture with religion. On the line of the European form of nationalism, they thought that there should be one culture or religion for making a nation. In this connection, Gandhi had to face a blunt question from the 'reader' what he also considered "serious one, and yet, on careful consideration".[20] The 'reader' asked, ".... now we have Mohammedans, Parsis, and Christians. How can they be one nation? Hindus and Mohammedans are old enemies. Our very proverbs prove it. Mohammedans turn to the West for worship, whilst Hindus turn to the East. The former look down on the Hindus as idolaters. The Hindus worship the cow, the Mohammedans kill her. The Hindus believe in the doctrine of non-killing, the Mohammedans do not. We thus meet with differences at every step. How can India be one nation?"[21]

Gandhi recognizes the factual differences between Hindu and Muslims but he does not consider them serious enough to prevent the growth of nationalism. He argues that "India cannot cease to be one nation because people belonging to different religions"[22].

Gandhi argues that the difference between Hindu and Muslim has been created by British colonials. When the 'reader' argues that "Hindus and Mohammedans are old enemies" and there is an "inborn enmity" between Hindu and Muslim, Gandhi replies, "that phrase has been invented by our mutual enemy". By coining "mutual enemy" Gandhi is referring to the British. Taking help from the historical narratives and using instrumental reasoning, he argues that although "Hindu and Muslim fought against each other" but "they have long since ceased to fight". Not only this but "the Hindu flourished under Moslem sovereigns, and Moslims under Hindu" as well as they "recognized that mutual fighting will be suicidal" therefore "decided to live in peace." Further, Gandhi accuses the British of creating such a problem as "with the English advent the quarrels recommenced".[23]

Gandhi also accuses that the enmity between Hindu and Muslin have also been created by selfish and religious teachers. It is also not that Hindu are non-violent and Muslims are violent as propagated by many. He notes "these thoughts are put into our minds by selfish and false religious teachers. The English put the finishing touch".[24] For Gandhi, institutional religion was not and could not be the basis of 'nation' and 'nationalism' in India. For Gandhi religion was a personal matter—as a quest for liberation and in this connection, he asserted, "In reality, there are as many religions as there are individuals." But "those who are conscious of the spirit of nationality do not interfere with one another's religion. If they do they are not fit for the nation".[25]

Challenging the ideologies of such nationalists whose nationalism was based on institutionalized religion as Hinduism Gandhi stated, "If the Hindus believe that India should be peopled only by Hindus, they are living in dreamland".[26] Furthermore, he asserted, "In no part of the world are one nationality and one religion synonymous terms: nor has it ever been so in India".[27] For him, the presence of Muslims and Christians, Sikhs, and Parsis did not put the challenge to Indian culture but rather they were manifesting their accommodative potential in Indian culture. Gandhi writes, "The Hindu, the Mahomedans, the Parsees and the Christians who have made India their country are fellow country-men and they will have to live in unity only for their own interest".[28] Further, "India cannot cease to be one nation because people belonging to different religions live in it".[29] Further, Gandhi offers a realistic argument stating that it was natural that Hindu and Muslim fought as "two brothers living together often do so" but when they fought they certainly did not "engage counsel and to resort to English or any law courts".[30]

In short, Gandhi's position in respect to the relation between the nation and the religion goes beyond extremists and moderates views on it. Gandhi does not identify the nation with the sociological formation of religion as extremists were attempting. On the other hand, Gandhi was also not neutral on the issue of religion in national life like moderates. In fact, Gandhi recognizes religion as ethics on which Indian nationalism could be erected.

Discussion on nationalism in *Hind Swaraj* also emerges when the reader and the editor argue over the issue of India as a nation and type of *Swaraj* that has to be achieved. Let us first see how *Hind Swaraj* describes India as a nation. The text makes a striking argument that India was made a 'nation' before the British came. Gandhi describes, in detail, how India was a nation much before the British came to India in spite of many differences. He writes, "I do not wish to suggest that because we were one nation we had no differences, but it is submitted that *our leading men* travelled throughout India either on foot or in bullock-carts. They learned one another's languages and there was no aloofness between them. What do you think could have been the intention of those *farseeing ancestors of ours* who established *Setubandha* (Rameshwaram) in the South, Jagannath in the East and Hardwar in the North as places of pilgrimage? You will admit they were no fools. They knew that worship of God could have been performed just as well at home. They taught us that those whose hearts were aglow with righteousness had the Ganges in their own homes. But they saw that India was *one undivided land* so made by nature. They, therefore, argued that it must be one nation. Arguing thus, they established holy places in various parts of India and fired the people with an *idea of nationality* in a manner unknown in other parts of the world. And we Indians are one as no two Englishmen are. Only you and I and others who consider ourselves civilized and superior persons imagine that we are many nations".[31]

Here, Gandhi's stresses upon the activities of those whom he calls "our leading man" or "the foreseeing ancestors of ours". By these, he is referring to the *acharyas* of ancient Indian culture. These individuals, he points out, travelled the length and breadth of India "either on foot or on bullock carts," and their activities had the effect of creating a common consciousness. It enabled them to come to know the people among whom they moved and to establish among them a sense of community. One very surprising thing in this dialogue is that Gandhi credits saint/learned person for being India's "nation builder". It is worth mentioning that he does not mention the role of kings and emperors in the whole text. In fact, Gandhi seems highly critical of the role of *rajas* and *maharajas* in history. On the contrary, there "tyranny", he says "was greater than that of English".[32] On the other hand, by stating that, "...they saw that India was *one undivided land* so made by nature. They, therefore, argued that it must be one nation", Gandhi makes a geographical argument that India has been a nation like other modern nation for which a territory is needed. Thus for him, India not only culturally but geographically too has been a nation. Thus, for Gandhi India has been a nation because of "one undivided India", "one thought", "same mode of life", and "faculty of assimilation". On the other hand, Gandhi in his text severely criticizes the 'modern' European notion of the nation which is, according to him, is based on violence or "brute force". In this connection, one may note; Gandhi defines modernity in *Hind Swaraj,* not as an objective phenomenon but a deluded state of mind characterized by selfishness and violence. Thus, through a discursive analysis, Gandhi argues that colonial imagination of India that represents itself as 'modern' is out of tune with the spirit of Indian traditions and its vision of India as a nation. On the contrary, he suggests that the true nationhood is impossible under the condition of modernity. Assuming a link between the virtues of non-violence, tolerance, morality and "true and genuine nationhood" what India as a nation represents, Gandhi argues 'modern' but morally underdeveloped European countries have not yet earned the distinction of being true nations. Extending this argument, he persistently calls in *Hind Swaraj* to "drive out modern civilization in order to return India to its nation-bestowing spiritual essence".[33] It is this link that provides the justification to his rejection of the "suicidal policies" of Indian radical nationalists who have mistakenly adopted "modern civilization and modern methods of violence to drive out the English".[34] In accordance with the idea of the nation as *Praja,* Gandhi's home-rule seems to depend upon the transformation of modernity by means of a different type of nationalism, which according to him should not be 'fixed' in modern civilization and its reliance on violence. The political purpose of such a nationalism which Gandhi provides was not to give an another modern nation-state like European nation-state but to build an exemplary nation guided by its own pre-modern tradition of performing duty and observing morality.

It is here the notion of *Swaraj* can be comprehended in relation to nationalism. *Hind Swaraj* claims, "Real Home Rule is self-rule or self-control".[35] But what is the true nature of Gandhi's *Swaraj*? In fact, Gandhi accepts the difficulty of the notion of *Swaraj* as there were many definitions and connotations which were related to this term. Discussing with the Reader in the chapter IV of the text titled as "What is *Swaraj*?", Gandhi accepts, "It is difficult for me to understand the true nature of *Swaraj*".[36] It seems that throughout the text *Swaraj* is a working hypothesis for Gandhi, which he mends time to time according to the context and discussion with the 'reader'. In the final paragraph of *Hind Swaraj*, Gandhi confesses, "we have used this term '*Swaraj*' without understanding its real significance". And "I have endeavoured to explain it as I understand it".[37] The debate on the nature and meaning of *Swaraj* between the 'reader' and the 'editor' also exposes the ideological limitation of Indian nationalists' consciousness. Gandhi argues that *Swaraj* defined only in terms of anti-colonial discourse, shows what Indian nationalist are against, but not what they are for. Consequently, Gandhi views the agenda of both the moderates and extremists factions of nationalists as seeking merely "English rule without the Englishman". He writes, "You want the tiger's nature, but not the tiger; that is to say, you would make India English and when it becomes English, it will be called not Hindustan but Englishtan. This is not the *Swaraj* that I want".[38]

The term 'English rule' is noteworthy here, as it was based on the idea of 'other' and 'difference'. Thus, 'English rule' in India 'without English' means retaining or constructing the 'other' and 'difference' within India by the Indians rulers, henceforth creating an "internal colonization" within India. Second, this statement also shows that Gandhi's view of nationalism, what he envisions in *Swaraj*, is entirely different from the conventional political nationalism that moderates and extremists envisioned.

Gandhi's version of *Swaraj* and its corresponding nationalism again emerges in the text when the editor and reader discuss the role of the national elite.

In fact, how the emerging Indian elite might achieve this *Swaraj* became the focus of the final argument in *Hind Swaraj*. Moreover, this argument is introduced with great artistic flair. "What will you say to the nation?" the 'reader' asks. The 'editor' responds with a question, "Who is the nation?" It is as if Gandhi wanted to emphasize the point that the elite were the nation in a special sense. If up to the last chapter Gandhi had been talking of nation in general sense as *Praja* then, in the concluding chapter, he took it in the narrower sense. Through the mouth of the 'reader' he conveyed this narrower meaning: "For our purposes it is the nation that you and I have been thinking of, that is those of us who are affected by European civilization, and who are eager to have Home Rule".[39]

Thus, *Hind Swaraj* submits the thesis that nationals tasks lay before the national elite. The most important corollary to this Gandhian theorem is that the fate of India as a nation depends on the moral character of the Indian professional classes, i.e. the character of its lawyers, doctors, and wealthy. It is interesting to note that Gandhi put a vehement critique of this professional in Chapters XI and XII of his text. Gandhi laments that professional classes, who exerts tremendous influence on the general masses, are hypnotized by greed and are victims of caste, creed and status considerations, which affected the unity and integrity of the nation.

One might notice here a striking resemblance between Gandhi's idea to that of Plato who said there was a link between the health of the soul and the health of the city, and the maintenance of the health of the city depends, in practical terms, on the moral character of the 'guardian' class. Similarly, Gandhi suggests that national elites as the 'guardians' must undergo a moral transformation and serve others. Here, Gandhi deconstructs the binary opposition of professional life and personal life and suggests that liberation of the nation depends upon the replacement of greed, power, and wealth by selfless love and service to others.

To bring about this mental transformation of the Indian elite, Gandhi proposes 19 points in the final chapter of *Hind Swaraj*. Of the 19 points, three were addressed to doctors, four to lawyers, and the rest to what Gandhi calls 'wealthy'. Gandhi thought that only such moral transformation could give Indian elite the necessary moral strength essential for *Swaraj*.

It needs to be mentioned that in Gandhi's analysis it is this lack of "moral strength" that has made India the subject nation under the British. In the chapter, "Why India was Lost", he wrote a long passage with many supportive arguments,

> "The English have not taken India; we have given it to them. They are not in India because of their strength, but because we keep them. Let us now see whether these propositions can be sustained. They came to our country originally for purposes of trade. Recall the Company Bahadur. Who made it Bahadur? They had not the slightest intention at the time of establishing a kingdom. Who assisted the Company's officers'? Who was tempted at the sight of their silver? Who bought their goods? History testifies that we did all this...when our Princes fought among themselves; they sought the assistance of Company Bahadur. That corporation was versed alike in commerce and war. It was unhampered by questions of morality. Its object was to increase its commerce and to make money. It accepted our assistance and increased the number of its warehouses. To protect the latter it employed an army which was utilized by us also. Is it not then useless to blame the English for what we did at that time?.... Hence, it is truer to say that we gave India to the English than that India was lost".[40]

Thus, it was the *moral failure on parts of Indian* that led to the conquest of India. In other words, Gandhi rejected those arguments that viewed that the backwardness or lack of modernity in Indian culture had made India subject nation.

Moreover, the editor argues that many Indians have accepted foreign rule for the purely materialistic reason. "We keep the English in India for our base self-interest. We like their commerce; they please us by their subtle methods and get what they want from us. To blame them for this is to perpetuate their power".[41] Gandhi here seems following Tolstoy's argument, who asserted in "Letter to the Hindu" that only possible explanation for the strange phenomenon of 30,000 "rather weak and ill looking" Britons enslaving 200 million of 'vigorous, clever, strong, and freedom loving people' was that Indian had to come to embrace the materialist values of their colonizers.[42]

Hence, Gandhi's all political effort to achieve Indian "home rule" i.e., *Swaraj* goes together with a rigorous programme of moral transformation of the individual. As Chatterjee (1986) points out, "Gandhi's entire political project of national liberation can, therefore, be understood as predicated upon his commitment to identify, address, and rectify the moral failure on the part of modern Indians".[43]

Thus, for Gandhi, nationalism is more a moral category than political. His argument is that Indians have handed over control of their nation to the foreign exponents of a materialistic lifestyle and have turned into timid sycophants and willing servants of the empire. Thus, they themselves prove to the world that they are morally "unfit to serve the country". It is not surprising the 'editor' never hesitates to drive his stern message to his fellow countrymen that they have become lazy and 'effeminate'.

Suppose Indians become morally fit for the nation, yet one of the significant questions remained unanswered as to how can Indians overcome of the British rule? Given that violence is ethically wrong and strategically imperfect then what is Gandhi's solution? For Gandhi, answer lies in the new language of resistance, what he calls Passive resistance in his text. It is noteworthy that Gandhi, later on, changed the term passive résistance to *Satyagraha*. Let us see how passive resistance can be alternative to revolutionary violence in overcoming British rule in India. The crux of passive resistance is that ruling is possible only if ruled obeys the ruler. In other words, British can govern Indians so long Indians obey the laws of British. How can it be operated in practice?

Gandhi writes, "Passive resistance is a method of securing rights by personal suffering; it is the reverse of resistance by arms. When I refuse to do a thing that is repugnant to my conscience, I use soul-force. For instance, the Government of the day has passed a law, which is applicable to me. I do not like it. If by using violence I, force the Government to repeal the law, I am employing what may be termed body force. If I do not obey the law and accept the penalty for its breach, I use soul-force. It involves the sacrifice of self".[44]

It needs to be pointed out that Passive resistance depends upon the distinction between "manmade laws" and "higher laws".[45] Moreover, Gandhi challenges the new notion of political obedience as 'effeminate' if it goes against one's own conscience. In his view, such thing is against the 'manhood' and 'religion' that means 'slavery'. Further 'manmade laws are not binding on him' who fears only God.[46]

Another important aspect of Gandhi's definition of Passive resistance or *Satyagraha* is that it makes a difference between 'force' and 'violence'. In *Hind Swaraj*, Gandhi distinguishes between the two types of forces. First, according to him, is the force of arms or "force of violence". And second is the force of soul or love or force of non-violence or *Satyagraha*. It might be noted, Gandhi does not reject the importance of force but it is the type of force, which is important for him. One may recall here how he criticized the moderates' practice of petitioning in Indian freedom struggle arguing that, "It is a fact beyond dispute that a petition, without the backing of *force* is useless".[47]

Then, which type of force did Gandhi suggest? Trying to define the force, Gandhi writes, "If you do not concede our demand, we shall be no longer your petitioners. You can govern us only so long as we remain the governed; we shall no longer have any dealings with you. The force implied in this may be described as love-force, soul-force, or, more popularly but less accurately, passive resistance. This force is indestructible".[48] It is significant to note that in *Hind Swaraj* Gandhi writes on *Satyagraha* in the context of colonial rule and his assertion that "You can govern us only so long as we remain the governed" has a serious implication. As one may note, it proposes another way to look at the dynamics of power inherent in the power structure comprised by the governing and the governed. Then it attempts to debase the power structure and making governing impossible through the disobedience of governed. Here, it should also be noted that *Satyagraha* was not only a political theory or an ideological move but it was a politically tested device that had the South African background. Discussion in the *Hind Swaraj* also tries to make *Satyagraha* central in the nationalist mobilization against British rule in India also.

Satyagraha, for Gandhi, is a forceful way of engaging in non-violent struggle. As a force both "on and for truth", Gandhi's *Satyagraha* requires an absolute commitment to struggle. Obviously, everything hinges on precise nature of the kind of force involved in *Satyagraha*. However, if the truth is something that must be fought over, why Gandhi rule out the use of violence *a priori*? Gandhi writes, "To use brute force, to use gunpowder, is contrary to passive resistance, for it means that we want our opponent to do by force that which we desire but he does not.

And if such a use of force is justifiable surely he is entitled to do likewise by us. And so we should never come to an agreement. We may simply fancy, like the blind horse moving in a circle round a mill, that we are making progress".[49]

But why one should use soul force in *Satyagraha*? Gandhi's reply is ethical and pragmatic, "No man can claim that he is absolutely in the right or that particular thing is wrong because he thinks so, but it is wrong for him so long as that is his deliberate judgement. It is, therefore, meet that he should not do that which he knows to be wrong, and suffer the consequence whatever it may be. This is the key to the use of soul-force."

Moreover, Gandhi also believes, as discussed above, that resorting to violence is also politically and strategically foolish. Although, it is difficult to separate what is moral and what is practical in Gandhi's *Satyagraha,* but Gandhi was well aware that adopting "methods of violence to drive out the English" would be a "suicidal policy".[50] In the *Hind Swaraj* there are numerous examples that suggest "violence begets violence"; hence, *Satyagraha* based on non-violence is the best answer to fighting against the British colonialism in India.

As *Satyagraha* is based on love force, Gandhi shows its strategic significance. He observes in *Hind Swaraj*, "*Satyagraha* is an all-sided sword; it can be used anyhow; it blesses him who uses it and him against whom it is used".[51] However, he argues that to become *Satyagrahi* one needs to "control over the mind". And when it is attained, Gandhi notes "man is free like the king of the forest, and his very glance withers enemy".[52]

Thus, on the discourse of nationalism, we notice that *Hind Swaraj* facilitates the possibility of making alliances across the varieties of social and political interests. In *Hind Swaraj* Gandhi attempts to provide an authentic ideological basis of Indian nationalism. Gandhi tried to resolve simultaneously the issue of social reform without allowing the modern colonial State to violate India's civilizational 'core' as well as he made efforts to solve the problem of social divisions prevalent within Indian elite. He also tackled another crucial problem. Moderates politics based on elite constitutionalism had reached to the dead end and Gandhi tried to offer new rules of engagement as a form of political negotiation with the colonial State. Moreover, Gandhi as an experienced political manager with *Satyagraha* experience in South Africa presented a new discourse that was capable of passing through the idioms of modern politics to 'masses' to whom modern political concepts were unfamiliar. By emphasizing the people, their needs, and aspirations, he at one stroke cut through the Gokhale/Tilak or the Rationalism/Tradition, or the Reform/Revival antitheses. Gandhi's reconciliatory strategies had the definite outcome. For conservative and progressive, his discourse suggested a way forward out of their ideological deadlock and merit in mass mobilization. His discourse, not only, gave the British a strong response to their critique of Indian society but a viable reason for giving India its independence. To the traditional authorities, it demonstrated that social reform could be made without loss of cultural identity. To the revolutionary, the *Hind Swaraj* suggested an alternative to Constitutional politics on a basis other than inefficient and ultimately incidental acts of revolutionary violence. Finally, it appealed to the groups hitherto excluded, in order to make them understand and identify the language of nationalism. In sum, Gandhi's *Hind Swaraj's* ultimate task was to tackle all those factors, which excluded the transition from an elite Constitutional field to the mass field of political participation. But, such a transition was difficult as there was the limited scope of "public sphere" in which such a politics could be located. In this connection, the political lessons from South Africa proved useful as he recognized that to adequately contest the colonial politics, it was essential to go beyond the constitutional field where political counter takes place of colonizer terms. Not strange, in the *Hind Swaraj* Gandhi exposed the wider field of power where the terms of engagement favoures the nationalists. Thus, Gandhi pioneered his own brand of extra-constitutional politics, writing a new language of resistance, by fully utilizing the public sphere available to him. It is in South Africa where Gandhi sharpened his sense of publicity and journalistic skill that made him a distinct modern politician, keenly aware that medium was as important as the message.

Notes and References

1. Gandhi, M.K., 1927. *An Autobiography or My Experiments With Truth.* Ahmedabad: Navajivan, pp. 211-212.

2. Webb Miller. 1938. *I Found No Peace*, New York: Garden City, p. 238.
3. *CWMG*, Vol. 71, p. 238.
4. *See* Parel, A.J., 1997, *Hind Swaraj and Other Writings*. New Delhi: Foundation Books, pp. xiv-xvi.
5. *CWMG*, Vol. 71, p. 238.
6. Gandhi, M.K., 2008. *Hind Swaraj or Indian Home Rule*, Ahmedabad: Navajivan, pp. 23-24.
7. *Ibid.*, pp. 19-20.
8. *Ibid.*, p. 20.
9. *Ibid.*
10. *Ibid.* p. 21.
11. *Ibid.*
12. *Ibid.*, p. 65.
13. *Ibid.*
14. *CWMG*, 19:277.
15. *Op. cit.*, *Hind Swaraj*, p. 59.
16. *Ibid.*, p. 59.
17. *Ibid.*
18. *CWMG*, 8, p. 374
19. *Hind Swaraj*, p. 20.
20. *Ibid.*
21. *Ibid.*, p. 41.
22. *Ibid.*, pp. 42-43.
23. *Ibid.*, p. 43.
24. *Ibid.*, p. 45.
25. *Ibid.*, p. 43.
26. *Ibid.*
27. *Ibid.*
28. *Ibid.*
29. *Ibid.*
30. *Ibid.*, p. 47.
31. *Ibid.*, p. 76.
32. *Ibid.*, p. 59.
33. *Ibid.*, p. 80.
34. *Op. cit.*, Parel, p. 7.
35. *Op. cit.*, *Hind Swaraj*, p. 90.
36. *Ibid.*, p. 27.
37. *Ibid.*, p. 86.
38. *Ibid.*, p. 26.
39. *Ibid.*, p. 87.
40. *Ibid.*, p. 37.
41. *Ibid.*, pp. 35-36.
42. *See* Chadha, Yogesh, 1999. *Gandhi: A Life*. New York: John Wiley & Sons, p. 156.

43. Chatterjee, Parth. 1986. *Nationalist Thought and the Colonial World: A Derivative Discourses?* London: Zed Books, p. 85.
44. *Op. cit., Hind Swaraj*, p. 69.
45. *Ibid.*
46. *Ibid.*, p. 70.
47. *Ibid.*, p. 65.
48. *Ibid.*
49. *Ibid.*, p. 70.
50. *Ibid.*, p. 69.
51. *Ibid.*, p. 71.
52. *Ibid.*

6

Bipin Chandra Pal's The Spirit of Indian Nationalism (1910)

The Spirit of Indian Nationalism, a long essay containing 58 pages, was written by Bipin Chandra Pal (1858-1932) in 1910.[1] The essay is set in the background of the *Swadeshi* movement and growing extremist nationalism in India. The central project that the text seems to accomplish is to provide the philosophical and cultural justification to the emerging extremist nationalism in India and put a vehement criticism of moderate politics carried out by Indian National Congress since 1885. Pal also presents a new reading of *Swadeshi* Movement in his text and claims that after *Swadeshi* movement nationalism in India became at once the name of a "common ideal, a common purpose, one general spirit, and impulse that moved the classes and the masses alike in more than one Indian province". Further, in his text, he also points out to the goal of "national destiny" that was to be achieved by Indian 'nationalists' through the methods of Boycott. He also argues that the method of Boycott was more than the economic and political significance *generally perceived.* Further, what India needed was, in his view, to train people on "national lines" to realize the "national destiny". Pal in his text also calls for "National Civil Volunteering" and a "new manhood" in national life, not for narrow and selfish interest but to make "special contribution in culture and character to the larger life of universal humanity".

Author's clear stand on extremist nationalism and its justification may be understood from the fact that along with Lala Lajpat Rai (1865-1928) and Bal Gangadhar Tilak (1856-1920) he belonged to the famous Lal, Bal and Pal trio that was associated with revolutionary activities in India. The trio was termed as 'extremists' as they stood for the ideal of *Swaraj* or complete political freedom to be achieved through courage, self-help, and self-sacrifice. The trio also advocated radical means to get their message across to the British, like boycotting British manufactured goods, burning Western clothes made in the mills of Manchester or strikes and lockouts of British owned businesses and industrial concerns. During the first decade of the twentieth century, along with Aurobindo Ghosh, Pal was also recognized as the chief exponents of a new national movement revolving around the ideals of *Purna Swaraj, Swadeshi,* and National education. For more than twenty years, he remained a major figure in the Indian nationalist movement, a leader of the extremist wing of the Congress party who advocated a more militant line against British Imperialism. An active politician, he also used his pen to great effect in furthering the nationalist cause. Looking his contribution to Indian freedom movement, it is not surprising, he was called "mightiest prophets of Indian Nationalism" by Sri Aurobindo, and "father of revolutionary thought" by many Indian nationalists.

I

Bipin Chandra Pal was born on 7th November, 1858 in Poil Village, Habiganj District, now a part of Bangladesh, in a wealthy Hindu Vaishnava family. The only son of his parents, Bipin Chandra Pal took his early education from a Maulvi in Sylhet town. He had his formal education at Sylhet Government High School from where he passed the Entrance Examination. In 1875, he was admitted to Presidency College in Calcutta but unfortunately could not complete his education and started his career as a headmaster. In the later years, while Bipin was working as a librarian in Calcutta public library he met many political leaders like Shivnath Shastri, S.N. Banerjee, and B.K. Goswami. He was influenced to quit teaching and start up a career in politics. He was further inspired by the work, philosophy, spiritual ideas and patriotism of Bal Gangadhar Tilak, Lala Lajpat Rai and Sri Aurobindo. Being highly influenced and inspired by all these political leaders, Bipin decided to devote himself to the freedom struggle. He also went to England to study comparative ideology in 1898. In a span of one year he returned to India and since then he started preaching local Indians with the idea of *Swaraj*. Being a good journalist and orator he always used articles, speeches and other write-ups to spread nationalism, humanity and social awareness and the need for complete independence. Pal had "never say die" attitude and with great courage, he participated in Bombay session of Indian National Congress in 1904, Partition of Bengal in 1905, *Swadeshi* Movement, Non-Cooperation Movement and Bengal Pact in 1923.[2]

In his youth, Bipin Chandra Pal was inspired by his political *Guru*, Surendra Nath Banerjee. He started taking interest in politics in the early eighties of the nineteenth century. He shared the views of the Moderate leaders of the Congress. There was a certain change in him during 1904, due to the official announcement that Bengal was going to be partitioned. There was an anti-partition agitation which cropped up against the decision of the government. Bipin Chandra like a true leader flung himself into the movement. He laid stress on the futility of the old methods of agitation through prayers, petitions, and protests and became the chief propagator of the *Swadeshi* Movement.

As far as his political thinking is concerned, even though he understood the positive aspects of Empire as a "great idea", he was radical in his approach. At the time of B.G. Tilak's arrest and government repression in 1907, he left for England, where he was briefly associated with the radical India House and founded the *Swaraj* journal. However, political repercussions in the wake of Curson Wyllie's assassination in 1909 by Madanlal Dhingra lead to the collapse of this publication, driving Pal to penury and mental collapse in London. In the aftermath, he totally moved away from his 'extremist' phase and even nationalism, as he contemplated an association of free nations as the great federal-idea. His plea for a transcendence to a broader entity than nation derived from the notion of the sociability of human beings, which he thought would create a common bond between nations.

It is important to note that he was among the first to criticize Gandhi or the "Gandhi cult" since it "sought to replace the present government by no government or by the priestly autocracy of the Mahatma." His criticism of Gandhi was persistent since the arrival of Gandhi in India but it became open in 1921 session of the Indian National Congress. In his presidential speech, he mentioned that Gandhi's ideas were based on magic rather than logic. He told, "You wanted magic. I tried to give you logic. But logic is in bad odour when the popular mind is excited. You wanted *mantaram*, I am not a *Rishi* and cannot give *Mantaram*... I have never spoken a half-truth when I know the truth... I have never tried to lead people in faith blind-folded." Pal also criticized Gandhi for his priestly, pontifical tendencies' and his alliance with pan-Islamism during the *Khilafat* movement. This led to Pal's eclipse from political life from 1922 till his death in 1932 under conditions of abject poverty. Comparing Gandhi with Leo Tolstoy during the year he died, Pal noted that Tolstoy "was an honest philosophical anarchist" while Gandhi was "a papal autocrat" firm and ethically grounded. Not only did he perceive the "Congress Babel" in terms of its shortsightedness in late 1920s or, Congress as an instance of repudiating debt's folly, composed of a generation "that knows no Joseph", Pal's critical comments should be located in context, since nobody can jump out of his skin of time. An estimation of Bipin Chandra Pal's entire corpus and the depth of his published writing cannot produce a fair idea or provide due justice if that is produced with the benefit of post-Independence hindsight. Though there are many articles and books written about him from India and Europe, most of which is not hagiographical, his "pen played not an inconsiderable part in the political and social ferments that have stirred the altars of Indian life", as the Earl of Ronaldshay wrote in 1925, what Nehru said in a speech during Pal's birth centenary in 1958 surmises "a great man who functioned on a high level on both religious and political planes opens a gate for enquiring this high-minded yet anomalous persona".

What was unique with Pal was his fierce Journalism and oration. A journalist himself, Pal used his profession in spreading patriotic feelings and social awareness. He had also published a lot of journals, weekly and books to spread nationalism and the idea of *Swaraj*. Most prominent books of Pal include Indian Nationalism, Nationality and Empire, *Swaraj* and the Present Situation, The Basis of Social Reform, The Soul of India, The New Spirit and Studies in Hinduism. He was the editor of the '*Democrat*', the '*Independent*' and many other journals and newspapers. "*Paridarsak*" (1886—Bengali weekly), "*New India*" (1902—English weekly) and "*Bande Mataram*" (1906—Bengali daily) and "*Swaraj*" are some of the prominent journals started by him.

Pal's writings are highly contextual and it is journalistic in nature. His aim seems to make people aware of the political happenings of the country and take a particular position. It is factual and concrete and away from the emotional appeal.

II

The book *The Spirit of Indian Nationalism* includes six essays first one with the same title besides other essays titled as Boycott Movement, The Partition of Bengal, National education, The national volunteers and Brief sketch of the Leaders of Nationalist Movement of Bengal. The book was published by The Hind Nationalist Agency, West Kensington, London in 1910. The book includes the preface by the author that runs into four pages besides the introduction of the book by W.T. Stead that runs into next four pages in the first edition.

As discussed, *The Spirit of Indian Nationalism* (1910) was written in the background of the ideology of the *Swadeshi* movement and growing nationalism in India. In the preface of the book *The Spirit of Indian Nationalism* (1910) Pal writes that "The object of this book is to help both the people and the Government in India to work out a peaceful settlement of the issues that face them, for in such a settlement lies the highest good of both".[3] In the preface he also mentions that "What the situation really demands are neither concessions nor repressions, but a larger synthesis which will harmonise, under a broad and universal philosophy of life, the conflicting ideals and cultures that have come face to face in modern India. The real work in India is thus not of the mere politician or publicist, be he Indian or British, but of the philosopher and statesman".[4]

In the preface, Pal also quotes Mr. Chirol who had started writing a series of Article in "The Times" with the title "The Indian Unrest" before the publication of the book. Pal's emphasis on Chirol's claim is significant as Chirol's raises the very important question as to what is the real nature of the problem of India. Pal writes, "Mr. Chirol admits that the present upheaval in India is essentially social and religious. It is really due to a keen conflict of two different types of civilisations".[5] Pal's response is very quick and strategic, he writes "If this be true, then it will have to be admitted that a conflict of ethical and spiritual ideals can never be overcome by any sort of political remedies".[6] One may note that it is the binary of two domains spiritual and material/political that serves as a framework in which Pal sets his work.

The text is a compilation of articles that justifies extremists' nationalism in India. Pal begins his text with an assertion that nationalism is a "new cry" and a "new school" in Indian politics. He asserts that this new school "came first into prominence in 1905, after the partition of Bengal into two administrative divisions, against the wishes of the people, and the declaration of a boycott of British goods, by their leaders, as a practical protest against that wanton outrage". He argues that this school proclaimed absolute autonomy as its ultimate ideal, and self-help and self-reliance as its methods.

Pal is referring here to *Swadeshi* movement and its significance in Indian politics. He claims that after *Swadeshi* movement nationalism became at once the name of a "common ideal, a common purpose, one general spirit and impulse that moved the classes and the masses alike in more than one Indian province".

Pal points out to the goal of "national destiny" that was to be achieved by nationalists through the methods of Boycott. In his view, this method was more than the economic and political significance. It was also aimed to train people on 'national lines' to realize the "national destiny". Pal tells us about the method of Nationalist school that included National Civil Volunteering. It aimed to impart a healthy civic training to the people in regard to rural sanitation, economic or medical relief, popular education, preventive police duties, settlement of civil and non-cognisable criminal disputes by means of arbitration committees etc. Pal argues that ......" The end pursued by these means was essentially moral. The object was to create in the community an interest larger and higher than the narrow and more or less selfish interest of personal preferment or family advancement."[7] These methods and works had higher objective. Pal writes that "it was really to develop a new manhood in the country, realising itself through the self-controlled activities of the national life, and gradually, through that life, making its special contributions in culture and character to the larger life of universal humanity".[8]

He claims that "no movement in any country had perhaps been inspired with a loftier ideal than this, or had tried to follow more peaceful methods for working out the political emancipation of a subject people".

Pal mentions that success of *Swadeshi* movement revealed before the British that secret of India lies in India's moral power, not in its physical power. Pal argues that *Swadeshi* movement also pointed out that the British conquered India by "sheer good luck" and they rule here through 'hypnotism'. In his words, "their authority rests entirely upon the willing acquiescence of the people in their rule and not upon the 75,000 British soldiers in the country. A hundred times that number would not be sufficient, as an army of occupation, in a continent about half as large as Europe, and with a population counting fully one-fifth of the known human race. The British did not conquer India by the sword, and they do not rule there now on the authority of the sword. They acquired the country by sheer good luck, they rule it through hypnotism. But however peaceful the new methods might be, they struck directly against this hypnotic spell".[9] To much extent Pal's argument is similar to Gandhi who wrote in the *Hind Swaraj* that British have not conquered India, we have given it to them. Pal also recognizes in the text that the method of violence or terror by Indians would be the strategic failure and only a peaceful propaganda, keeping itself within the limits of the law, and slowly quickening and organizing the latent moral and spiritual forces of the people, would be absolutely irresistible.

After describing *Swadeshi* movement Pal tells us about the ultimate ideal of Indian nationalism. He writes, "......*Swaraj* is still the ultimate ideal of Indian Nationalism. It is the far-off object of the Nationalist Movement. It does imply absolute autonomy. But no one can definitely forecast what will be the practical settlement of this claim, and in what position Great Britain may finally stand in relation to a self-governing India".[10]

Elaborating it he argues "....It presented an intelligible ideal, that of swaraj or national autonomy; and prescribed a definite and practical method which every man, and even every woman, might at once adopt in his or her own sphere of life, for the furtherance of this ideal, the method, namely of self-help and passive resistance".[11]

On the other hand, Pal asserts the nature of *Swadeshi* movement. In his view, British Government had failed to understand this movement and its strength. Further, the *Swadeshi* movement was not only an independent political event as British viewed it, but, it was really the continuation of the process of social evolution in India. Pal also notes that "the new Nationalist Movement was not a class movement" and it integrated "classes and masses" to the Nationalist platforms in which women also took part actively. He also makes a contrast between the Congress propaganda and new nationalist movement. "The Congress propaganda practically failed to draw the masses, first because it was conducted mainly in a foreign tongue; next, because its ideas and ideals had no reference to the thoughts and traditions of the people, were not expressed in the terms of national history and literature; and, lastly and chiefly, because it had no religious reference or inspiration in it. The failure of the Congress was entirely due to its pronounced secular character."

It is interesting to analyze Pal's argument here. He mentions that the failure of the Congress was entirely due to its pronounced secular character. As we may observe, secular is understood here in the terms of "foreign tongue", "no reference to the thoughts and traditions of the people", "no religious reference or inspiration". This shows Pal's emphasis on Indian tradition and its cultural history and the Hindu tradition and history. It is not surprising to note that Pal's book's title page begins with *OM* and *Bande Mataram* and after that, the title of the book appears to the readers.

Providing some sort of religious identification (read Hindu identification) to the movement, Pal notes that new National Movement came into being with the cry of "*Bande Mataram*". He observes,

> "This salutation imparted to it a religious inspiration which the National Congress never had. It drove the new ideals deep down into the very heart and soul of the land and introduced a new sacrament of nationality and patriotism among the people. "*Bande Mataram*" is not really "Hail, Motherland," but "Hail, Mother." This "Mother", as applied to the Divine, is an old ...word and an old idea in Hinduism, which recognises not merely the fatherhood but also the motherhood of God. The term "Father" applied to the Divine, signifies his protective providence; the word "Mother" specially symbolises his creative energy. It is the common designation of all the goddesses worshipped by the Hindus. Kali, Durga, Lakshmi, Sarasvati—all these have always been addressed as "Mother." This "Mother" in "*Bande Mataram*" combined

> them all in a new synthesis, and applied the old, the sacred, the dearly-beloved term, to a new concept, that of the Motherland. Through this salutation has come into being a *new cult in the land, the cult of patriotism.* This new patriotism is thus filiated to the *Pitris*, or the line of immortal ancestors; to the *Devas*, or the ancient and traditional deities presiding over nature; to the *Rishis*, or the saints and sages of the race, to whom society owes its special culture and character. And, last of all, this new patriotism has also become filiated to Universal Humanity, which is symbolised by *Maha-Vishnu* or *Narayana* in orthodox Hindu thought."[12]

The symbolic effect of *Bande Mataram* and emphasizing the nation as 'mother' and its affiliation with religious dimension (Hindu dimension) of the nation was more than the strategy of the movement. It was not an alternative strategy in response to the earlier failure of Indian National Congress (1885) propaganda which was based on "prayer and protest" which was in Pal's view offered the method of "political mendicancy, though miscalled, constitutional" but it was also showing a radical departure from the "earlier secular agenda" of nationalist movement to the beginning of "religious or Hindu agenda" of nationalism.

The religious or Hindu agenda of nationalism by Pal is not sketchy but deliberate as he defines nation and patriotism through it. He clearly admits that Bankim Chandra Chatterjee is the discoverer of this new salutation "*Bande Mataram*"; and his symbolic presentation of the "Mother" is significant. Here the essential and permanent form of the "Mother" rests eternally on the lap of Maha-Vishnu. This is her real form,—*the nation eternally resting in Humanity*. And by all these means the new patriotism in India has become really a new religion to vast numbers of its people.[13]

Equating new patriotism with a new religion and, as we have noted, this new religion was more a Hindu religion, Pal strikes a new chord in Indian Nationalism that made the far-reaching effect in coming time. Pal lambasts those who were in favour of constitutionalism or liberal secular form of nationalism. As history suggests, the new middle class was more inclined to this form of nationalism in the early twentieth century under the impression of English education. Pal writes, "The modern half-educated European is peculiarly *lacking in imagination and insight.* He cannot understand anything that does not fall into the narrow grooves of his thoughts and predilections. Inflated with the conceit of superior colour and culture, he cannot form any correct estimate of what he contemptuously brushes aside as barbarism and superstition. *Lacking to a very large extent the spirit of religion himself,* he cannot adequately assess the worth of the religious impulse, especially when expressed through unfamiliar symbols and ideas, as a motive power in human affairs. Not that he is not apprehensive of what he calls fanatical outbursts, especially among people considered *low in the scale of civilization;* but his apprehensions are very much like those of the skilful and intrepid sportsman shooting big game in the wilds of India or Africa. To this lack of imagination and insight is added, in the case of the Indian Bureaucracy, a general ignorance of the inner thoughts and sentiments of the people they are set to rule. They do not even know the language of the country, and without an intimate acquaintance with the literature of the people, they are necessarily unable to understand the real inwardness and strength of the nationalist upheaval".[14]

Pal also suggests that how language is important in the national awareness. Moreover, how the language and literature are the important part of nation building and awakening nationalism. On the other hand, he also emphasizes that how nationalist feeling may create an atmosphere conducive to vernacular language. He argues that "the political agitations of the past generations in India have left practically no mark upon any of the vernacular literature of the country" but the "present movement" which has generated "new patriotism" within "the last six or seven years, created a special and inspiring literature of its own patriotism". In his words, "Indeed, what may be called the hymnology of this new patriotism offers a most striking proof of the depth and reality of the new movement, especially in Bengal."

Pal asserts that British are totally unaware about this development that developed during the movement and most significant thing is that songs composed during the movement had "strong messianic hope". But the so called responsible rulers of the country have little knowledge and less appreciation of this. Moreover, "this messianic idea is the last refuge of downtrodden and despairing peoples, with a supremely religious turn of mind".[15]

This messianic idea, Pal claims, has been so with the Hindus, almost at every period of political ferment in the past. Pal cites two examples of great political upheavals in the eighteenth century; first was the protest of the Hindu consciousness against Moslem domination, and second the rise of the Sikhs in the west and that of the Mahrattas in the south. Pal recognizes it as "a new religious upheaval". Here the use of term 'Hindu' is again noteworthy. Pal repeatedly uses this word in his text to justify his position. Moreover, Pal employs the theory of *Karma* to describe the condition of individual and nation. "He [Hindu] believes in the inexorable law of *karma,* which is only another name for the law of causation as applied in the moral world. Nations, like individuals, are equally subject to this law."

It is this theory of *Karma* by which Pal depicts the history of India. In his words, "They [nations], too, have to work out their respective *karmas,* both good and bad. Through their good *karma,* the Hindu came to prominence and power, colonised new regions of the earth, conquered new peoples, spread culture and civilisation in the world."

The theory of *karma* which is the significant part of Hindu religion is the basis of Pal's argument of nation and nationalism. In a more powerful form, Pal narrates the history of "*Hindu India*" on the basis of the theory of *Karma* in more detail in his text. Interesting thing is that when Pal depicts India he takes it as "*Hindu India*". How this Hindu India has been surviving and how Hindu mythological story has worked in popular unconsciousness is worth mentioning here. Pal narrates the story of *Brahma* and argues that how this story has influenced the popular unconsciousness in India. "Even *Brahma,* the first progenitor, and ruler of the universe, so runs the sacred tradition, having created the worlds, could not eternally keep or rule them. Night came, the night of universal dissolution and the worlds passed away; and with them passed away even *Brahma* himself into that Eternal Silence, whence he and all his wondrous worlds had come to being".[16] Pal notes, "... though the story may be treated as mythical, the idea underlying it has no feebler hold on the popular consciousness today than what it had in the old unsophisticated days." This story, according to Pal, "is repeated even now from a hundred thousand platforms by Brahmin preachers and reciters of legendary lore, all over *Hindu India*". The effect of this story is that "it quickens the natural intuitions of the people concerning the absolute impermanence of earthly life and fortune. This is the real meaning of the so called fatalism of the race." In Pal's view, "This is the explanation of their placid acquiescence to the successive changes of political government in the country".[17]

On this religious ground, Pal explains the political events occurred in Indian history and to some extent justifies the Hindu silence while facing Muslims. Central to this explanation is that when the Hindus had exhausted their good *karma* they went down and the Mahomedans came-up. When they gathered some good *karma*, as in the case of Maratha and Sikh, they got sovereignty, although, for a short period.

In his words, "This is how, when the *Mahomedans* came and commenced to break down Hindu thrones and desecrate Hindu temples with impunity, people saw that it was *the will of God* that this should be so. Such sacrileges would be impossible without divine sanction. It was, therefore, that *Mahomedan rule was accepted by the people as a divine ordering*, not sullenly, but with calm resignation, and even with good grace. They helped it, they cooperated with it, they bore no ill will towards it, until in its own time it, too, commenced to fall into decay and disrepute, and signs of a new turn of the Wheel of Providence became evident. *When the Hindus had exhausted their good karmas they went down and the Mahomedans came-up*. When the Mahomedans also had exhausted their own *karma*, and had served their special purpose in the divine scheme, they too went down. The Hindus had gathered a little *karma* under *Moslem* subjection, and they came up once again for a little while to rule the destinies of the country. The sovereignty of the *Mahrattas* in the south, and of the Sikh Commonwealth in the west, was the fruit of this *karma*. But this *karma* was feeble; the fruit thereof was, consequently, very short-lived".[18]

Viewing again the colonial rule as a result of "evil *karma*" of Indian (Hindu), Pal argues that people know that this phase will soon disappear with the "another turn of the Wheel of Providence". "And thus, in the ordering of Providence, another, and a new race, came in and took the reins of government away from the paralysed hands of the Moghuls, pushing aside both the Sikhs and the Mahrattas. The masses now accepted them also as a new dispensation of Providence. The time had not yet come for India to come to her own. *The sins of past generations, the evil karma of the nation, had not yet completely worked themselves out.* A new subjection and a new penance were necessary to wash and work these out. This is how the national consciousness almost intuitively interpreted the new turn of events. This is the meaning, really, of the quiet and willing acquiescence of the people in this rule. But while doing so, they knew all the while, in their inner consciousness, that it was, like all else in this world, only a passing phase of their history and evolution. And as before in the past, so equally also in the future, there will be another turn of the Wheel of Providence; and when the signs of a fresh change become evident this quiet and willing acquiescence of the people in the existing political order will also begin to wane. And then a demand will be made upon the deepest spiritual forces of India and the highest statesmanship of England to save the situation".[19]

Thus, Pal is optimistic about the change of political order but as he mentions it will be spiritual in nature. Pal views *Swadeshi* movement as a sign of this spiritual force which India is getting. Depicting the nature of *Swadeshi* as "essentially religious and spiritual", "a fervent religious spirit", "the new nationalist sentiments". Pal writes that "It has created new symbols,—a new form of idolatry, as some perhaps would call it,—representing the apotheosis of the geographical habitat of the race. And it is this intensely religious note which constitutes the reality and the gravity of the present situation".[20]

Pal condemns those who do not understand the true meaning of the *Swadeshi* movement. Commenting on the Europeans and their Indian counterparts, Pal writes that lacking true spiritual perceptions themselves, they are interpreting a deep spiritual upheaval as a mere economic unrest or political ferment.

Pal finds that in India there is a birth of "new exegesis", which is reconstructing the old beliefs and trying to adjust them to the demands of the modern life and thought. The result is that it has revived the faith of the educated classes of the country in national institutions and scriptures. Further, this phenomenon is rapidly bridging over the gulf between educated class and the general masses of India which was created by the foreign ideas and ideals. Pal also recognizes that "it is this religious spirit, at once so real and so conservative, which differentiates the new National Movement from the old, purely secular, political movements in British India."

It is important to note that Pal observes that this religious tone has the "messianic aspiration" since the beginning of the movement. Moreover, he strikingly recognizes that this "messianic idea" exists in Hinduism which can be found in the fullest expression in the well-known verses of the *Bhagavad Gita*.

Pal quotes one of the very popular verses of *Bhagavad Gita* (IV. 7-8) and provides its meaning to show that how Hinduism has "messianic idea".

> *Yada yada hi dharmasya glanirbhavati bharata,*
> *Abhyutthanamadharmasya tadatmanam srijamyaham.*
> *Paritranaya sadhunam vinashayachadushkritam,*
> *Dharma samsthapanarthaya sambhavami yuge yuge.*
>
> Whenever, O Bharata, there is decadence of *Dharma* and prevalence of *Adharma*, I always incarnate myself.
> For the protection of the good, for the extirpation of evil-doers, and for the establishment of *Dharma*, I am born from age to age.

This shows how Pal views the nationalist movement against colonialism as the struggle between *dharma* and *adharma* in India and how he gets inspiration from the ancient religious text (Hindu text).

Pal further argues that it was Bankim Chandra who revived this old "Hindu messianic idea" to Bengali people. He writes "To him we owe a new interpretation of the life and character of Sri Krishna as a great nation-builder in ancient India, and as a divine exemplar to the Hindu people for all time to come".[21]

However, Pal asserts that Bankim's influence was confined to educated class only. On the other hand the Indian masses, he writes, have always believed in Sri Krishna, and they do not need new exegesis or interpretation to revive their lost faith. Moreover, he asserts that what people wanted was a practical application of that faith. This was not to be only religious or spiritual force but was to be a social, and, perhaps, even as a political inspiration.

Pal interprets the message of *Gita "Dharma samsthapanarthaya sambhavami yuge yuge"* in then nationalist context and writes, "He had incarnated himself repeatedly, from age to age, for the protection of the good, for the extermination of evil-doers, for the re-establishment of decadent *Dharma*. A fresh cry now went up from the heart of his chosen people for a fresh advent of the Saviour. This cry is a peculiar feature of the present ferment in India, and more particularly in Bengal, which is, in some sense, the native home of the new Nationalist Movement".[22]

Thus Pal interprets *Swadeshi* movement in the terms of *Gita* and its "messianic message". This interpretation also compels him to make a difference between older liberal political agitation and extremist politics what he terms as the "new nationalist movement". In Pal's view earlier agitation was secular while "new nationalist movement" was "religious and spiritual" in nature. Further, earlier agitation was 'imitative' and 'imaginative' while "new nationalist movement is realistic" and shows the "actualities of Indian life and thought". Again the older generations drew their inspirations of freedom and progress from European, and especially British, history and literature while "new movement" gets inspiration from Indian religious ideas.

Pal mentions several examples of patriotic hymens and songs that developed during the new movement and argues that these compositions are full of spirit and close to the Indian political reality. He writes that "It showed that the mind of the nation had commenced to turn to higher powers for strength and inspiration. It was no longer a prayer for justice or generosity from man, but a cry for strength and illumination from God. No political conjurer can call up such a cry from a nation's heart".[23]

Further, he notes, "The immense popularity of these hymns is a proof of the depth of the new patriotic sentiment in the country". Pal suggests that songs and hymns have penetrated to remote villages and they are in "extensive circulation in spite of the police and the magistracy". Pal also tells that these songs are "half political" and "half religious" and "it is in this way that the new National Movement has been working itself into the very heart and soul of the people".[24]

On the foundation of "new movement", Pal notes that new movement is a new interpretation of old philosophical foundation of the Hindu race. In his words, "Behind the new nationalism in India stands the old Vedantism of the Hindus. This ancient Indian philosophy, divided into many schools, has one general idea running through it from end to end. It is the idea of the essential unity of man and God".[25]

Yet Pal mentions that old Vedantic thought has been revived what he calls the neo-Vedantism and argues that this may be called Neo-Hinduism. In his view, this neo-Vedantism is not about the monkish negation but it demands to a socio-political reconstruction of life to help to achieve highest spiritual life not only to individual but community also. "Neo-Vedantism, which forms the very soul and essence of what may be called Neo-Hinduism, has been seeking to realise the old spiritual ideals of the race, not through monkish negations or medieval abstractions, but by the idealisation and the spiritualisation of the concrete contents and actual relations of life. It demands, consequently, a social, an economic, and a political reconstruction, such as will be helpful to the highest spiritual life of every individual member of the community. The spiritual note of the present Nationalist Movement in India is entirely derived from this revived Vedantic thought".[26]

Pal also mentions that how this movement has brought a new transformation in the Hindu society. This created a new space for non-Brahmins. He writes that in the new movement, old and orthodox Brahmins are rendering "open respect" to the heterodox and non-Brahmin teachers. On the other hand, this movement did not only develop a strong spiritual note, but it also struck a strong note of reality in Indian politics also, which it never had before. This movement also subjected the British policy in India to a rigorous analysis, and thus revealed its true character with almost cruel candour. It has completely demolished the idea that England is and always been, in India mainly for good of the Indian. Above all, the Nationalist Movement has approached the central political problem in India from a new standpoint, namely, that of psychology.

It is interesting to note here that Pal is referring to the psychology of people. In fact, Pal boldly asserts in his text the "real political problem in India is not a strictly political, but essentially a psychological problem". Pal gives a strong proof to support his arguments. "The miracle of British rule in India,—the government of 3,00,000,000 peoples, spread over a whole continent, by a couple of hundred thousand foreigners, civil and military, all told,—was due neither to the physical nor to the intellectual, nor to the moral superiority of the rulers over the ruled, but to pure hypnotism". This argument is close to Gandhi's who held the same position arguing that Indians are in *'moha'*.

The people were hypnotized to believe in the altruism of the foreign rulers. As we may note that this was the result of the civilization mission argument proposed by colonials. Pal indirectly mentions this civilization mission argument and writes, "They had been told that the people of India were unfitted to manage their own affairs, and they believed it to be true. They had been told that the people were weak and the foreign Government was strong, and they believed it to be true. They had been told that India stood on a lower plane of humanity, and England's mission was to civilise the semi-barbarous native, and people believed that they were really low in the scale of civilisation." Pal asserts that the nationalist school not only exposed the hollowness of all these arguments but also broke the hypnotism, and made Indian aware about their own strength and their own glorious culture. This resulted in a new conviction that and Indians, too, like the other races of the world, have a distinct mission and destiny.

Pal also analyses the earlier religious and social movement in the light of Nationalist movement and European influence. He admits that earlier movements of religious and social revolt rose under the influence of European thoughts and ideals. "This revolt was the direct result of the application of the canons of the dominant rationalistic thought of Europe of the later eighteenth and the early nineteenth century to the social and religious life of India".[27] Pal terms it as "the outer movement of the modern Indian consciousness" which "represented really the return of the national consciousness to itself". But in Pal's view this was not the conflict between "the progressive and conservative elements of Indian society, as superficial observers have tried to make it out, but a conflict between aggressive European and progressive Indian culture." In Pal's view, "It was India's mental and moral protest against the intellectual and ethical domination of Europe". Pal also observes that like Christian missionaries, Hindu and Buddhist missionaries' activities in Europe and America have revealed India's place in the evolution of modern world culture that resulted into create a new pride of Hindu race; and "in this pride of race was really born the new National Spirit in the country". Thus, Pal writes, "by all these various means the old hypnotism was slowly breaking away. What was needed was only the bold declaration of the new political ideal to complete this work." The Nationalist School came into being, "as a new political party in India, with such a declaration". This declaration was national autonomy – absolutely free from British control.

Pal elaborates this declaration writing that as "in religion and social life, India had commenced to *claim her right to determine her own course of evolution herself, in the light of her own past,* untrammeled by, overbearing foreign thoughts and ideals; so, in politics also, she claimed her legitimate right of self-control and self-determination, to work out her own problems in her own way, freed from the bondage of European economic or political philosophy. Not self-government, whether colonial or otherwise, which expressed the idea of political freedom in terms of European thought.and experience, but SWARAJ was proclaimed as the new ideal".[28]

SWARAJ, as defined by Pal, is worth mentioning. Pal argues that SWARAJ is basically a "highest philosophical concept" that has been borrowed by politics. It is more than "political freedom" or "self-government" generally understood. It is also "larger than the English word freedom". In his view, Freedom is an essentially negative while *Swaraj* is a positive concept.

He mentions, "The term is used in the *Vedanta* to indicate the highest spiritual state, wherein the individual, having realised his identity with the Universal, is not merely freed from all bondage, but is established in perfect harmony with all else in the world. *Swaraj* means cessation of all conflicts".[29]

Pal also describes the political implication of the term *Swaraj*. "Politically, it means not merely the absence of bondage, but also the settlement of all disputes due to conflict of interests, either national or international. The concept involves not merely national freedom, but universal federation also, without which nations can never be established in perfect harmony with one another".[30]

Pal gives a very specific meaning of *Swaraj* and relates it with Indian nationalism. He argues that it "fully represents the spirit of Indian nationalism".[31] In his view, *Swaraj* is a relational notion and it is not about only individual freedom but about the recognition of Unity of self that looks "One Life, One Mind, One Will, One Spirit".

Pal mentions that *Swaraj* is the spiritual reference point of Indian national movement. "Viewing life and all its relations and activities from this supremely spiritual standpoint", he notes "the Indian Nationalist recognises a spiritual reference as much in religion proper as in his social economy and political laws and institutions". "Politics is, with him, part of his larger religion; it is a department of the science or philosophy of salvation. And, it is therefore, that the word which signifies the highest spiritual end represents also the highest political ideal".

It is interesting to note that how Pal locates the basis of Indian political ideal in the spiritual realm. It is also worth noting that the inseparability of political and spiritual is one of the characteristics that one finds in his discourse on nationalism. In his discourse of nationalism, Pal argues that social and political life is a means to achieve the end of *Swaraj*. In his words, "This is the real spirit of Indian Nationalism. It is an essentially religious spirit. Its end is the realisation of God-life in and through the activities of the social and the political life. That end is absolutely assured, but whether it will be reached by peaceful means or not will be determined by the capacity or incapacity of British statesmanship to work out the problem that faces it in India".[32]

Because of this spiritual reference point, Pal insists that "the conditions of peaceful progress towards political freedom are present in India to an extent in which these have never been present, perhaps, in any other country struggling for national freedom."

Pal in his text criticizes the secret revolutionaries, who believed in physical forces, and argues that how their works are harming Indian national movement. Pal calls these revolutionaries "immature, impatient, irresponsible men" who has no "real appreciation of the culture of their country" and "any intimate knowledge of the real character of their people". Pal alleges that these people are working in secret or from the safety of foreign lands, are "trying to drive the movement beyond the limits of law and order".[33]

He notes that like the earlier methods of political agitation, miscalled constitutional, these new methods of revolutionary propaganda are also imitative and European, without any reference to the life and culture of the people, and having no inspiring message for them.

In his words, "It is not our own creation. It is not of our own seeking. We have always been anxious for peaceful, lawful, orderly evolution. But we desire freedom". "We desire to be in our own country as other peoples are in their country. We claim the right of controlling the course of our historic evolution ourselves. We desire our own good and our own place in the universal scheme of things, and bear no ill-will towards any other people or country. We are against all violent methods, because we know that these will defeat the high ends that we have in view, namely the revelation of God in men through due regulation of the social and civic relations and activities".[34]

He further notes, what is wanted is freedom of thought and speech for the education of the people in their own national ideal and culture; freedom of association for the promotion of public good, and the organisation of public life—freedom within the limits of the law".[35] On the other hand, Pal argues why the violent method is appearing in the movement and how it is against both the Great Britain and India. This authority is based upon the general acquiescence of the people in their rule, and as long as this acquiescence lasts it is not only a political, but an essentially moral, authority.

In Pal's view, it is recent repressions in India by Britain which openly attacked the primary rights of the Indian people are entirely responsible for the appearance of revolutionary violence in a movement of lawful, self-reliant activities and peaceful, passive resistance. However, Pal does not support the violent method. The greatest risk, he writes, to India would be a further loss of her old spirit, a decadence of her revived moral and spiritual life, a diversion, for a time at least, from her God-appointed mission as the spiritual teacher of modern humanity. For England, he argues, the meaning of violent method will be "far more serious" and 'permanent'. He observes that although the revolutionary may not upset the British government but they may very easily paralyse the administration, by undermining the moral hold of the Government upon the governed. Moreover, "Governments, whose authority is based essentially upon their hypnotic influence over the people, are peculiarly liable to be paralysed by revolutionary violence."[36] Besides "there are very serious economic risks also involved in the increase or continuance of this kind of political unrest. Thus, the continuance of this revolutionary unrest will inevitably depreciate every form of Indian stock, to the financial embarrassment of many British families who derive their subsistence from the industrial and commercial exploitation of India".[37]

Yet Pal's view on revolutionary violence should not be considered only from strategic points of view. He clearly argues that revolutionary violence is destructive "do not have, as a rule, any constructive programme, and capable of practical realization".[38]

Thus, Pal views that "From whatever point of view it may be approached, an early and radical settlement of this revolutionary unrest in India will seem to be extremely urgent, equally in the interest of India as of England".

Pal summarizes his argument in the following way:

> "If British statesmen realised the depth of the present upheaval in India, if they knew how it has affected not merely the English-educated classes but even the ignorant and inert masses as well, how even the women have caught the infection of this new national spirit, how it has become even as a new religion to vast numbers of people, how it is transforming the old fatalism of the race into a mighty political force, developing a new stoicism in the people, such as makes them absolutely indifferent to physical pain, privation, or even to death itself,—if British statesmen could calmly think of the infectious character of all patrioneracnfice and revolutionary heroism,—they would understand the utter folly of trying repressive measures for putting down the surging aspirations for freedom of teeming multitudes. Repression has failed everywhere: it will not succeed in India".[39]

Notes and References

1. Pal, Bipin Chandra. 1910. *The Spirit of Indian Nationalism.* West Kensington; London: The Hind Nationalist Agency.
2. *Encyclopaedia of Indian War of Independence 1857-1947* (Vols. 1 to 19). New Delhi: Anmol Publisher, 2009.
3. *Op. cit.,* Pal. *The Spirit of Indian Nationalism,* p. iv.
4. *Ibid.,* p. iii.
5. *Ibid.*
6. *Ibid.*
7. *Ibid.,* p. 3.
8. *Ibid.*

9. *Ibid.*, p. 5.
10. *Ibid.*, p. 6.
11. *Ibid.*, p. 7.
12. *Ibid.*, p. 13.
13. *Ibid.*, pp. 13-14.
14. *Ibid.*, pp. 14-15.
15. *Ibid.* p. 16.
16. *Ibid.*, p. 18.
17. *Ibid.*, p. 19.
18. *Ibid.*
19. *Ibid.*, pp. 20-12.
20. *Ibid.*, p. 22
21. *Ibid.*, p. 28.
22. *Ibid.*, pp. 28-29
23. *Ibid.*, p. 33.
24. *Ibid.*, p. 34.
25. *Ibid.*, p. 38.
26. *Ibid.*, p. 40.
27. *Ibid.* p. 39.
28. *Ibid.*, pp. 45-46.
29. *Ibid.*, p. 46.
30. *Ibid.*, pp. 46-47.
31. *Ibid.*, p. 47.
32. *Ibid.*, p. 48.
33. *Ibid.*, p. 50.
34. *Ibid.*
35. *Ibid.*, p. 51.
36. *Ibid.*, p. 53.
37. *Ibid.*, p. 54.
38. *Ibid.*
39. *Ibid.*, p. 56.

7
Rabindranath Tagore's Nationalism (1917)

> "The last sun of the century sets amidst the blood-red clouds of the West and the whirlwind of hatred.
> The naked passion of self-love of Nations, in its drunken delirium of greed, is dancing to the clash of steel and the howling verses of vengeance.
> The hungry self of the Nation shall burst in a violence of fury from its own shameless feeding.
> For it has made the world its food,
> And licking it, crunching it and swallowing it in big morsels,
> It swells and swells
> Till in the midst of its unholy feast descends the sudden shaft of heaven piercing its heart of grossness...."[1]

This is beginning of the poem 'The Sunset of the Century', written by Rabindranath Tagore (1861-1941) on the last day of the nineteenth century. This poem is included in his book *'Nationalism'* published in 1917. As it appears it tells us the core of poet's views on nationalism. This anti-nationalism sentiment depicted in the poem conveys that nationalism is a source of war and carnage; death, destruction, and divisiveness. These ideas remain at the core of Tagore's most of his writings on nationalism.

Tagore was a highly sensitive poet who left an indelible mark on literary and social/political thought in India in particular and the world in general. Combined with his poetic temperament, his voice on nationalism was not confined to one particular country or tradition. It was cosmopolitan in nature based on human love. Through his text *Nationalism,* he reinforced his faith in the eternal and everlasting reason and goodness of human being which is universal qualities.

Although Tagore's anti-nationalist views get an abstract form and content in his text *Nationalism*, yet one may find the echo of these abstractions in his earlier novels besides the poem mentioned above. Some poems of *Gitanjali* (1910) also show his anti-nationalist position. His two novels *Gora* (1909) and *The Home and the World* (1916) can be considered here briefly to show that how Tagore had visualized nationalism before the publication of his text Nationalism (1917).

Tagore's novel *Gora* (1909) shows the theme of anti-colonial nationalism and suggests that freedom movement should not ignore human quality in day to day social life. The novel is set in Bengal where the skin colour of most of the people is dark. The protagonist of the novel is the believer of staunch Hinduism. His nationalistic sentiment was restricted to rituals, symbols, and superstitions of Hindu religion. He believes that every Hindu should sacrifice his life for the attainment of freedom. When he comes to know about his Irish lineage and his identity, he gets shocked that transforms the whole course of his life and thought process. His ideas towards the concept of nationalism are badly shattered. He feels that he belongs to no one and nowhere and senses the feelings of rootlessness.

Similarly, Tagore's *The Home and the World* (1916) expresses the various facets of the anti-colonial nationalist struggle in India against the colonial regime. The novel is set in 1905 colonial India and describes the particular context of the partition of Bengal. There are three main characters Nikhil, Sandip, and Bimla and they represent various aspects of nationalism from their own perspective. According to Nikhil, ultra-nationalism is exclusive and it is against the idea of equality. Sandip believes in aggressive nationalism and he wants to attain independence by every means. Bimala, the wife of Nikhil is caught between the two approaches towards nationalism.

We may note that Tagore's view on nation and nationalism is complex in these novels. The reason of complexity is that he defies the traditional definition of nation and nationalism. This complexity reaches to its height in his text *Nationalism* (1917). His views on nation and nationalism, in the text, emerge in the context of his overall reading of Indian history, development of the modern nation and development of nationalism in Europe and its corresponding relation to the materialism.

I

A brief review of Tagore's life, his intellectual formation, and his literary work is essential before engaging into his text *Nationalism* (1917). Born in 1861, Tagore was the fourteenth and youngest son of Debendranath Tagore. His father was the leader of the Brahmo Samaj which was a new religious sect in nineteenth century Bengal. It focused on the revival of the ultimate monistic basis of Hinduism as laid down in the *Upanishads*. In the age of eleven, Tagore accompanied his father on a tour across India. In 1878, he moved to Brighton, East Sussex, England, to study law. He attended the University College London for some time, following which he started studying the works of Shakespeare. He returned to Bengal in 1880 without a degree, with the aspiration of fusing the elements of Bengali and European traditions in his literary works. In 1890, while on a visit to his ancestral estate in Shelaidaha, his collection of poems, *'Manasi'*, was released. The period between 1891 and 1895 proved to be fruitful during which, he authored a massive three-volume collection of short stories, *Galpaguchchha*. By then, several of his works were published and he had gained immense popularity among Bengali readers.

In the late 19th and early 20th centuries, Tagore gradually turned from philosophical reflections in his poetry to more personal themes—the celebration of nature, lyrical love, man's social responsibility. In several poems, he called on the Bengalis to rally in the struggle against tyranny. *The Instant* (1900), for example, is suffused with a spirit of rebellion against middle-class philistinism, and in *The Gifts* (1901) social themes are intertwined with religious and philosophical motifs. In his novels on social mores, *The Grain of Sand* (1902) and *The Wreck* (1905), as well as in the novella *Broken Nest* (1903), Tagore described the conflict between feudal family morality and democratic ideas.

However, the death of Tagore's wife, son, and father, all within a brief period, caused the poet to pour out his grief in three collections, *In Memoriam* (1903), *The Child* (1903), and *The Crossing* (1906). During this time, as India's movement for national liberation underwent a revival, especially after the partition of Bengal in 1905,

Tagore emerged as one of its leaders, writing patriotic songs and editing the socio-political periodical *Bhandar.* However, when the movement went beyond non-violence, he broke with it and devoted himself instead to education. In the novel *Gora* (1907–10), whose protagonist fights for freedom and social and economic progress, Tagore appealed to all Indians, regardless of caste or religion, to join in the struggle for national liberation. How to carry on such a struggle was the question pondered in *Atonement* (1909), a play in which the author anticipated the ideas behind the movement of non-cooperation with the colonial authorities. In the satirical play *The Castle of Conservatism* (1911), he assailed the conformism of a society steeped in Hindu traditions.

In 1912, he went to England and took a collection of his translated works with him. There he introduced his works to some of the prominent writers of that era, including William Butler Yeats, Ezra Pound, Robert Bridges, Ernest Rhys, and Thomas Sturge Moore. His popularity in English speaking nations grew manifold after the publication of *Gitanjali: Song Offerings* and later in 1913, he was awarded the Nobel Prize in Literature. In 1915, he was also granted knighthood by the British Crown, which he renounced after the 1919 *Jalianwala Bagh* massacre. In the 1920s and 1930s, he travelled extensively around the world; visiting Latin America, Europe, and South-East Asia. During his extensive tours, he earned a cult following and endless admirers.

Tagore's political views became more radical in the late 1920s. In *Four Chapters* (1934), a novel written in response to the national liberation movement's renewed activity in 1929–1934, he returned to the question of the legitimacy of violence as a means of social struggle. His prose works of this period include the psychological novella *Two Sisters* (1933), the novel *The Flower Garden* (1934) and a number of short stories. The poem collections *Mahuya* (1929), *The Message of the Forest* (1931), *Completion* (1932), *Once Again* (1932), and *The Last Octave* (1935), and the poem *Motley Things* (1933) are somewhat introspective. Tagore also published the collections *Leaves* (1936), *The Borderland* (1938), *Evening Lamp* (1938), *Newly Born* (1940), *From the Sickbed* (1940), *Recovery* (1941), *On the Birthday* (1941), and *Last Poems* (1941). In *The Story of a Muslim Woman* (1941), he again warned about the danger of religious and communal fanaticism.

From the literature point of view, through his works, Tagore strongly influenced the development of Bengali literature in particular and Indian literature in general. But what is less recognized is Tagore's social, political and contextual concern that he has shown in some of his novels and poems mentioned earlier. Yet, one may ask; what was the force behind such writings?

As far as Tagore's intellectual formation is concerned Collins (2008) notes that "His travels to the West and his numerous high profile Western friends appear to be evidence for some of an indelible mark upon the Tagore's mind".[2] But it does not mean that he was influenced only by Western scholars. In fact, Indian lineage was more profound than this international tour and friendship. As Kalyan Sen Gupta (2005) notes, "... he [Tagore] was... receptive to ideas associated with the Bauls and *Sufis* of Bengal, as well as to Hindu Vaishnavism and to Buddhism, it was always to the *Upanishadic* endeavour to relate everything to a single ultimate reality that he remained most faithful".[3]

Influence of Indian philosophy on Tagore may also be found in his family background that was influenced by the *Upanishads* and the *Bhagavad Gita*. It can be also noted that when Rabindranath was twelve and went to the Himalayas with his father, they chanted the *Upanishads* together. His father insisted that he should know the verses by heart. Not Surprizing in his poem and later on in his views on nationalism we find a kind of unity of human being.

In short, Tagore developed a spiritual humanism that connected ancient Indian philosophical ideas with Western ideas and gave them his own original twist. He believed that human beings could fulfil their potential and find freedom and fulfilment through love, knowledge, and freedom if they succeeded in connecting their narrow self with the universal Being. Not Surprizing not only Tagore's poetry and novels but his abstract and concrete text *Nationalism* also reflects this view.

Now, we consider the book *Nationalism* in some detail before engaging in it. As historian Ramchandra Guha (2009) notes, "In 1916, a speaking bureau based in New York offered Tagore $ 12,000 to undertake a lecture tour in the United States. He agreed because it would allow him to raise money for his school in Santiniketan. That he would go via Japan was an added attraction".[4] Thus, from May, 1916 to April 1917, he stayed in Japan and the U.S. where he delivered lectures on '*Nationalism*' and on 'Personality'. The book *Nationalism* is the collection of revised form of these lectures.

It is interesting to note that when Tagore's lectures were published in book form, they were subjected to a blistering attack in print by the Yale geographer Ellsworth Huntington. Noted historian Ramchandra Guha (2009) beautifully summarizes these attacks. He notes, "The geographer admired the poet's inimitable style"; as he put it, "it is wonderful that a man who uses English which is ungrammatical can hold the reader's attention so steadily".[5] But he had less patience with the contents. "Stripped of its fascinating imagery and rhythmical language", remarked Huntington, "Tagore's book is merely a protest against the way in which the energy of the West imposes itself upon the indolence of the tropics". After he had read through half the book, the reviewer wrote a note to himself describing it as "a vivid appeal of the weak, impotent, but the brainy man of the tropics against the overmastering power of the "nations" which live in the temperate zone". In Huntington's view, "Tagore seems to oppose the idea of a nation because he belongs to a race which has no nation of its own. Such a race is to be pitied, not blamed".[6] Thus, Tagore's nationalism invited the hostile response from Europeans.

II

Tagore's *Nationalism* comprises three chapters—"Nationalism in the West", "Nationalism in Japan" and "Nationalism in India" and a poem "The Sunset of the Century" mentioned above. "Nationalism in the West" is one of the series of the lectures delivered throughout the United States during the winter of 1916-17. While "Nationalism in Japan" is based upon his two lectures delivered in Japan before the Imperial University and Keio Gijuku University in June and July 1916. "Nationalism in India" written in the United States in late 1916, is the poet's reflection upon the state of India that also gives worldwide completeness to the discussion of nationalism. This book was written in 1917 and it is about the nation state and how the East should adjust to modernization. It is a well thought out work and presents a balanced view of society that reads more like poetry than political philosophy. The book also offers a very radical view on nation and nationalism. It also tells that how the poet engaged himself in the biggest question of his time that is the problematic of nation and nationalism. His answer to this question is not straightforward and it has been located in a very discursive way. Exploring the issue of nation and nationalism, Tagore digs up the history of India and its formation and posits it against the formation of the nation in the history of Europe. This might be seen in his constructed dichotomy of the East and West and their progress towards the realization of humanity. This dichotomy soon takes the form of spiritual and material domain respectively in which he locates his idea of nation and nationalism. Tagore's own approach to nation and nationalism is spiritual and he finds spirituality in beauty, nature, and simplicity. While discussing nation and nationalism, he finds and highlights major shortcomings in the history of India and a terrible contradiction in the history of Europe in regard to their formation. What Tagore finally seems to suggest is that the East and America must evolve in a way that should not be mechanical but moral and human.

Tagore, in the first chapter of his book '*Nationalism*' titled as '*Nationalism in the West*', argues that the history of India is not about the "political supremacy" or "the rise and fall of kingdoms" as history is generally perceived. In his views, Indian history is "about the attainment of spiritual ideas". He wrote, "In fact, our history has not been on the rise and fall of kingdoms, of fights for political supremacy. In our country records of these days have been despised and forgotten. For they in no way represent the true history of our people. Our history is that of our social life and attainment of spiritual ideals".[7]

He further argues that although there were conflicts in Indian society but India has always remained aloof from such conflicts because of the typical nature of its society as it is based on simplicity and self-governance. In his words, "Through all the fights and intrigues and deceptions of her earlier history, India had remained aloof. Because her homes, her fields, her temples of worship, her schools, where her teachers and students lived together in the atmosphere of simplicity and devotion and learning, her village self-government with its simple laws and peaceful administration—all these truly belonged to her. But her thrones were not her concern. They passed over her head like clouds, now tinged with purple gorgeousness, now black with the threat of thunder. Often they brought devastation in their wake, but they were like catastrophes of nature whose traces are soon forgotten".[8]

In his interpretation of history, Tagore also makes an interesting contrast between Mughals, Pathans on the one hand and British on the other who invaded India one after one. He writes that Mughals and Pathans who invaded India were human races, with their own religions and customs, likes and dislikes. He asserts that "We loved and hated them as occasions arose; we fought for them and against them, talked with them in a language which was theirs as well as our own, and guided the destiny of the Empire in which we had our active share".[9] He emphatically mentions that they were not a 'nation' but 'race'. On the other hand, in his view British presence in India is different. In the case of British, he writes that "we had to deal, not with kings, not with human races, but with a nation, — we, who are no nation ourselves".

Tagore assertion that India is 'nonation' is significant. Here Tagore views nation in the term of organized politics with a specific aim. The nation and its aim that developed in Europe are different from Indian situation. Tagore writes that India has a different aim and it has been devoid of politics. He points out, ".... here is India, of about fifty centuries at least, who tried to live peacefully and think deeply, the India devoid of all politics, the India of no nations, whose one ambition has been to know this world as of soul, to live here every moment of her life in the meek spirit of adoration, in the glad consciousness of an eternal and personal relationship with it".[10]

At this point what surprises us is Tagore's view on Nation. Tagore directly answers the question of what is Nation? In his view, "A nation, in the sense of the *political and economic union of a people*, is that aspect which a whole population assumes when organized for a mechanical purpose. Society as such has no ulterior purpose. It is an end in itself. It is a spontaneous self-expression of man as a social being. It is a natural regulation of human relationships so that men can develop ideals of life in cooperation with one another. It has also a political side, but this is only for a special purpose. It is for self-preservation. It is merely the side of power, not of human ideals".[11]

This view of Tagore is radical in the sense that it makes a difference between the society and nation. As mentioned, nation, for him, is an organized mechanical entity and it is merely an economic and political union. Moreover, it is a means. While society is a "spontaneous self-expression of man" and an organization for "natural regulation of human relationships".

Tagore in his historical analysis of nation also argues that how society changed into a nation and how nation developed in due course of time. In his view, the organization of nation developed because of science and technology. Behind the development of nation, there was a greed and power. He also mentions that how this development of nation has created a very inhumane world system that has created competition, mutual jealousy, and supremacy. He writes, "with the help of science and the perfecting of organization this power begins to grow and brings in harvests of wealth, then it crosses its boundaries with amazing rapidity. For then it goads all its neighbouring societies with the greed of material prosperity, and consequent mutual jealousy, and by the fear of each other's growth into powerfulness. The time comes when it can stop no longer, for the competition grows keener, organization grows vaster, and selfishness attains supremacy. Trading upon the greed and fear of man, it occupies more and more space in society, and at last becomes its ruling force".[12]

In a very radical way, Tagore argues that power is central to the very notion of the nation that has become today too abstract. He defines power as "a scientific product made in the political laboratory of the Nation, through the dissolution of the personal humanity".[13] Thus, he mentions that nation is nothing but "an organization of politics and commerce that has become all powerful at the cost of the harmony of the higher social life, then it is an evil day for humanity".[14] Moreover, in the Indian context, Tagore claims that "Nation as abstract being is ruling India".[15]

As it appears, Tagore looks the question of the nation from the human point of view rather than political. In his view nation represents the "organized self-interest of whole people and it is the least human and least spiritual". Like Gandhi, Tagore also looks modern nation as "soulless organization" and views nationalism as "cruel epidemic of evil". He is worried about the moral part of human being that does not get a place in the notion of nation. He laments that the history has come to a stage when the moral man, the complete man, is more-and-more giving way, almost without knowing it, to make room for the political and the commercial man. Further, he writes that how progress in science is helping to the formation of the nation which is causing the upset of man's moral balance and obscuring man's human side under the shadow of the soulless organization. It is in this context, Tagore recognizes nationalism as a bigger problem. He argues, "Its iron grip we have felt at the root of our life, and for the sake of humanity we must stand up and give warning to all, that this nationalism is a *cruel epidemic of evil* that is sweeping over the human world of the present age, eating into its moral vitality".[16] Relating the idea of the nation with the spirit of nationalism he argues that "... the idea of the Nation is one of the *most powerful anesthetics* that man has invented. Under the influence of its fumes the whole people can carry out its systematic programme of the most virulent self-seeking without being in the least aware of its moral perversion, fact feeling dangerously resentful if it is pointed out".[17]

Tagore's critique of nation and nationalism, as seen above, is based on his human approach. Coming directly to the Western nationalism, Tagore also examines it again through his humanistic approach. In a more radical way, Tagore claims that the spirit of conflict and conquest is at the centre of western nationalism. Furthermore, in his view, the basis of Western nationalism is not social cooperation or spiritual idealism but it is the power that has evolved to a perfect organization of nation.

It is important to note that in his text '*Nationalism*' Tagore makes a difference between "the spirit of the West" and the "Nation of the West". Elaborating it he points out that "while the spirit of the West marches under its banner of freedom, the Nation of the West forges its iron chains of organization which are the most relentless and unbreakable that have ever been manufactured in the whole history of man".[18]

The distinction between the "spirit of the West" and "Nation of the West" is interesting. This distinction is also applied to distinguish between British 'as a race' and as 'a nation' also. It is by this distinction Tagore praises the British 'as a race' and points out that he has a deep love and a great respect for the British race as human beings as it has produced great-hearted men, thinkers of great thoughts, doers of great deeds and great literature. On the other hand, 'as a nation' British Government is nothing but "an applied science and therefore more or less similar in its principles wherever it is used". It is important to note here that Tagore is not against only the British nation but he is against any kind of nation as he considers the nation as mechanical and scientific in itself. As he mentions, "Our government might have been Dutch, or French, or Portuguese, and its essential features would have remained much the same as they are now. Only perhaps, in some cases, the organization might not have been so densely perfect, and, therefore, some shreds of the human might still have been clinging to the wreck, allowing us to deal with something which resembles our own throbbing heart".[19]

Locating the contrast of "spirit of the West" and "Nation of the West" in Indian context, he argues that India is suffering because it has become the battleground of the conflict between the "Spirit of the West" and the "Nation of the West". In his words, "The benefit of the Western civilization is doled out to us in a miserly measure by the Nation trying to regulate the degree of nutrition as near the zero point of vitality as possible".[20]

At this point, it is significant to note that Tagore also makes a difference between the government and Nation (British). He argues that although the government is also mechanical but the nature of government in India earlier the British and after the British are different. He points out that before the [British] Nation came to rule over us we had other governments which were foreign, and these, like all governments, had some element of the machine in them. But the difference between them and the government by the Nation is like the difference between the "handloom" and the "power loom". In his view, in the products of the hand loom the magic of man's living fingers finds its expression. But the "power loom" is relentlessly lifeless and accurate and monotonous in its production.

But, Tagore is not blind to the typical Indian problems and he admires the spirit of West that has been employed in India although in a very limited amount. He admits that during the personal government of the former days in India there have been instances of tyranny, injustice, and extortion. They caused sufferings and unrest from which because of "spirit of the West" Indian people are rescued. This "spirit of the West", he views in the idea of protection of the law. This point, at face value, seems contradictory but Tagore's position is apparently clear from this view: "We must admit that the protection of the law is not only a boon, but it is a valuable lesson to us. It is teaching us the discipline which is necessary for the stability of civilization and continuity of progress. We are realizing through it that there is a universal standard of justice to which all men irrespective of their caste and colour have their equal claim".[21] Moreover, "This reign of law in our present

Government in India has established order in this vast land inhabited by peoples different in their races and customs. It has made it possible for these peoples to come in closer touch with one another and cultivate a communion of aspiration".[22]

As it appears the universal element of the spirit of West is being admired by Tagore and he does not look any problem in accepting its significance in the Indian context. At the same time, he complains that Western Nation is coming in India's way to stop such spirit of West. He claims that Western Nation "acts like a dam to check the free flow of the Western civilization into the country of the No-Nation". He argues that because Western civilization is the civilization of power, therefore, it is exclusive, thus, it is naturally unwilling to open its sources of power to those whom it has selected for its purposes of exploitation. It is important to note that Tagore views India as no Nation. Here 'no-nation' suggests that how India is different from the West.

As mentioned above, Tagore is not against only the British nation in India but the very idea of nation. The reason is that he finds the very idea of the nation against the humanity. In his words, "The Nation has thriven long upon mutilated humanity. Men, the fairest creations of God, came out of the National manufactory in huge numbers as war-making and money-making puppets, ludicrously vain of their pitiful perfection of the mechanism. Human society grew more and more into a marionette show of politicians, soldiers, manufacturers and bureaucrats, pulled by wire arrangements of wonderful efficiency".[23]

Tagore's view on nationalism and nation is centred on the individual. He observes that the aim of the nation and the individual is different. He argues that Nation is abstract entity and individuality is the freedom which cannot be fully realized in such abstract entity as the nation. Like Gandhi who criticized modern nation because it was against the individuality, Tagore too finds the same reason against the Nation. In his words, "Those who have any faith in Man cannot but fervently hope that the tyranny of the Nation will not be restored to all its former teeth and claws, to its far-reaching iron arms and its immense inner cavity, all stomach and no heart; that man will have his new birth, in the freedom of his individuality, from the enveloping vagueness of abstraction".[24]

Instead of the nation, Tagore finds the solution in the Indian tradition of 'no nation' in which the individuality can be fully realized. Furthermore, he finds that India as 'nonation' has potential to show the world a new way. In a very poetic way, he concludes the chapter "Nationalism in the West" by stating that "And we of no nations of the world, whose heads have been bowed to the dust, will know that his dust is more sacred than the bricks which build the pride of power. For this dust is fertile of life, and of beauty and worship. We shall thank God that we were made to wait in silence through the night of despair, had to bear the insult of the proud and the strong man's burden, yet all through it, though our hearts quaked with doubt and fear, never could we blindly believe in the salvation which machinery offered to man, but we held fast to our trust in God and the truth of the human soul. And we can still cherish the hope, that, when power becomes ashamed to occupy its throne and is ready to make way for love, when the morning comes for cleansing the bloodstained steps of the Nation along the highroad of humanity, we shall be called upon to bring our own vessel of sacred water—the water of worship—to sweeten the history of man into purity, and with its sprinkling make the trampled dust of the centuries blessed with fruitfulness".[25]

In the second chapter "Nationalism in Japan" of the book *Nationalism*, Tagore opens an argument that shows the difference between the East and the West. It also attempts to answers the colonial charges against the Eastern people. First of all, he puts the West's view on Asia. "We have been repeatedly told, with some justification, that Asia lives in the past—it is like a rich mausoleum which displays all its magnificence in trying to immortalize the dead. It was said of Asia that it could never move in the path of progress, its face was so inevitably turned backward".[26] This was the very common and prevalent colonial discourse of late nineteenth century and early twentieth century known as "Civilization mission" with which nationalists like Bipin Chandra, Aurobindo and Gandhi had also to wrestle. Like Gandhi, Tagore also finds that some Indian and Asian elite are accepting these views under the "hypnotic spell" of Western ideas. Tagore challenges the colonial discourse of civilization mission arguing that, "We forgot that in Asia great kingdoms were founded, philosophy, science, arts and literature flourished, and all the great religions of the world had their cradles. Therefore, it cannot be said, that there is anything inherent in the soil and climate of Asia that produces mental inactivity and atrophies the faculties which impel men to go forward. For centuries we did hold torches of civilization in the East when the West slumbered in darkness, and that could never be the sign of sluggish mind or narrowness of vision".[27]

In this background, Tagore praises Japan for its rise but he tells us that it did not occur because of *imitation* of West. He tells us that "We cannot imitate life, we cannot simulate strength for long, nay, what is more, a mere imitation is a source of weakness".[28] He mentions that Japan has imported her food from the West, but not her vital nature. Further, "If it be a mere reproduction of the West, then the great expectation she has raised will remain unfulfilled". Tagore also points out the problems that Western civilization has presented before the humanity. Moreover, they have no answer to these questions.

In his words, "The conflict between the individual and the state, labour and capital, the man and the woman; the conflict between the greed of material gain and the spiritual life of man, the organized selfishness of nations and the higher ideals of humanity; the conflict between all the ugly complexities inseparable from giant organizations of commerce and state and the natural instincts of man crying for simplicity and beauty and fullness of leisure, — all these have to be brought to a harmony in a manner not yet dreamt of".[29]

Thus, Tagore highlights the inherent contradiction of the Western civilization. Like Gandhi's critique of modern civilization, Tagore writes, "We have seen this great stream of civilization choking itself from debris carried by its innumerable channels. We have seen that with all its vaunted love of humanity it has proved itself the greatest menace to Man, far worse than the sudden outbursts of nomadic barbarism from which men suffered in the early ages of history. We have seen that, in spite of its boasted love of freedom, it has produced worse forms of slavery than ever were current in earlier societies,—slavery whose chains are unbreakable, either because they are unseen, or because they assume the names and appearance of freedom. We have seen, under the spell of its gigantic sordidness, man losing faith in all the heroic ideals of life which have made him great".[30]

He warns that modern civilization cannot be accepted as a

full package. What we need is Eastern touch to modern means. "Therefore, you cannot with a light heart accept the modern civilization with all its tendencies, methods and structures, and dream that they are inevitable. You must apply your Eastern mind, your spiritual strength, your love of simplicity, your recognition of social obligation, in order to cut out a new path for this great unwieldy car of progress, shrieking out its loud discords as it run".[31]

Tagore argues that what we are facing is a political civilization that has sprung up from the soil of Europe. Moreover, it is overrunning the whole world and it is based on 'exclusiveness'. He highlights the basic feature of this political civilization. "It is always watchful to keep at bay the aliens or to exterminate them. It is carnivorous and cannibalistic in its tendencies; it feeds upon the resources of other peoples and tries to swallow their whole future. It is always afraid of other races achieving eminence, naming it as a peril, and tries to thwart all symptoms of greatness outside its own boundaries, forcing down races of men who are weaker, to be eternally fixed in their weakness".[32] On the nature of this political civilization he writes, "This political civilization is scientific, not human. It is powerful because it concentrates all its forces upon one purpose, like a millionaire acquiring money at the cost of his soul. It betrays its trust, it weaves its meshes of lies without shame, it enshrines gigantic idols of greed in its temples, taking great pride in the costly ceremonials of its worship, calling this patriotism".[33]

Exposing the real nature of Western civilization, Tagore also responds to the argument of civilization mission made by colonials in India. "But the charge is brought against us that the ideals we cherish in the East are static, that they have not the impetus in them to move, to open out new vistas of knowledge and power, that the systems of philosophy which are the mainstays of the time-worn civilizations of the East despite all outward proofs, remaining solidly satisfied in their subjective certainty. This proves that when our knowledge is vague, we are apt to accuse of vagueness our object of knowledge itself. To a Western observer, our civilization appears as all metaphysics, as to a deaf man piano playing appears to be mere movements of fingers and no music. He cannot think that we have found some deep basis of reality upon which we have built our institutions".[34]

On the other hand, Tagore defends Eastern civilization. He states that "unfortunately all proofs of reality are in realization". "The reality of the scene before you depends only upon the fact that you can see, and it is difficult for us to prove to an unbeliever that our civilization is not a nebulous system of abstract speculations, that it has achieved something which is a positive truth—a truth that can give man's heart its shelter and sustenance. It has evolved an inner sense—a sense of vision, the vision of the infinite reality in all finite things".[35]

The question of progress central to colonial's "civilization mission" is responded by Tagore in a very rhetoric way. He does not see 'progress' in a linear materialistic way. He writes, "But he [Colonial] says, "You do not make any progress, there is no movement in you." I ask him, "How do you know it? You have to judge progress according to its aim. A railway train makes its progress towards the terminus station—it is movement. But a full-grown tree has no definite movement of that kind; its progress is the inward progress of life. It lives, with its aspiration towards light tingling in its leaves and creeping in its silent sap." We also have lived for centuries, "we still live, and we have our aspiration for a reality that has no end to its realization—a reality that goes beyond death, giving it a meaning, that rises above all evils of life, bringing its peace and purity, its cheerful renunciation of self. The product of this inner life is a living product".[36]

Thus contrary to the political civilization of the West, Tagore asserts that Eastern Asia has been pursuing its own path, evolving its own civilization, which is not political but social, not predatory and mechanically efficient, but spiritual and based upon all the varied and deeper relations of humanity. He makes a contrast between Europe and Japan on the basis of his vision of civilization. "All particular civilization is the interpretation of particular human experience. Europe seems to have felt emphatically the conflict of things in the universe, which can only be brought under control by conquest. Therefore, she is ever-ready for the fight, and the best portion of her attention is occupied by organizing forces. But, Japan has felt, in her world, the touch of some presence, which has evoked in her soul a feeling of reverent adoration. She does not boast of her mastery of nature, but to her she brings, with infinite care and joy, her offerings of love. Her relationship with the world is the deeper relationship of heart".[37] As we may note in the chapter "Nationalism in Japan", Tagore praises Japanese approach towards the development which is not separated from humanity and morality.

Yet Europe in itself is not like that Tagore mentions above. It is significant to note that Tagore condemns the "political civilization" that Europe has developed but not the Europe. In fact, he praises Europe in a very glorifying manner; "I must not hesitate to acknowledge where Europe is great, for great she is without a doubt. We cannot help loving her with all our heart, and paying her the best homage of our admiration—the Europe who, in her literature and art, is pouring an inexhaustible cascade of beauty and truth fertilizing all countries and all time; the Europe who, with a mind which is titanic in its untiring power, is sweeping the height and the depth of the universe, winning her homage of knowledge from the infinitely great and the infinitely small, applying all the resources of her great intellect and heart in healing the sick and alleviating those miseries of man which up till now we were contented to accept in a spirit of hopeless resignation; the Europe who is making the earth yield more fruit than seemed possible, coaxing and compelling the great forces of nature into man's service".[38]

Tagore suggests that the East can learn a lot from the Europe—both in terms of material and moral. "The East has instinctively felt, even though her aversion, that she has a great deal to learn from Europe, not merely about the materials of power, but about its inner source, which is of mind and of the moral nature of man. Europe has been teaching us the higher obligations of public good above those of the family and the clan, and the sacredness of law, which makes society independent of individual caprice, secures for it continuity of progress, and guarantees justice to all men of all positions in life. Above all things Europe has held high before our minds the banner of liberty, through centuries of martyrdom and achievement, liberty of conscience, liberty of thought and action, liberty in the ideals of art and literature".[39]

Tagore's Third Chapter "Nationalism in India" begins with a striking analysis of "real problem" of India and Europe. He argues that the real problem in India is not political but social. On the other hand, he points out that Europe developed in a very different way. He argues that in Europe peoples had their racial unity from the beginning, on the other hand, natural resources were insufficient for the inhabitants, and thus, the civilization had naturally taken the character of political and commercial aggressiveness. He mentions that they [European countries] had no internal complication, thus, they had to deal with strong and rapacious neighbours, therefore, they developed a watchful attitude of hostility against 'others' as the solution to their problems. Consequently, Tagore asserts that in former days they [European countries] organized and plundered neighbours, in the present age the same spirit continues—and they organize and exploit the whole world.

On the other hand, in Tagore's view, the Constitution of India has been different. Tagore asserts that since the beginning of the history India had to suffer from a serious problem that is the race problem. Tagore argues that India has tried to solve this problem by making an adjustment of races and acknowledging the real differences between them. Moreover, India has tried to construct some basis of unity. "This basis has come through our saints, like Nanak, Kabir, Chaitanya and others, preaching one God to all races of India".[40]

Tagore claims that what India has been doing is worth imitating by the world as the whole world is becoming one country through the scientific facility, thus what we need today is a non-political solution of the problem of racial difference. He claims that "There is only one history—the history of man. All national histories are merely chapters in the larger one. And we are content in India to suffer for such a great cause".[41]

Tagore extends this point further. In his words, "The most important fact of the present age is that all the different races of men have come close together. And again we are confronted with two alternatives. The problem is whether the different groups of peoples shall go on fighting with one another or find out some true basis of reconciliation and mutual help; whether it will be interminable competition or cooperation".[42]

Tagore gives a solution of this problem that might be seen as the role of India in the modern world. He asserts that "those who are gifted with the moral power of love and vision of spiritual unity, who have the least feeling of enmity against aliens, and the sympathetic insight to place themselves in the position of others will be the fittest to take their permanent place in the age that is lying before us". Tagore argues that mere political and commercial basis of unity among races is insufficient and claims only spiritual unity would solve the differences of race.

Tagore laments that Indian elite class is trying to absorb some lessons from the history of Europe contrary to the lessons of our ancestors. He is against such imitation. In his view, "The East, in fact, is attempting to take unto itself a history which is not the outcome of its own living. Japan, for example, thinks she is getting powerful through adopting Western methods, but, after she has exhausted her inheritance, only the borrowed weapons of civilization will remain to her. She will not have developed herself from within".

Like Gandhi, who argues that India will perish if it follows the path of West, Tagore too argues that Europe's strength, therefore, lies in her history and India should not borrow the European interpretation of history. Thus, "We, in India, must make-up our minds that we cannot borrow other people's history, and that if we stifle our own, we are committing suicide. When you borrow things that do not belong to your life, they only serve to crush your life. And, therefore, I believe that it does India no good to compete with Western civilization in its own field. But we shall be more than compensated if, in spite of the insults heaped upon us, we follow our own destiny".[43]

In spite of the difference between Europe and India, Tagore admits that there is always a possibility to bridge the gulf between them. He argues that how East can help the West. He asserts that "We must, however, know it is providential that the West has come to India. Yet, someone must show the East to the West, and convince the West that the East has her contribution to making in the history of civilization. India is no beggar of the West. And yet even though the West may think she is, I am not for thrusting off Western civilization and becoming segregated in our independence. Let us have a deep association".[44]

On the other hand, Tagore suggests that how the West can help East. "The West must not make herself a curse to the world by using her power for her own selfish needs, but by teaching the ignorant and helping the weak, by saving herself from the worst danger that the strong is liable to incur by making the feeble to acquire power enough to resist her intrusion. And also she must not make her materialism to be the final thing but must realize that she is doing a service in freeing the spiritual being from the tyranny of matter".[45]

It is in this broad canvass Tagore views the question of nation and nationalism in India. Tagore repeats in the chapter "Nationalism in India" that nation is organized power and it is an organization that incessantly keeps up the insistence of the population on becoming strong and efficient. His basic objection against the nation is that this strenuous effort after strength and efficiency drains man's energy from his higher nature where he is self-sacrificing and creative. As discussed earlier, for Tagore, man is central. He finds that nation is a mechanical organization whereas man is moral by nature and in the process of nation in making man gets diverted form the higher objective of creativity and sacrifice.

This is the reason Tagore views nationalism as "a great menace".[46] Moreover, he expresses his concern that this particular thing has been at the bottom of India's troubles for years. To support his argument Tagore reviews the nationalist agenda in India. He points out that in the beginning of the history of political agitation in India there was no conflict between parties. He is, in fact, referring to Indian National Congress about which he tells that it had no real programme. "They had a few grievances for redress by the authorities. They wanted larger representation in the Council House and more freedom in the Municipal government. They wanted scraps of things, but they had no constructive ideal. Therefore, I was lacking in enthusiasm for their methods".[47] Tagore's frustration towards the Congress is not difficult to understand as Congress was mainly an elitist organization in its early days. Tagore's personal conviction was that what India most needed was constructive work coming from within herself. He also points out to the nature of constructive work. "In this work we must take all risks and go on doing our duties which by right are ours, though in the teeth of persecution; winning moral victory at every step, by our failure, and suffering. We must show those who are over us that we have the strength of moral power in ourselves, the power to suffer for the truth. Where we have nothing to show, we only have to beg. It would be mischievous if the gifts we wish for were granted to us right now, and I have told my countrymen, time and time again, to combine the work of creating opportunities to give vent to our spirit of self-sacrifice, and not for the purpose of begging".[48]

On the other hand, Tagore also criticizes extremist faction of nationalists and their methods. He writes, "The party split, and there arrived the Extremists, who advocated independence of action, and discarded the begging method—the easiest method of relieving one's mind from his responsibility towards his country".[49] Tagore's objection to the extremist's, politics, what he terms 'nationalist' politics, is that their ideas are based on the imitation of Western history. He also argues that these nationalists had no sympathy with the special problems of India. Moreover, they do not recognize the apparent fact that there were causes in our social organization which made the Indian incapable of coping with the alien. He is more concerned with the social organization of the Indian society than the only transformation of political power from British to Indian. He, like Gandhi, argues that "What would we do if, for any reason, England was driven away? We should simply be victims for other nations. The same social weaknesses would prevail. The thing we, in India, have to think of is this—to remove those social customs and ideals which have generated a want of self-respect and a complete dependence on those above us,—a state of affairs which has been brought about entirely by the domination in India of the caste system, and the blind and lazy habit of relying upon the authority of traditions that are incongruous anachronisms in the present age".[50]

After this discussion, Tagore comes to the crucial question of the early twentieth century; the problem of race. Tagore argues that the attitude towards solving the problem of race has been different in the East and the West. He highlights the fundamental difference between Europe and India in tackling this problem on the basis of the evolution. He further observes that India has a typical condition in comparison to Europe in this regard. India represents "many countries in one" while Europe "one into many countries". Thus, he argues that the problem of race in India may be seen as the "problem of the world in miniature" because India is too vast in its area and too diverse in its races. In other words, like the world, India symbolizes "many countries packed in one geographical receptacle", on the other hand, "Europe truly is, namely, one country made into many". He finds this condition a kind of advantage for Europe and a suffering for India. In his words, "Europe in its culture and growth has had the advantage of the strength of the many, as well as the strength of the one. But

India, on the contrary, being naturally many, yet adventitiously one has all along suffered from the looseness of its diversity and the feebleness of its unity".[51]

However, Tagore gives credit to India to solve the problem of race. He argues that although diversity was not India's own creation but it has accepted diversity as a fact from the beginning of her history. In his view, India has tried to solve this problem of diversity by 'toleration' and "caste system is the outcome of this spirit of toleration".

He writes, "For India has all along been trying experiments in evolving a social unity within which all the different peoples could be held together, yet fully enjoying the freedom of maintaining their own differences. The tie has been as loose as possible, yet as close as the circumstances permitted".[52] But Tagore also highlights the problem that emerged in this caste system. In his view, although caste regulations in India recognized differences, but it did not permit mutability which is the law of life. Further, in trying to avoid collisions, the caste system in India set-up boundaries of immovable walls among castes but by doing so it resulted in "the negative benefit of peace and order" among numerous races but "not the positive opportunity of expansion and movement".

On the other hand, Tagore argues that the West has solved this problem of race in a very different way. He writes that the West, being more favourably situated as to homogeneity of races, has never given her attention to this problem, and whenever confronted with it she has tried to make it easy by ignoring it altogether. On the issue of how the West solved the problem of the race, he points out, "...Either you shut your doors against the aliens or reduce them into slavery. And this is your solution of the problem of race conflict. Whatever may be its merits you will have to admit that it does not spring from the higher impulses of civilization, but from the lower passions of greed and hatred".[53] Nationalism in modern times has much to do with the power and freedom as it emerged in the context of colonial subjugation. Any nationalists, who worked under colonialism, could not ignore this and Tagore is no exception. Thus he also, in his text, discusses the nature of political freedom and power in his discourse on nationalism. He makes a point when he argues that people who have got their political freedom are not necessarily free. In fact, "they are merely powerful". He again points out the contradiction between the modern form of huge organization that is the state and the individual freedom. "Passions which are unbridled in them are creating huge organizations of slavery in the disguise of freedom". Thus, Tagore finds a deeper problem in this kind of discourse. Writing on this problem Tagore argues, "Those who are enamoured of their political power and gloat over their extension of dominion over foreign races gradually surrender their own freedom and humanity to the organizations necessary for holding other peoples in slavery. In the so-called free countries, the majority of the people are not free, they are driven by the minority to a goal which is not even known to them. This becomes possible only because people do not acknowledge moral and spiritual freedom as their object".[54] Tagore laments that those of us in India who have come under the delusion that mere political freedom will make us free have accepted their lessons from the West as the gospel truth and lost their faith in humanity. "We must remember whatever weakness we cherish in our society will become the source of danger in politics. The same inertia which leads us to our idolatry of dead forms in social institutions will create in our politics prison houses with immovable walls".[55]

It is on this conviction Tagore reviews the problem of then Indian nationalism existing".[56]

He clearly notes that political freedom is not everything. It is a kind of "delusion that merely political freedom will solve our real problem".[56] He is more concerned about the social, economic and political regeneration of India. He, like Gandhi, argues that India should adopt its own way rather than imitating the West. For example, referring India's India background of good economic development that was suppressed by British, Tagore suggests, "We had good industries before the British but under the British rule these industries were suppressed. Furthermore, since then, India has not met with any real help or encouragement to enable itself to make a stand against the monster commercial organizations of the world".[57]

Like Gandhi, Tagore was against the modern industrialization, commercialization and modern big machinery. However, there seems a basic difference between them. Gandhi criticized them on the 'moral' ground while Tagore criticized them on 'aesthetic' ground. He writes, "I personally do not believe in the unwieldy organizations of the present day. The very fact that they are ugly shows that they are in discordance with the whole creation. The vast powers of nature do not reveal their truth in hideousness but in beauty. Beauty is the signature which the Creator stamps upon his works when he is satisfied with them. All our products that insolently ignore the laws of perfection and are unashamed in their display of ungainliness bear the perpetual weight of God's displeasure. So far as your commerce lacks the dignity of grace it is untrue. Beauty and her twin brother Truth require leisure, and self-control for their growth. But the greed of gain has no time or limit to its capaciousness. Its one object is to produce and consume".[58]

Extending this argument, he writes, "It is this ugly vulgarity of commerce which brought upon it the censure of contempt in our earlier days when men had the leisure to have an unclouded vision of perfection in humanity. Men in those times were rightly ashamed of the instinct of mere money-making. But in this scientific age money, by its very abnormal bulk, has won its throne. And when from its eminence of piled-up things it insults the higher instincts of man, banishing beauty and noble sentiments from its surroundings, we submit".[59]

"This commercialism with its barbarity of ugly decorations is a terrible menace to all humanity. Because it is setting up the ideal of power over that of perfection. It is making the cult of self-seeking exult in its naked shamelessness".[60] Again, "The temptation which is fatal for the strong is still more so for the weak. And I do not welcome it in our Indian life even though it be sent by the lord of the Immortals. Let our life be simple in its outer aspect and rich in its inner gain. Let our civilization take its firm stand upon its basis of social cooperation and not upon that of economic exploitation and conflict".[61]

In short, Tagore's book *Nationalism* opens a new discourse in debating nationalim. He argues that a mutually-built society is much more humane in essence than the so called artificially created nationhood. He clearly rejects the term 'nationalism' as understood in the Western sense. He also questions the idea of political nation, if it does not bring freedom of mind. His text raises a fundsmental question; does world community need 'Nationalism' or 'Humanism'? He categorically rejects the idea of 'national history' also. In Indian context, he comes heavily on national Jingoism. As we noted, his text *Nationalism* provides a bold rational and humane critique of the idea of nationalism.

Notes and References

1. Tagore, Rabindranath. 1917. *Nationalism*. San Fransico USA: Macmillan.
2. Collins, Michael. Empire, 2012. Nationalism and the Postcolonial World. *Rabindranath Tagore's Writings on History, Politics, and Society*. London and New York: Routledge, p. 3.
3. Gupta, Kalyan Sen. 2005. *The Philosophy of Rabindranath Tagore*. Aldershot: Ashgate, p. 9.
4. Guha, Ramachandra (ed.): 2009. *Nationalism*. India: Penguin, p. 10.
5. *Ibid.*
6. *Ibid.*, p. 14.
7. Tagore, Rabindranath. 1917. *Nationalism*. San Fransico USA: Macmillan, p. 16.
8. *Ibid.*, p. 17.
9. *Ibid.*, p. 19.
10. *Ibid.*, p. 17.
11. *Ibid.*, pp. 19-20.
12. *Ibid.* p. 20.
13. *Ibid.*, p. 22
14. *Ibid.*, p. 23.
15. *Ibid.*, p. 24.
16. *Ibid.*, pp. 23-24.
17. *Ibid.*, p. 57.
18. *Ibid.*, p. 37.
19. *Ibid.*, p. 29.
20. *Ibid.*, p. 31.
21. *Ibid.*, p. 30.
22. *Ibid.*, p. 23.
23. *Ibid.*, p. 58.
24. *Ibid.*, p. 59.
25. *Ibid.*, p. 61.
26. *Ibid.*, p. 65.
27. *Ibid.*, p. 66.
28. *Ibid.*, p. 70.
29. *Ibid.*, p. 72.
30. *Ibid.*, p. 73.
31. *Ibid.*
32. *Ibid*, p. 77.
33. *Ibid.*
34. *Ibid.*, p. 79.
35. *Ibid.*, p. 80.
36. *Ibid.*
37. *Ibid.*, p. 90.
38. *Ibid.*, pp. 82-83.

39. *Ibid.*, p. 110.
40. *Ibid.*, p. 119.
41. *Ibid.*
42. *Ibid.*, p. 121.
43. *Ibid.*, p. 128.
44. *Ibid.*, p. 130.
45. *Ibid.*
46. *Ibid.*, p. 133
47. *Ibid.*, p. 143.
48. *Ibid.*, p. 134.
49. *Ibid.*, p. 135.
50. *Ibid.*
51. *Ibid.*, p. 136.
52. *Ibid.*, p. 137.
53. *Ibid.*, p. 140.
54. *Ibid.*, p. 143.
55. *Ibid.*, p. 145.
56. *Ibid.*
57. *Ibid.*, p. 149.
58. *Ibid.*, p. 150.
59. *Ibid.*, p. 150-151.
60. *Ibid.*, p. 152.
61. *Ibid.*, p. 153.

8

V.D. Savarkar's Essentials of Hindutva (1923)

The text *Essentials of Hindutva* written in 1923, by Vinayak Damodar Savarkar (1883-1966) has taken a place of Classic in the literature of *Hindutva* and Hindu nationalism. The text attempts to construct and define the idea of Hindu, Hinduism, and *Hindutva* through a new interpretation of Indian history. His concept of *Hindutva,* what he considers a political concept in his text, meticulously attempts to portrait a "collective Indian/Hindu identity" and its corresponding imagined Indian/Hindu nation. In fact, through this book, Savarkar tried to give a new shape to Indian nationalism on the basis of the idea of *Hindutva*. The text also shows the lofty idea of Hindu nation and nationalism and justify them with the example of ancient Indian past that was, in Savarkar's view, essentially Hindu in its form and content. No doubt Savarkar's version of nationalism, during his time and afterward, came in conflict with other versions of nationalism including Gandhi's non-violent and inclusive nationalism and modern secular nationalism. This conflict still echoes in contemporary Indian political scenario, both at the level of practice and discourse.

Essentials of Hindutva was not Savarkar's first book. What is remarkable is the shift that Savarkar takes in this book. His first influential text *The Indian war of independence* (1908) that interprets Indian history in modern times shows his nationalist orientation against colonialism rather than "*Hindutva* reference" that we find in his text *Hindutva*. Giving a sign of passionate nationalists, in *The Indian war of independence,* he refuted the claims of British historians that the revolt of 1857 was just a Sepoy mutiny having nothing to with the general mass of the country. He argued that fundamental motive of 1987 revolt was the liberation of the country from the clutches of British rule. It is difficult to provide a correct explanation for Savarkar's ideological shift from violent Indian revolutionary nationalism to the concept of exclusive Hindu nationalism within the time span of 15 years. His biographer Keer (1988) suggests that his experience of Muslim prisoners, while he was in prison in Andaman, was largely responsible for that.[1] However, his published prison letters to his brother during 1918-20, as Grover (1993) informs us do not mention any such thing what Keer argues.[2] Whatever be the reason of Savarkar's paradigm shift, his text *Hindutva* had its own strength and power to construct an altogether different discourse on nationalism.

I

To find the undercurrent of Savarkar's *Hindutva* it is essential to have a look at his life, work and intellectual formation in brief. Born on 28 May, 1883, in the village of Bhagur near Nasik in Chitpavan Brahmin family, Savarkar had his initial education at the Shivaji School, Nasik. During his high school days, he used to organize *Shivaji Utsava* and *Ganesh Utsava*, started by Bal Gangadhar Tilak and used these occasions to put up plays on nationalistic themes. In 1902, Savarkar joined Fergusson College in Pune where he founded the "Abhinav Bharat Society" (1904). He was also involved in the *Swadeshi* movement and later joined Tilak's *Swaraj* Party. In June 1906, with the help of Shyam Krishna Varma, he left for London to become Barrister where he united and inflamed the Indian students in England against British rule in India. He stayed at the India House in London which was a thriving centre for student political and intellectual activity, and with Savarkar's addition, it soon became a hot-bed of revolutionary thought and activities. In 1908, Savarkar completed "the History of the War of Indian Independence." The text was banned by the British even before it was published for being "revolutionary, explosive and seditious."

In 1910, Savarkar was arrested in London and charged with five serious offenses, including conspiracy against the king's government and abetting murder. Extradited to India for trial, he was subsequently convicted and taken in 1911 to serve two life terms on the Andaman Islands. Savarkar was repatriated to an

Indian jail in 1921. He remained imprisoned in Ratnagiri Jail and then in Yeravada Jail until 6 January, 1924, when he was freed under the condition that he would not leave Ratnagiri district and abstain from political activity for the next five years. At the end of his five-year confinement in Ratnagiri, Savarkar joined Tilak's *Swaraj* Party and the Hindu Mahasabha. On 10 December, 1937, he was Elected as President of Akhil Bharat Hindu Mahasabha at its 19th Session at Karnavati (Ahmedabad) and continued to be re-elected President for the next seven years. He propagated Hindu Nationalism and later joined the Quit India movement. Savarkar was arrested and indicted by the Government of India in the Mahatma Gandhi assassination case. But he was acquitted by the Supreme Court of India, for reasons of lack of evidence. Savarkar died on 26 February, 1966, at the age of 83.

Savarkar's political life can be divided into two phases. In the first phase of childhood to 1910, he was an ardent revolutionary nationalist who was devoted to eliminating British rule. Afterward, during his imprisonment years (1911-1924) to his death, he stood as a prophet of Hindu nationalism who propagated the political philosophy of *Hindutva* through his writings and action. Close study of his writings suggests that, although, he derived his basic idea of the *Hindutva* both from Indian and foreign sources, however, he received motivation, direction and realistic suggestion from the writings and activities of political and social thinkers of Europe. In this connection, Sharma (2003) argues that Savarkar had little time for studying all the different schools of Hinduism, and moreover he was deeply suspicious of philosophical tenets founded on Holy Scriptures.[3] On the other hand, he was deeply influenced by the European philosophers. Sharma (2003) further informs, Savarkar studied the philosophy and ideas of Political Economy of James Mill (1773-1836) and J. Stuart Mill (1806-1876) in detail.[4] Especially, their notions of liberalism, individual freedom, and ideas on democracy had a deep impact on his mind. Further, as Sharma (2003) mentions, he was impressed with the philosophy of evolution proposed by Herbert Spencer (1820-1903).[5] As Woolf (2010) notes, from Herbert Spencer and Charles Darwin (1809-1882) he adopted the controversial idea of the "survival of the fittest" which is, without the doubt, the underlying theorem of Savarkar's "*Panchsheela*" towards the social and political transformation of the Indian society.[6] His philosophical outlook also got strengthened by studying the works of Jeremy Bentham (1748-1832). Savarkar himself wrote, "From then on I began to acknowledge this principle of morality as the touchstone of all my pursuits, of my ethical standards, and of my behaviour".[7]

In addition, as Lederle (1976) notes it is possible to find remarkable elements of Auguste Comte (1798-1857) in his political and social thoughts, for example, the importance given to the service of humanity as the best of human ends.[8] From all these European authors he studied the basic principles of social and political life, interpreted them through Indian eyes, and used them to propose his best approach towards the social and political problems of India.

Influenced by these European philosophers, Savarkar developed peculiar views on the God, universe and human being. According to him, human beings live in this world and not in a transcendental one, thus, the universe had nothing to do with the people and how they arranged their worldly life. Moreover, he claimed that the forces in the universe are to a little degree for Man, but to a greater extent, they are against him. From this Savarkar developed an exceptionally utilitarian ethics that seems the bedrock of his political thought, as he claims, "We must say that what is beneficial for mankind is good and what makes us suffer is bad. It is absurd to say what God likes is beneficial for the man or *vice versa*, because they are false notions. We live in the Universe but the Universe does not belong to us. To a great extent, it is unfavourable and to a very small extent favourable to us. We must appreciate this and face the heavenly occurrences. That is true Nature. That is the real worship of the God of the universe".[9]

Thus, he reached to a position that stated that "Man is the maker of his fortune and cause of his misfortunes. No divine power does any good or evil to human life. Man himself is responsible for the successes and failures, sweets and bitters of his life. Reason and intelligence lead one to light and ignorance to darkness.[10]

In his socio-political analysis, Savarkar was in favour of scientific reason than religious dogmatism. He argued that all religious scriptures are man-made. In his view, "What does not stand the test of scientific reason ought to be verily discarded even if it appears in the *Vedas, Avesta, Quran, Bible, Book of Moses* and the like. It is not true that an age of your is necessarily an age of truth! It is incorrect to think that everything that is ancient is necessarily sacred and worthy of worship".[11]

Thus, for him, no religious scripture is valid for all times. He did not consider any religious scripture to be unchangeable and valid for all times. Further, "I shall apply the test of present day science to all the wisdom and ignorance present in these scriptures. Only then shall I unreservedly practice and update what is essential for upholding and rejuvenating the nation![12] Apart from this scientific temper, Savarkar incorporated many other Western theories in Hinduism and developed a peculiar notion of *Hindutva* employing them in the Indian context. Wolf states, "Savarkar interpreted various concepts like utilitarianism, rationalism, humanism (universalism), pragmatism and realism and tried to apply them in the Indian context as cornerstones for the progress of his countrymen. He attempted to compose a worldly philosophy of life consisting of a portfolio of elements drawn from "classical Indian thought", western social and political philosophy and his own experience and observations".[13]

Savarkar's writing can be divided into three categories: non-political literature, historical studies, and political statement. If his historical studies *The Indian War of Independence* (1908), and *Six Glorious Epochs* narrates his specific view on Indian History, his political writings, *Essentials of Hindutva* (1923), *Hindu-pad-paadshaahi* (1925), and *Hindu-Rashtra Darshan* (Six lectures given in Hindu Mahasabha from 1937 to 1942) present his focused view on *Hindutva,* Hindu polity and Hindu *Sangathan* respectively.

As noted above, it is very surprising to the readers of Savarkar that his first influential text *The Indian War of Independence* that published in 1908 that interprets Indian history in modern times shows his nationalist orientation against colonialism rather than *"Hindutva reference"*. Savarkar argued in this book that the revolt of 1857 was India's first war of independence owing to fact that it essentially, was the natural manifestation of the feeling of independence visiting the hearts and minds of the patriotic soldiers' right from the western to the eastern part of the country. Savarkar had tremendous admiration for this sense of innate freedom of the sepoys, as it was rooted in the indigenous ideals of *Swadharma* and *Swaraj*.

No doubt, this book had the tremendous effect on Indian nationalists. In fact, at political level, his conclusion about a general state of war, fired by an intuitive but coherent idea of a nation, and overriding communitarian difference, gave a radical genealogy to the Extremists and revolutionary terrorists, who could now turn for inspiration to the violently anti-colonial and—indeed nationalist-resistance of an earlier generation. Thus, Savarkar's interpretation of Indian history was fully nationalist that challenged both colonial conceptions of India and re-vitalized nationalist sentiments.

Interesting point of his writing in this book is that his account of the War of Independence of 1857 makes a strong case for "feelings of mutual friendship" between the Hindus and the Muslims. There is acknowledgement in it of the enmity between Hindus and Muslims, but that is brushed aside as being "born out of ignorance". In fact, there are lyrical passages in it where Savarkar talks about members of the two antagonistic faiths partaking of the "same milk of the breasts of the Motherland" and becoming one. However, these views drastically change in his book *Hindutva*.

II

The first edition of the book titled as *Essentials of Hindutva* published in May 1923 does not mention the name of Savarkar as its author. Instead of the author of the text, it mentions "A Maratha'. The reason is given in the second edition of the book as "Veer Savarkar was still in prison the author's name was not published". The first edition also informs us that it was published by Sri V.V. Kelkar who was from Nagpur and it was printed at Poona city. The publisher in his notes, writes that book's "forcible style" and "convincing arguments", "passionate pleading" and "able survey" will attract even those "who hold different views from the author". The publisher, does not introduce the subject of the book to the readers "as the author is going to do it so beautifully in coming pages". The first edition does not inform us anything about the author and context in which the book was written. It is also interesting to note that the first edition of the book was also translated into Hindi after three years and published in 1926 by Sri Lakshmannarayan Garde from Calcutta.

The Preface by the Publisher of the second edition of the book tells us about its discursive history. It notes that it was during his stay from 1906 to 1910 in England that the attention of Veer Savarkar was drawn pointedly to the question as to who can be precisely called a 'Hindu'.[14] After years of study, he found the confusion lay in only identifying 'Hindu' with religious aspects. Savarkar decided to approach this question historically. Savarkar wrote this book in prison, after he had come in contact with *Khilafatists* whose attitude apparently convinced him—a revolutionary till then—that Muslims were the real enemies, not the British.

The text begins with the problem and anxiety of naming. Thus, one may notice in the text that there is a rather strained, complex, confused and confusing argument for preferring Hindu rather than Bharat, and later a contemporary, transcendental political *Hindutva* rather than the hitherto diverse/sectarian polymorphous Hinduism.

Savarkar begins his text with the "Fair maid of Verona" asking, "What's in a name?" And the central aim of his book is to answer the question "Who is a Hindu". He writes, "To this category of names which have been to mankind a subtle source of life and inspiration belongs the word *Hindutva,* the essential nature and significance of which we have to investigate into".[15] The other difficulty with defining *Hindutva* is that as Savarkar points out "The ideas and ideals, the systems and societies, the thoughts and sentiments which have centred around this name are so varied and rich, so powerful and so subtle, so elusive and yet so vivid that the term *Hindutva* defies all attempts at analysis". Thus, he claims that, "*Hindutva* is not a word but a history".[16] This history is not only the spiritual or religious history but a "history in full". He makes a distinction between *Hindutva* and Hinduism. "Hinduism is only a derivative, a fraction, a part of *Hindutva*".[17] Make it a little bit more clear he argues, "By an 'ism' it is generally meant a theory or a code more or less based on spiritual or religious dogma or creed. Had not linguistic usage stood in our way then 'Hinduness' would have certainly been a better word than Hinduism as a near parallel to *Hindutva. Hindutva* embraces all the departments of thought and activity of the whole Being of our Hindu race".[18] Thus, Savarkar concern is that "ism"s represents dogmas or creeds. *Hindutva* does not. He writes that he is not attempting a definition of the more limited term Hinduism (which has dogma and creed). But what his project is to understand Hindu to understand *Hindutva.*

Thus, Savarkar finds it difficult to define who is Hindu and argues that "Failure to distinguish between these two terms has given rise to much misunderstanding and mutual suspicion between some of those sister communities that have inherited this inestimable and common treasure of our Hindu civilization".[19]

Savarkar in the sub-section of this text "what is a Hindu" presents the historical view on the term 'Hindu'. He also claims that it is based on "solid recorded facts". He makes it clear that "We do not know exactly when the first intrepid Aryans made it to the Sindhu, the Indus river, but it was before the Egyptians and Babylonians." He further notes, "By the time the Aryans got to Indus, they had developed a sense of nationality and given it a name, "*Sapta Sindus*." The *Rigveda* records this as applying to all of Vedic India. Sindu is a variation on Indus river and the S and H being interchanged in Sanskrit, Sindu indicates Hindu. Savarkar also claims that other nations also recognized the Hindus. The Persians designated Vedic Aryans as Hindus. Local tribes, "who contacted Persians, must have also known the Aryans as Hindus".

Later in the text Savarkar argues "it is quite probable that the great Indus was known as Hindu to the original inhabitants of our land and owing to vocal peculiarity of the Aryans it got changed into Sindhu when they adopted it by the operation of the same rule that S is the Sanskritised equivalent of H. Thus, Hindu would be the name that this land and the people that inhabited it bore from time so immemorial that even the Vedic name Sindhu is but a later and secondary form of it".[20] Thus, Savarkar insists that the term Hindu goes back to the beginning of mythology.

Savarkar then goes to describe Hindu as the nation. The activities of so intrepid a people as the Sindhus or Hindus could no longer be kept cooped or cabined within the narrow compass of the *Panchanad* or the Punjab. Thus, The Hindus spread "led by the consciousness of a great mission and their Sacrificial Fire that was the symbol thereof"[21] and "they soon reclaimed the vast, waste and but very thinly populated lands. Forests were felled, agriculture flourished, cities rose, kingdoms thrived,—the touch of the human hand changed the whole face of the wild and unkemp nature".[22]

Elaborating further, Savarkar argues that cities arose and kingdoms thrived. But due to the Aryan's individualistic tendencies, their polities were loosely centralized. As their reach increased they brought other highly developed folks into their orbit. Keeping distant from locals, new names such as Kurus, Kashis, and Magadhas emerged while the old generic term of Sindhus or Hindus was almost forgotten. Thus not that the conception of national and cultural unity vanished, it just took other names. This growth peaked when "the valorous Prince of Ayodhya made a triumphant entry in Ceylon and actually brought the whole land from the Himalayas to the Seas under one sovereign sway".[23]

Savarkar gives a poetic description in his book and writes how the event of home coming of Ram Chandra to Ayodhya was "the real birthday of our Hindu people" and "truly our national day". He writes, "The day when the Horse of Victory returned to Ayodhya unchallenged and unchallengeable, the great white Umbrella of Sovereignty was unfurled over that Imperial throne of Ram Chandra, the brave, Ram Chandra the good, and a loving allegiance to him was sworn, not only by the Princes of Aryan blood but Hanuman, Sugriva, Vibhishana from the south that day was the real birthday of our Hindu people. It was truly our national day: for Aryans and Anaryans knitting themselves into a people were born as a nation. It summed-up and politically crowned the efforts of all the generations that preceded it and it handed down a new and common mission, a common banner, a common cause which all the generations after it had consciously or unconsciously fought and died to defend".[24]

Savarkar further gives another historical proof of Indian antiquity in a sub-section titled 'other name'. Savarkar argues that the terms Aryavarta or Bramhavarta were not so suitable as to express the vast synthesis that embraced the whole continent from the Indus to the sea and aimed to weld it into a nation. Although Aryavarta was best suited to the circumstances which gave it birth, however, it could not serve as a common name to a people that had welded Aryans and non-Aryans into a common race and had carried their culture-empire far beyond the bending summits of Vindhyadri. Thus, a suitable alternative name was found to indicate the Indian Nation "when the House of Bharat came to exercise its sway over the entire world".[25] Savarkar argues that there is no need to debate whether he was Vedic or a Jain or the exact dates of his rule, however, the subordinate groups took up the term "Bharatakhanda". According to Savarkar, "Bharatakhanda" indicated "politically grander expression"—from the Himalayas to the sea – as well as "common cultural empire".[25] He quotes *Vishnu Purana* arguing that we have met with no better attempt to define our position as a people than the terse little couplet in the *Vishnu Purana*, "The land which is to the north of the sea and to the south of the Himalaya mountain is named Bharata inhabited by the descendants of are Bharata".[27]

However the name Bharata did not totally suppress the name Hindu or Sindu although it seems like that The epithet Bharatakhand succeeded in almost overshadowing the cradle name of our nation in India. Yet the foreign nations seem to have cared little for it and as our frontier provinces continued to be known by their ancient name, so even our immediate neighbours—the Avestic Persians, the Jews, the Greeks and others clung to our ancient name Sindhus or Hindus. They did not merely indicate the borderland of Indus by this term as in days gone by, but the whole nation into which the ancient Sindhus by expansion and assimilation had grown. The Jews and Greeks continued to call us Sindhus or Hindus. Even Huentsang, Savarkar writes, who lived so long with us persists in calling us Shindus or Hindus. Down to this day, he further mentions, "the whole world knows us as 'Hindus' and our land as 'Hindusthan' as if in fulfillment of the wishes of our Vedic fathers who were the first to make that choice."

Giving a twist to his argument Savarkar notes that names are for others, more than ourselves. Thus, when wars and contact with the world happened, the word Hindu expressed "Bharatakhanda." In his words, "This fact added to the circumstances which brought us first into contact and then into a fierce conflict with the world at large, soon enabled the epithet Hindu to assert itself once more and so vigorously as to push into the background even the well-beloved name of Bharatakhanda itself".[28]

Reflecting on the name of Bharatakhand, Savarkar then turns to international acceptance of the name. In his view, though Hindusthan was by no means cut off from the world when Buddhism entered, this entry shows an international character. At this time, Hindusthan had filled up its land. And, India, he argues, "had become the heart and soul of almost the whole then known world. The outsiders who poured in to learn and trade came to call us Hindus too. Buddhism helped the name to grow in prominence throughout the world and made us more conscious of ourselves as Hindus."

Savarkar raises certain questions on the fall of Buddhism. "Can it be that philosophical differences alone could have made our nation turn against Buddhism?" "Can it be the inanitation and demoralization of the Buddhistic Church itself?"[29] "Note wholly', he argues and tells us that such shortcomings "would not have attracted such fierce attention and proved fatal to Buddhistic power in India had not the political consequences of the Buddhistic expansion been so disastrous to the national virility and even the national existence of our race".[30] He asserts that the Buddhist faith made people too passive and thus facilitated the Huns taking over India. But Hindus "could not drink with equanimity this cup of bitterness and political servitude at the hands of those whose barbarous violence could still be soothed by the mealy-mouthed formulas of *Ahimsa* and spiritual brotherhood".[31] He does not mean to rebuke Buddhism, "We yield to none in our love, admiration, and respect for the Buddha – the *Dharma* – the *Sangha*. They are all ours. Their glories are ours and ours their failures".[32] But, even holier things preceded the Buddhists, Hindu statesmen that allowed Buddhism to become what it became. "So, we do not think that the political virility or the manly nobility of our race began and ended with the Mauryas alone – or was a consequence of their embracing Buddhism. But Hindus could not be otherworldly while dominated by Huns whose whole creed could be summed in two words, "Fire and Sword".[33] And Buddhism had no "logic and no argument" that could counter the Fire and Sword doctrine. "So the leaders of thought and action of our race had to rekindle their Sacrificial Fire to oppose the sacrilegious one and to re-open the Vedic fields for steel, to get it sharpened on the altar of Kali".[34] The Hindus drove the invaders back to Tartary and Mongolia. On the other hand, "Back to the *Vedas*! The national cry grew louder and louder, more and more imperative because this was essentially a political necessity".[35]

In spite of this, Savarkar praises Buddhism. One of the subtitles of his text reads, Buddhism – A universal religion. He writes,

> "Buddhism had made the first and yet the greatest attempt to propagate a universal religion. "Go, ye Bhikkhus, to all the ten directions of the world and preach the law of Righteousness!" Truly, it was a law of Righteousness. It had no ulterior end in view, no lust for land or lucre

> quickening its steps; but grand though its achievements were it could not eradicate the seeds of animal passions nor of political ambitions nor of individual aggrandizement in the minds of all men to such an extent as to make it safe for India to change her sword for a rosary".[36]

Yet, he argues that grand though its achievements were, Buddhism "could not eradicate the seeds of animal passions nor of political ambitions nor of individual aggrandisement". India did try to incorporate and live up to Buddhist precepts to the best of its ability, "Nobly did she try to kill killing by getting killed – and at last found out that palm leaves at times are too fragile for steel!" "The leaders of thought and action grew sick of repeating the mumbos and jumbos of universal brotherhood".[37]

"Then came reaction", Savarkar claims and notes, "The reaction against universal tendencies of Buddhism only grew more insistent and powerful as the attempt to re-establish the Buddhist power in India began to assume a more threatening attitude".[38] We were aware of people in our ranks who sympathized with the enemy. Buddhist armies, stationed in China readied for an attack but they lost. And "They had to formally renounce all ulterior national aims against India and give a pledge that they would never again enter India with any political end in view".[39] Savarkar quotes *Bhavishya Purana, Pratisarga Parva* and writes, "All the Buddhists swore there and then that they would not come to the Aryadesh with any territorial designs". However, Savarkar writes, "The Buddhists as individuals had nothing to fear from India, the land of toleration, but they should give-up all dreams of endangering the national life of India and her independence".[40]

Savarkar then informs us that as a part of this retrenching in the face of the Buddhist some institutions were revived in which one of the institutions; the system of four *varnas* grew in popularity. His argument is that "From this, it was a natural step to prohibit our people from visiting shores which were uncongenial– in some cases fiercely hostile – to such peculiar institutions".[41]

On the other hand, the nation became stronger in self-knowledge to fight off the Buddhists. But in our North-Western borders, there was a commingling of races that were "growing rather too unceremonious to be healthy and our frontiers too shift to be safe". Thus, a boundary was drawn. And it was Sindhu River.

Savarkar again quotes *Bhavishya Purana, Pratisarga Parva* and writes, "The best country of the Aryans is known as *Sindhusthan* whereas the *Mleccha* country lies beyond the Indus. This demarcation was made by the great king (Shalivahan the grandson of the great Vikramaditya). Thus, "The day on which the patriarchs of our race had crossed that stream they ceased to belong to the people they had left behind and laid the foundation of a new nation".[42] They assimilated and expanded and created "a race and a new polity that could only be most fittingly and feelingly described as Sindhu or Hindu".

Savarkar then highlights the advantage of the term *Sindhusthan*. He notes in his text that *Bharatavarsha* is and must be a latter designation besides being personal in its appeal. It refers to a particular King. Emperor Bharata is gone, but Sindhu goes on for ever. In his words, "It is the vital spinal cord that connects the remotest past to the remotest future".[43] This must be why the leaders must have restored the "ancient Vedic name of our land and nation Sindhusthan – the best nation of Aryans." Another advantage of the name is that "Sindhu in Sanskrit does not only mean the Indus but also the Sea which girdles the Souther peninsula." Savarkar points to the geographical significance of the terms and writes "the epithet Sindhusthan calls up the image of our whole Motherland: the land that lies between Sindhu and Sindhu—from the Indus to the Seas".

Yet, in Savarkar's formulation of Sindhusthan does not only refer to geography. In his view, "the concept expressed by this word was 'national' and not merely 'geographical'." "Sindhusthan was not merely a piece of land but it was a nation which was ideally if not always actually a state (*rajnah-rashtram*)".[44] Further, Sindhusthan refers to the culture. Sindhusthan was the "Best nation of the Aryas". Elaborating it he notes, the term "is not based on any theological hair-splitting or fanaticism". The word Arya expressly refers to all who "have inherited a common culture, common blood, common country and common polity, while Mlechcha also by the very fact of its being put in opposition to Sindhusthan meant foreigners nationally and racially and not necessarily religiously."

Savarkar's source of history by which he depicts his views is ancient Hindu texts. He writes that we owe a debt of gratitude to these *Puranas* and Epics for having preserved all ancient and venerable records of our people through revolutions which had effaced the very traces of whole nations and whole civilizations elsewhere in the world. For after all, these records of our ancient and patriotic *Puranas* and Historis (*Itihasas*) are at any rate more faithful, more accurate and more reliable than the modern up-to-date western *Puranas* that have such convincing discoveries to their credit as the one which assures us that *Ramayana* sings of the foundation of Vijayanagar or the other which asserts that Gautam the Buddha was merely the Sun or the Dawn personified !

Savarkar then turns to the question of language. His argument is that the rise and fall of Buddhism were accompanied by a remarkable spread and growth of the vernacular and Sanskrit being shut-up in a classical fortress. "*Prakrit*" (Hindi) which better fit the living thoughts of the people. While Sanskrit writers generally preferred the word '*Bharat*' in being more in consonance with the established canons of elegance. But Hindusthan stuck in popular and living culture. While Sanskrit is the linguistic and cultural backbone, *Prakrit* (Hindi) – an elder daughter of Sanskrit – is the living spoken tongue. Centuries prior to the British Hindi or Hindustani was the mother tongue for those crossing the nation."

In his words, "Hindusthani is par excellence the language of Hindusthan or Sindhusthan. The attempt to raise Hindi to the pedestal of our national tongue is neither new nor forced. Centuries before the advent of British rule in India we find it recorded in our annals that this was the medium of expression throughout India. A *sadhu* or a merchant starting from Rameshwaram and proceeding to Hardwar, could make himself understood in all parts of India through this tongue. Sanskrit might have introduced him to circles of *pandits* and princes, but Hindusthani was a safe and sure passport to the *Rajsabhas* as well as to the *bazaars*. A Nanak, a Chaitanya, a Ramdas could and did travel up and down the country as freely as they would have done in their own provinces teaching and preaching in this tongue. As the growth and development of this our genuine national tongue was parallel to and almost simultaneous with the revival and popularization of the ancient names Sindhusthan or Sindhus or Hindusthan or Hindus it was but a matter, of course, that language being the common possession of the whole nation should be called Hindusthani or Hindi".[45]

It is this common bondage, Savarkar argues, that after the Huns were expelled, nearly a thousand years of peace and prosperity took place India. He provides a picture of political unity in India. He writes:

> "From Ceylon to Kashmir the Rajputs—a single family of princes—ruled, often connected closely by marriages and more closely by the tradition of chivalry and culture handed down by a common law. The whole life of the nation was being brought into a harmony as rich as divine, and the growth of the national language was but an outward expression of this inward unity of our national life".[46]

Savarkar then comes to the foreign invader. He notes, "The Mohammedans had crossed that stream even under Kasim, but it was a wound only skin-deep, for the heart of our people was not hurt and was not even aimed at. The contest began in the grim earnestness with Mohammad and ended, shall we say, with Abdalli ? From year to year, decade to decade, century to century, the contest continued. Arabia ceased to be what Arabia was; Iran annihilated; Egypt, Syria, Afghanistan, Baluchistan, Tartary,—from Granada to Gazni—nations, and civilizations fell in heaps before the sword of Islam of Peace!! But here for the first time, the sword succeeded in striking but not in killing ...The contrast was not only grim but it was monstrously unequal. It was not a race, a nation or a people India had to struggle with. It was nearly all Asia, quickly to be followed by nearly all Europe. ...Day after day, decade after decade, century after century, the ghastly conflict continued and India single-handed kept up the fight morally and militarily. The moral victory was won when Akbar came to the throne, and Darashikoh was born".[47]

It is in this background Savarkar puts his view on "*Hindutva* at work." He writes that in this prolonged furious conflict our people became intensely conscious of ourselves as Hindus and were welded into a nation to an extent unknown in our history. There was no divide between sects. "It must not be forgotten that we have all along referred to the progress of the Hindu movement as a whole and not to that of any particular creed or religious section thereof—of *Hindutva* and not Hinduism only. Sanatanists, Satnamis, Sikhs, Aryas, Anaryas, Marathas and Madrasis, Brahmins and Panchamas—all suffered as Hindus and triumphed as Hindus.

Both friends and foes contributed equally to enable the words Hindu and Hindusthan to supersede all other designations of our land and our people".[48]

Further, "All those on this side of the Indus who claimed the land from Sindhu to Sindhu, from the Indus to the seas, as the land of their birth, felt that they were directly mentioned by that one single expression, Hindusthan. The enemies hated us as Hindus and the whole family of peoples and races, of sects and creeds that flourished from Attock to Cuttack was suddenly individualised into a single Being".[49]

Thus, Savarkar argues that *Hindutva*, again, refers to all as a unit who suffered under the invaders. Those who fought did so as *Hindutva*. "This one word, *Hindutva*, ran like a vital spinal cord through our whole body politic and made the Nayars of Malabar weep over the sufferings of the Brahmins of Kashmir. Our bards bewailed the fall of Hindus, our seers roused the feelings of Hindus, our heroes fought the battles of Hindus, our saints blessed the efforts of Hindus, our statesmen moulded the fate of Hindus, our mothers wept over the wounds and gloried over the triumphs of Hindus".[50]

All the testimonials to those who cultivated and fought in the name of *Hindutva* would take volumes, he writes but offers a few examples in his text. After setting different examples and making analysis of history of Hindu and Hidusthan, Savarkar in the subtitle "stupid notion must go" writes that "having thus tried to trace the successive chapters of the history of the words Hindu and Hindusthan from the earliest Vedic period to the fall of the last of our Hindu empire in 1818 A.D., we are now in a position to address ourselves to the main task of determining the essentials of Hindutva".[51]

Thus, as we may note almost in half of the book he traces the history of word Hindu and Hindusthan as well as support and refutation of arguments. He then mentions, "The first result of this enquiry is to explore the baseless suspicion which has crept into the minds of some of our well-meaning but hasty countrymen that the origin of the words Hindu and Hindusthan is to be traced to the malice of the Mohammedans![52]

He makes his arguments by stating that "Long before Mohammad was born, nay, long before the Arabians were heard of as a people, this ancient nation was known to ourselves as well as to the foreign world by the proud epithet Sindhu or Hindu and Arabians could not have invented this term, any more than they could have invented the Indus itself".[53]

Savarkar then makes his own position; "Now, we are fairly in a position to try to analyse the contents of one of the most comprehensive and bewilderingly synthetic concepts known to human tongue. *Hindutva* is a derivative word from Hindu, we have seen that the earliest and the most sacred records of our race show that the appellation, *Saptasindhu* or *Hapt-Hindu* was applied to a region in which the Vedic nation flourished. The geographical sense being the primary one has, now contracting, now expanding, but always persistently been associated with the words Hindu and Hindus than till after the lapse of nearly 5,000 years if not more, Hindusthan has come to mean the whole continental country from the Sindhu to Sindhu from the Indus to the Seas".[54]

He further observes, "The most important factor that contributes to the cohesion, strength and the sense of unity of a people is that they should possess an internally well-connected and externally well-demarcated "local habitation," and a "name" that could, by its very mention, rouse the cherished image of their motherland as well as the loved memories of their past.[55]

He praises the land as follows, "We are happily blessed with both these important requisites for a strong and united nation. Our land is so vast and yet so well-knit, so well demarcated from others and yet so strongly entrenched that no country in the world is more closely marked out by the fingers of nature as a geographical unit beyond cavil or criticism, as also is the name Hindusthan or Hindu that it has come to bear".[56]

He further mentions that "The first image that it rouses in the mind is unmistakable of our motherland and by an express appeal to its geographical and physical features it vivifies it into a living Being. Hindusthan meaning the land of Hindus, the first essential of *Hindutva* must necessarily be this geographical one. A Hindu is primarily a citizen either in himself or through his forefathers of 'Hindusthan' and claims the land as his motherland".[57]

As we may note, Savarkar reaches to his original project only after half of the book.

The next project is to chalk out the essential implications of *Hindutva* that is the title of the book. He begins, "But throughout our inquiry we have been concerning ourselves more with what would have been or what should be. Not that to paint what should be is not a legitimate pursuit; nay, it is as necessary and at times more stimulating; but even that could be better done by first getting a firm hold of what actually is".[58]

In fact, in the subtitle "Essential Implications of *Hindutva*," he points out his original project that is essential of *Hindutva.* He writes, "We must try, therefore, to be on our guard so that in our attempt to determine the essentials of *Hindutva* we be guided entirely by the actual contents of the word as it stands at present".[59]

It is here Savarkar makes a difference between Hindu and Indian. He fears, "although the root-meaning of the word Hindu like the sister epithet Hindi may mean only an Indian, yet as it is we would be straining the usage of words too much—we fear, to the point of breaking if we call a Mohammedan a Hindu because of his being a resident of India".[60]

He argues that at some future time the word 'Hindu' may come to indicate a citizen of Hindusthan and nothing else; but it is possible if every other 'ism' has disowned its special dogmas and he/she adopted our culture and our history, inherited our blood and has come to look upon our land not only as the land of his love but even of his worship.

Thus in Savarkar's view, "the first requisite of *Hindutva* is that he be a citizen of Hindusthan either by himself or through his forefathers, yet it is not the only requisite qualification of it, as the term 'Hindu' has come to mean much more than its geographical significance".[61]

Savarkar makes another criterion to determine who should be called Hindu. He argues that Hindu cannot be synonymous with Bharatiya or Hindi and mean an Indian only. In his words, "The reason that explains why the term 'Hindu' cannot be synonymous with Bharatiya or Hindi and mean an Indian only, naturally introduces us to the second essential implication of that term. The Hindus are not merely the citizens of the Indian state because they are united not only by the bonds of the love they bear to a common motherland but also *by the bonds of a common blood*. They are not only a Nation but also a race—*jati*".[62]

He further elaborates his position by arguing that they [Hindu] are not only a Nation but also a race—jati. The word *jati* derived from the root *Jan* to produce, means a brotherhood, a race determined by a common origin,—possessing a common blood.

All Hindus claim to have in their veins the blood of the mighty race incorporated with and descended from the Vedic fathers, the Sindhus.

Savarkar's this position cannot be read only in relation to the Moslems. He was really responding to the colonial discourse that proposed that India cannot be a nation because it does not belong to one race.

He writes, "We are well aware of the not unoften interested objection that carpingly questions "but are you really a race?" Savarkar argues that if English, German, French, Chinese can claim in spite of the freely infusing foreign blood into their race by contracting marriages with other races then Hindu too. Giving his own version of interpretation of history, he makes a statement of the racial unity of Hindu.

> "No word can give full expression to this racial unity of our people as the epithet, Hindu, does. Some of us were Aryans and some Anaryans; but Ayars and Nayars—we were all Hindus and own a common blood. Some of us are *Brahmans* and some Namashudras or Panchamas; but *Brahmans* or Chandalas—we are all Hindus and own a common blood...... We feel we are a JATI, a race bound together by the dearest ties of blood and therefore, it must be so".[63]

He further supports his argument by stating that "And speaking relatively alone, no people in the world can more justly claim to get recognized as a racial unit than the Hindus and perhaps the Jews. A Hindu marrying a Hindu may lose his caste but not his *Hindutva*. A Hindu believing in any theoretical or philosophical or social system, orthodox or heterodox, provided it is unquestionably indigenous and founded by a Hindu may lose his sect but not his *Hindutva*—his Hinduness—because the most important essential which determines it is the inheritance of the Hindu blood. Therefore, all those who love the land that stretches from Sindhu to Sindhu—from the Indus to the Seas, as their fatherland consequently claim to inherit the blood of the race that has evolved, by incorporation and adaptation, from the ancient *Saptasindhus* can be said to possess two of the most essential requisites of *Hindutva*".[64]

The third criterion Savarkar sets to be called Hindu is Hindu culture. He writes, "Hindus are bound together not only by the tie of the love we bear to a common fatherland and by the common blood that courses through our veins and keeps our hearts throbbing and our affections warm, but also by the tie of the common homage we pay to our great civilization—our Hindu culture".[65] Thus he concludes, "We are one because we are a nation, a race and own a common *Sanskriti* (civilization)".[66]

Having established the criterion, Savarkar attempts to illustrate a fundamental issue of the twentieth century; the issue of civilization. In a chapter of the text What is civilization Savarkar elaborates his views on civilization. In his definition 'Civilization is the expression of the mind of man".[67] "Civilization is the account of what man has made of matter". Further, "If matter is the creation of the Lord, then civilization is the miniature secondary creation of man". "At its best it is the perfect triumph of the soul of man over matter and man alike".[68] Locating this definition of civilization in nation he writes, "The story of the civilization of a nation is the story of its thoughts, its actions, and its achievements. Literature and art tell us of its thoughts; history and social institutions of its actions and achievements".[69]

He is convinced that civilizations may borrow much, "yet their civilization is too characteristic to be mistaken for any other 'cultural unit'." His text lists cultural items that all Hindus and only Hindus understand. "We understood our Hindu heroes as people who fought and died for us". Savarkar also tells that wars among Hindus do not mean that Hindus are divided and separate as a people. "But what about the internecine wars amongst Hindus? We answer, what about the Wars of Roses amongst the English? What of the internecine struggle, of the state against state, sect against sect, class against class, each invoking foreign help against his own countrymen, in Italy, in Germany, in France, in America? Are they still a people, a nation and do they possess a common history? If they do, the Hindus do. If the Hindus do not possess a common history, then none in the world does".[70]

He further argues that "our history tells the story of the action of our race, so does our literature taken in its fullest sense tell the story of the thought of our race" and the works of art and architecture are also a common inheritance of our race, whether they be representative of *Vaidik* or *Avaidik* school of thought.

Savarkar further argues that common laws and rites among Hindu also proves its basic unity.

Common institutions and a common law that sanctions and sanctifies them, however, they may differ in details are nevertheless both the cause and the effect of the basic unity of our race.

"We have feasts and festivals in common. We have rites and rituals in common. The *Dasara* and the *Divali* the *Rakhi Bandhan* and the *Holi* are welcomed wherever a Hindu breathes, Sikhs and Jains, *Brahman*s and Panchams alike. You would find the whole Hindu kingdom enfete on the *Divali* day, not only Hindusthan, but the Greater Hindusthan that is fast growing in all the continents of the world".[71] Savarkar points out that :

> "These then in short—and the subject in hand does not permit us to be exhaustive on this point —constitute the essence of our civilization and mark us out a cultural unit. We Hindus are not only a *Rashtra*, a *Jati*, but as a consequence of being both, own a common *Sanskriti* expressed, preserved chiefly and originally through Sanskrit, the real mother tongue of our race. Everyone who is a Hindu inherits this *Sanskriti* and owes his spiritual being to it as truly as he owes his physical one to the land and the blood of his forefathers".[72]

This is why converts to Christianity and Islam are not to be recognized as countrymen, though they have much culturally in common.

"Hindusthan to them is Fatherland as to any other Hindu, yet it is not to them a Holyland too. Their holy land is far off in Arabia or Palestine".[73] Consequently, their names and their outlook smack of a foreign origin. Their love is divided. "They must set their Holyland above their Fatherland in their love and allegiance. That is but natural. We are not condemning nor are we lamenting. We are simply telling facts as they stand".[74]

Savarkar further suggests that reconversion to the Hindu fold is allowed. But those who speak of a distant Holy land cannot be part of *Hindutva*.

Savarkar finally reaches to his definition of who is a Hindu and writes that "A Hindu then is he who feels attachment to the land that extends from Sindhu to Sindhu as the land of his forefathers—as his Fatherland; who inherits the blood of the great race whose first and discernible source could be traced from the Himalayan altitudes of the *Vedic Saptasindhus* and which assimilating all that was incorporated and ennobling all that was assimilated has grown into and come to be known as the Hindu people; and who, as a consequence of the foregoing attributes, has inherited and claims as his own the *Hindu Sanskriti*, the Hindu civilization, as represented in a common history, common heroes, a common literature, common art, a common law and a common jurisprudence, common fairs and festivals, rites and rituals, ceremonies and sacraments".[75]

Savarkar also mentions, "The limits of this essay do not permit us to determine the nature or the essentials of Hinduism or to try to discuss it at any great length. As we have shown above the inquiry into what is Hinduism can only begin after the question "Who is a Hindu"? is rightly answered determining the essentials of *Hindutva*; and as it is only with these essentials of *Hindutva*, which enable us to know who is a Hindu, that this our present enquiry is concerned, the discussion of Hinduism falls necessarily outside of our scope".[76]

Savarkar clarifies the meaning of *Hindu dharma* in his own way. Hinduism, in his view, denotes the religion of the majority only. Either the word should be restored to its proper significance to denote the religions of all Hindus or if you fail to do that it should be dropped altogether. "This is *Hindu dharma*—the conclusion of the conclusions arrived at by harmonising the detailed experience of all the schools of religious thought—*Vaidika, Sanatani,* Jain, Bauddh, *Sikh* or *Devasamaji*. Each one and everyone of those systems or sects which are the direct descendants and developments of the religious beliefs—*Vaidik* and non-*Vaidik* that obtained in the land of the Saptasindhus or in the other unrecorded communities in other parts of India in the Vedic period, belongs to and is an integral part of *Hindu dharma*".[77]

Further, "Hinduism means the system of religious beliefs found common amongst the Hindu people. Hinduism means the "ism" of the Hindu. The word 'Hindu' comes from Sindu, the Indus. Thus, it means the religions that are peculiar and native to this land and these people. You might say these sects contradict each other. But they are all still of the Indus and as such "Hinduism".[78]

"*Hindutva* is not identical with *Hindu Dharma*; nor is *Hindu Dharma* identical with Hinduism. This twofold mistake that identifies *Hindutva* with *Hindu Dharma* and both with *Sanatani* sect is justly resented by our non-*Sanatani* sects or religious systems and goads a small section of people amongst them—not to explode this mistaken notion, but unfortunately to commit another grave and suicidal mistake in the opposite direction and disown their *Hindutva* itself".[79]

"This *Bharatbhumi*, this *Sindhusthan*, this land of ours that stretches from Sindhu to Sindhu is our *Punyabhumi*, for it was in this land that the Founders of our faith and the Seers to whom '*Veda*' the Knowledge was revealed, from *Vaidik* seers to Dayananda, from Jina to Mahavir, from Buddha to Nagasen, from Nanak to Govind, from Banda to Basava, from Chakradhar to Chaitanya, from Ramdas to Rammohan, our *Gurus* and Godmen were born and bred. The very dust of its paths echoes the footfalls of our Prophets and *Gurus*".[80] So to every Hindu, from the Santal to the *Sadhu* this *Bharata bhumi* this *Sindhusthan* is at once a *Pitribhu* and a *Punyabhu*—fatherland and a holy land.

After this definition, Savarkar gives a national call. He writes that who by race, by blood, by culture, by nationality possess almost all the essentials of *Hindutva* and had been forcibly snatched out of our ancestral home by the hand of violence—ye, have only to render wholehearted love to our common Mother and recognize her not only as Fatherland (*Pitribhu*) but even as a Holyland (*punyabhu*); and yet would be most welcome to the Hindu fold.

Savarkar reaches to the final section of his text what he terms as Unique Natural Blessings to Hindusthan.

The central question that Savarkar puts is this section is that "we found *Hindutva* to contribute towards the strength, cohesion, and progress of our people, but is it a ground strong enough to build a future that will repel attacks?"

He mentions that some ancient people built huge walls as to convert a whole country into a fortified castle. Today their walls are dust. But for Bharat, the Himalayas are Sindhusthan's ramparts, the oceans their moat.[81] "She is the richly endowed, daughter of God—this our Motherland."[82] He seems to write a beautiful poetry on Sindhusthan's natural endowments. And the second essential of Hindustan (beyond a land) "puts the estimate of our latent powers of national cohesion and greatness yet higher. No country in the world with the exception of China again is peopled by a race so homogeneous, yet so ancient".[83] Muslims and Christians are religious but not a race or national. The Hindus are! "And culture? The English and Americans feel they are kith and kin, because they possess a Shakespeare in common." The Hindus—a *Ramayana* and a *Mahabharata* and the *Vedas*. Americans have history in centuries. Hindus in *Kalpas*. "If people that had no past has no future, then writes the people that had produced an unending galaxy of heroes... [who] fought with and vanquished the forces whose might struck Greece and Rome".[84]

Beyond culture, the tie of common holy land has often seemed stronger than the bonds of Motherland. Muslims would sacrifice all India if that be to the glory of Islam or could save the city of their prophet. Look at the Jews through centuries abroad, they are still super attached to Israel, the land of their Prophets. If a Jewish state ever happens in Palestine, they would naturally set the interests of their Holyland above those of their Motherland in America and Europe. If war happened between their motherland and Holyland, they did sympathize with the latter. The crusades again attest to the wonderful influence that a common holy land exercises over a people widely separated in race, nationality, and language.[85]

The ideal conditions in which a nation can attain perfect solidarity and cohesion would, other things being equal, be found in the case of those people who inhabit the land they adore, the land of whose forefathers is also the land of their Gods, the scenes of their history and mythology. Only Arabia and Palestine (if it becomes Jewish) have this advantage. But Arabia is poorer in natural, cultural, and historical essentials of a great people. And the potential Zionist state too. China alone of the present comity of nations is almost as richly gifted with the geographical, racial, cultural essentials as the Hindus are.

Thus, the actual essentials of *Hindutva* are the ideal essentials of nationality. Great combinations are the order of the day the League of Nations, Pan-Islamism, Pan-Slavism are each little beings seeking to be incorporated into greater wholes, so as to be better fitted for the struggle for existence and power. "Who to those who have them already as their birth-right and know them not; or worse, despise them!" Can any one of you, Oh Hindus! Whether Jain or *Samaji* or Sikh or any other sub-section afford to cut yourselves off or fall out of the organic combination that already exists?

Strengthen these ties if you can: "pull down the barriers that have survived their utility, of castes, and custom, of sects and sections:... "inter-marriages between provinces and provinces, castes and castes, be encouraged where they do not exist." Where they do exist – "suicidal be the hand that tries to cut the nuptial tie." "Let the minorities remember they would be cutting the very branch on which they stand. Strengthen every tie that binds you to the main organism, whether of blood or language or common Motherland." Blend blood, "from vein to vein, from Attock to Cuttack till at last the Hindu people get fused and welded into an indivisible whole, till our race gets consolidated and strong sharp as steel." "We are trying our best, as we ought to do, to develop the consciousness of and a sense of attachment to the greater whole, whereby Hindus, Mohammedans, Parsis, Christians, and Jews would feel as Indians first and every other thing afterward. But whatever progress India may have made to that goal one thing remains almost axiomatically true – not only in India, but everywhere in the world—that a nation requires a foundation to stand upon and the essence of the life of a nation is the life of that portion of its citizens whose interest and history and aspirations are most closely bound-up with the land and who thus provide the real foundation to the structure of their national state."

He inspires Hindu saying, "Look at America whose Germans deserted during First World War. The "American State, in the last resort, must stand or fall with the fortunes of its Anglo-Saxon constituents." Hindus are India's bedrock. Therefore, "even from the point of Indian nationality, must ye, O Hindus, consolidate and strengthen Hindu nationality; not to give wanton offense to any of our non-Hindu compatriots... but in just and urgent defence of our race and land." Further,

> "As long as competition and pan – movements compete for the world, we must have our team in order. And someday India when will be able to dictate claims to the whole earth they cannot do so in terms so very different from the terms which the *Gita* dictates or the Buddha lays down."

Savarkar concludes the text with a bold confidence. He notes "Thirty crores of people, with India for their basis of operation, for their Fatherland and for their Holyland with such a history behind them, bound together by ties of a common blood and common culture can dictate their terms to the whole world. A day will come when mankind will have to face the force. Equally certain it is that whenever the Hindu come to hold such a position whence they could dictate terms to the whole world — those terms cannot be very different from the terms which *Gita* dictates' or the Buddha lays down—A Hindu is most intensely so, when he ceases to be Hindu; and with a Shankar claims the whole earth for a Benares "Waranasi Medini !" or with a Tukaram exclaims "my country ! Oh, brothers, "the limits of the Universe — there the frontiers of my country lie!"[86]

Notes and References

1. Keer, Dhananjay. 1988. *Veer Savarkar.* Bombay: Popular Prakashan, 1998, p. 234.
2. Grover, V., 1993. *V.D. Savarkar.* New Delhi, Deep and Deep, pp. 582-636.
3. Sharma, Jiotirmaya. 2003. *Hindutva: Exploring the Idea of Hindu Nationalism.* New Delhi: Viking/Penguin Book, p. 125.
4. *Ibid.*, p. 127.
5. *Ibid.*, p. 136.
6. Wolf. Heidelberg Papers in South Asian and Comparative Politics, *Vinayak Damodar Savarkar's 'Strategic Agnosticism': A Compilation of his Socio-political Philosophy and Worldview* by Siegfried O. Wolf, Working Paper No. 51, January 2010, archiv.ub.uni-heidelberg.de/ voll text server/.../HPSACP_Wolf.pdf, downloaded on 10-06-2012, p. 5.
7. *Samagra Savarkar Vangamaya* (Vol. 1). Pune: Prakashan Samiti, Maharashtra Prantik Hindu Sabha, 1963-65, p. 206.
8. Lederle, Mathew, 1976. *Philosophical Trends in Modern Maharashtra.* Bombay: Popular Prakashan, p. 138.
9. Keer, *op. cit.*, p. 204.
10. Quoted in Godbole, V.S., 2004. *Rationalism of Veer Savarkar.* Thane: Itihas Patrika Prakashangal,p. 338.
11. *Samagra Savarkar Vangmaya*, Vol. 4, 1936, p. 579.
12. *Ibid.*, Vol. 3, 1934, p. 364.
13. Wolf, *op. cit.*, p. 8.
14. This study employs the fifth edition of *Hindutva* for its analysis. Savarkar, V. D., 1969, *Essentials of Hindutva*, Bombay: Veer Savarkar Prakashan.
15. Savarkar, V. D. 1969, *Essentials of Hindutva*, Bombay: Veer Savarkar Prakashan, p. 3.
16. *Ibid.*, p. 3.

17. *Ibid.*
18. *Ibid.*, p. 4.
19. *Ibid.*, p. 3.
20. *Ibid.*, p. 10.
21. *Ibid.*
22. *Ibid.*, p. 11.
23. *Ibid.*
24. *Ibid.*, pp. 11-12.
25. *Ibid.*, p. 13.
26. *Ibid.*
27. *Ibid.*
28. *Ibid.*, p. 16.
29. *Ibid.*, p. 18.
30. *Ibid.*
31. *Ibid.*, p. 19.
32. *Ibid.*, p. 20.
33. *Ibid.*, p. 21.
34. *Ibid.*
35. *Ibid.*, p. 22.
36. *Ibid.*
37. *Ibid.*, p. 23.
38. *Ibid.*, p. 25.
39. *Ibid.*, p. 26.
40. *Ibid.*
41. *Ibid.*, p. 27.
42. *Ibid.*, p. 30.
43. *Ibid.*, p. 31.
44. *Ibid.*, p. 32.
45. *Ibid.*, p. 41.
46. *Ibid.*, p. 42.
47. *Ibid.*, p. 44.
48. *Ibid.*, p. 45.
49. *Ibid.*
50. *Ibid.*, p. 46.
51. *Ibid.*, p. 70.
52. *Ibid.*, pp. 70-71.
53. *Ibid.*, p. 71.
54. *Ibid.*, pp. 81-82.
55. *Ibid.*, p. 82.
56. *Ibid.*
57. *Ibid.*
58. *Ibid.*, p. 83.
59. *Ibid.*
60. *Ibid.*

61. *Ibid.*, p. 84.
62. *Ibid.*
63. *Ibid.*, pp. 89-90.
64. *Ibid.*, p. 90.
65. *Ibid.*, pp. 90-91.
66. *Ibid.*, p. 92.
67. *Ibid.*
68. *Ibid.*
69. *Ibid.*
70. *Ibid.*, p. 95.
71. *Ibid.*, p. 98.
72. *Ibid.*, p. 99.
73. *Ibid.*, p. 113.
74. *Ibid.*
75. *Ibid.*
76. *Ibid.*, p. 105.
77. *Ibid.*, p. 108.
78. *Ibid.*, p. 104.
79. *Ibid.*, p. 121.
80. *Ibid.*, p. 111.
81. *Ibid.*, p. 132.
82. *Ibid.*
83. *Ibid.*
84. *Ibid.*, p. 134.
85. *Ibid.*, p. 136.
86. *Ibid.*, p. 141.

9
Epilogue

As mentioned earlier in this study, the period from 1905 to 1923 was crucial one in the development of nationalism in India. Nationalism that was propagated previously (before 1905) took mature form in this period and it was scripted properly. It was also presented in coherent and cogent form. The scripted nationalism, although with variations, had lineage and were influenced by many other factors. As this study shows, Indian nationalism had a long background of more than one hundred years and it was conditioned both by the materiality and ideology of some forms of nationalist and colonial politics.

There are some important common themes that emerge in texts considered in this study. Themes that most prominently come up in these texts are: a particular essential nature of India in comparison to colonial Britain, notion of civilization, idea of nation as well as idea of India, and methods taken for solidarity among Indians. Yet, underneath the treatment of these common themes there exist serious variations. This chapter deals with the commonalities and variations emerging out of aforementioned themes.

Before we deal with these issues, it needs to be pointed out that the texts, which are under-consideration here, show a deep unification of "Indian culture" and "politics". The assumed and depicted Indian culture in these texts attempted to map out a site on which the complex struggle of Indian independence was to be waged. Not only this, these texts also carved out an imagined Indian identity by visualizing a nation which was free from British domination and one in which brotherhood and democracy will prevail among its citizens. These texts also invoke discourses that are important in implications.

This final chapter deals with these discourses. As these texts were written in the nationalist temperament one might argue; what were the nationalists' discourses and how they were put against colonials? What was common among them and what was different? How did they present their view on India? How did they imagine India? How are they affecting India today? How can they be located in broad debate of Indian nationalism?

These questions are discursive in nature. For the sake of clarity, let us consider some direct questions raised earlier in the study in the light of these texts that also throws light on the questions raised above. These questions were:

(i) How do these texts claim Indians rights to make their own self-definition, rather than being defined by the British? In other words, how do these texts construct *a difference* between India and Britain?
(ii) How do these texts *define civilization* in general and Indian civilization in particular?
(iii) How do these text *define nation* and offered *the idea of India*?
(iv) How do these texts offer the means by which divergent people within the India can construct *solidarity* across cultural and class differences?

These questions generate discourses that can be put respectively as discourse on essential nature of India, discourse of Indian civilization, discourse on nation and discourses on means of solidarity. Let us examine them separately.

Discourse on Essential Nature of India

We noticed that Sri Aurobindo's text *Bhawani Mandir* (1905) answer this question on the basis of Indian spiritualism. In other words, the spiritual power of India is basis by which Indian should assert their right under British colonialism and it is on this basis they should define themselves against colonial construction of India. As noted in chapter four of this study, *Bhawani Mandir* also claims that India was once a spiritual nation, but it has lost its power because of 'inaction' in *Jñāna, Bhakti* and *Karma*. Thus, India needs to 'reborn'. The texts emphasizes that Indian should accumulate 'strength' to establish their old glory. The strength that the text stresses on, is not only physical strength, but includes intellectual, moral and spiritual strength also. Like other nationalists, we find here that Aurobindo also sees real source of strength in spiritualism. As noted, he also finds this spiritual strength "inexhaustible and imperishable" source of all the other strengths. He also warns that Indian should not imitate the west, including the "western science" as it will not solve their problems. In his words, "we must strive to acquire before all others, is strength—strength physical, strength mental, strength moral, but above all strength spiritual which is the one inexhaustible and imperishable source of all the others".[1] Thus, it is through spiritual strength, Aurobindo attempts to give the self-definition of India. It is the spiritual strength by which Aurobindo maps out Indian nationalism.

Gandhi in his text *Hind Swaraj* (1909) also argues that Indians are entirely different from British people as their civilization is entirely different from the British. As discussed in chapter five of this study, in Gandhi's view, Indian civilization represents spiritual civilization while British represent modern civilization. Further, Indian civilization is not only *different* but *higher* than the British civilization. Gandhi is convinced that India's civilization is spiritual and superior, thus, it is different and higher than the Western civilization which is body centric and materialist. Not only this Indian civilization is 'true civilization' that is 'permanent' while British civilization that represents materialistic civilization is 'self-destructive' in nature. It is on this basis Gandhi argues that India does not need European form of violent nationalism that European civilization offers. Instead India needs its own form of nationalism that will reflect true spiritual essence of Indian civilization. This is highlighted by many set of dialogues between the 'reader' and the 'editor' in the text that confirms Gandhi's views on the correlation between Indian civilization and its true form of nationalism. Gandhi valorizes Indian civilization and notes that the civilization India has evolved "is not to be beaten in the world". Moreover, "Nothing can equal the seeds sown by our ancestors". He further mentions that "Rome went, Greece shared the same fate, the might of the Pharaohs was broken, Japan has become westernized, of China nothing can be said, but India is still, somehow or other, sound at the foundation".[2] In Gandhi's view, it is the spiritual nature of Indian civilization that is its foundation.

Bipin Chandra Pal in this text *The Spirit of Indian Nationalism* (1910), although not directly comes to the spiritual essence of India like Gandhi and Aurobindo, as his writing is highly contextual, yet he confirms that "secret of India lies in India's moral power not in its physical power". He also notes that in India "there is nothing really is purely secular. The sacred and secular are strangely blended together in every department of the comparatively primitive life and activities of the people".[3] He argues that Hindu has "endowed with exceptional spiritual discernment" by which he "recognizes the signs of coming changes in the political condition of his country". He also mentions that "deepest spiritual forces of India" must be recognized to save the world.[4]

It is important to note that when Pal mentions Indian culture in his text he emphasizes Hindu culture. Furthermore, he uses religion and spirituality interchangeably in his text. Interpreting *Swadeshi* spirit in terms of Indian spirituality (read Hindu spiritual tradition) he clearly notes that "new movement is new interpretation of old philosophical foundation of the Hindu race". Further, "Behind the new nationalism in India stands the old Vedantism of the Hindus." This ancient Indian philosophy, divided into many schools, has one general idea running through it from end to end. It is the idea of the essential unity of man and God".[5] Thus, Pal also recognizes the essential nature of India (read Hindu) as spiritual and by this he constructs a difference with British.

The spiritual nature of India again comes into the text when Pal discusses the idea of *Swaraj* in his text, which is in his views, is the spiritual reference point of Indian national movement. "Viewing life and all its relations and activities from this supremely spiritual standpoint", he notes "the Indian Nationalist recognises a spiritual reference as much in religion proper as in his social economy and political laws and institutions". "Politics is, with him, part of his larger religion; it is a department of the science or philosophy of salvation. And, it is therefore, that the word which signifies the highest spiritual end represents also the highest political ideal".

Thus, we find that Pal also locates the basis of Indian political ideal in the spiritual realm. It is also worth noting that the inseparability of political and spiritual is one of the characteristics that one finds in his discourse on nationalism.

Tagore in his text *Nationalism* (1917) also emphasizes on ths spiritual nature of India although differently from Aurobindo, Gandhi and Pal. We have noted earlier that exploring the issue of nation and nationalism, Tagore digs up the history of India and its formation and posits it against the formation of nation in the history of Europe. On this basis, he observes that "Our history is that of our social life and attainment of spiritual ideals".[6] He also points out, ".... here is India, of about fifty centuries at least, who tried to live peacefully and think deeply, the India devoid of all politics, the India of no nations, whose one ambition has been to know this world as of soul, to live here every moment of her life in the meek spirit of adoration, in the glad consciousness of an eternal and personal relationship with it".[7] In the text, he like Aurobindo, Gandhi and Pal, constructed a dichotomy of the East and the West and their progress towards the realization of humanity. This dichotomy, as noted earlier, soon takes the form of spiritual and material domain respectively in which he locates his idea of nation and nationalism. Tagore's own approach to nation and nationalism is essentially spiritual and he finds spirituality in beauty, nature and simplicity. While discussing nation and nationalism, he also finds and highlights major shortcomings in the history of India and a terrible contradiction in history of Europe in regard to their formation. What Tagore finally seems suggesting in his text that the East and America must evolve in a way that should not mechanical but moral and human. Thus, Tagore also highlights the spiritual essence of India and its formation in comparison to materialist West.

Similarly, Savarkar in his text *Essentials of Hindutva* (1923) also highlights the spiritual essence of India (Read *Hindu Rashtra*). We saw that in his attempt to evolve the concept of *Hindutva*, what he considered a political concept in his text, he meticulously attempted to portrait a "collective Indian/Hindu identity" and its corresponding "imagined Indian/Hindu nation". Through this exercise, we noted, Savarkar tried to give a new shape to Indian nationalism on the basis of idea of *Hindutva*. But underneath, the texts also shows lofty idea of Hindu nation and nationalism and justify them with the example of ancient glorious Indian past that was, in Savarkar's view, "essentially Hindu in its form and content". To quote him, "This Bharatabhumi, this Sindhusthan, this land of ours that stretches from Sindhu to Sindhu is our *Punyabhumi*, for it was in this land that the Founders of our faith and the Seers to whom '*Veda*' the Knowledge was revealed, from *Vaidika* seers to Dayananda, from Jaina to Mahavira, from Buddha to Nagasen, from Nanak to Govind, from Banda to Basava, from Chakradhar to Chaitanya, from Ramdas to Rammohun, our *Gurus* and Godmen were born and bred. *The very dust of its paths echoes the footfalls of our Prophets and Gurus*".[8] Thus his text also recognizes the spiritual essence of India (read *Hindu Rashtra*).

Thus, what we notice is that discourse on Indian nationalism was clearly connected with the assumed antiquity and spiritual nature of India. Therefore, it was the spiritual basis by which the nationalists tried to define India and constructed a difference with British colonials who were seen as materialist.

However, we can note the differences among these nationalists and in their texts on the issue of spiritual nature of India. Aurobindo's spiritual depiction of India shows Hindu masculinity while Gandhi locates spiritual nature of India in the cultural evolution of India. Pal's formulation of spiritual nature of India is based on his understanding and reading of Hindu religious texts. Tagore explores spiritual essence of India through his own understanding and interpretation of Indian History. Savarkar also recognizes the spiritual nature of India, but he does it through his own reading of Hindu past and Hindu texts.

Now, we turn to the second question raised earlier in the study; how do these texts define civilization in general and Indian civilization in particular?

Discourse of Indian Civilization

Sri Aurobindo's *Bhawani Mandir* (1905) does not have any direct reference to this question. However, the text gives the impression that civilization is about moral and spiritual strength (*shakti*). In his text, India is contrasted with 'other divisions of mankind' or civilization and in Aurobindo's view India is 'reserved', 'highest', and 'most splendid'. On the question of civilization, the text also constructs a binary opposition of *mlecchahood/aryanisation* and argues that India's mission is "to purge barbarism (*mlecchahood*) out of humanity and to *aryanise* the world". Here again we may note how 'others' are assumed as '*mleccha*' or barbaric and how India is assumed as civilized. In other words, civilization is seen in the term of *'aryaniztion'*. Thus, what we note is that India is velorized and 'other' needs spiritual guidance from India. Yet, this is not to happen automatic and what Aurobindo feels is that for such a great project India "must first re-*aryanise* herself".

Gandhi in his text *Hind Swaraj* (1909) defines civilization in moral terms. Gandhi devotes a full chapter in his text titled as 'civilization' arguing that "its true test lies in the fact that people living in it make bodily welfare the object of life". Gandhi here uses the term civilization in reference to modern civilization. He also argues that the modern civilization is 'irreligious' as it "takes note neither of morality nor of religion". On the other hand, "true civilization" is being represented by India. As mentioned previously, in his words, "I believe that the civilisation India has evolved is not to be beaten in the world. Nothing can equal the seeds sown by our ancestors". He also defines civilization in abstract terms in the following manner, "Civilisation is that mode of conduct which points out to man the path of duty. Performance of duty and observance of morality are convertible terms. To observe morality is to attain mastery over our mind and our passions". So doing, we know ourselves. The Gujarati equivalent for civilisation means "good conduct". If this definition be correct, then India, as so many writers have shown, has nothing to learn from anybody else, and this is as it should be".[9] Further, he mentions in his text,

> "The tendency of Indian civilization is to elevate the moral being, that of the Western civilization is to propagate immorality. The latter is godless, the former is based on a belief in God. So understanding and so believing, it behoves every lover of India to cling to the old Indian civilization even as a child clings to its mother's breast".[10] Not only this he notes that "....ancient civilization of India which, in my opinion, represents the best that the world has ever seen".[11] "In our own civilization, there will naturally be progress, retrogression, reforms and reactions; but one effort is required, and that is to drive out Western civilization".[12] "Indian civilization is the best, and that European is a nine days' wonder".[13] Again he mentions, "...ephemeral civilizations have often come and gone, and will continue to do so".[14] "I bear no enmity towards the English, but I do towards their civilization".[15]

Bipin Chandra Pal in his text *The Spirit of Indian Nationalism* (1911) does not provide any specific views on civilization. However, it does appear contextually. In the preface of his text he quotes Chirol who wrote series of Article in '*The Times*' with the title "The Indian Unrest" and indirectly tackles the question of civilization. Pal writes in preface, "Mr. Chirol admits that the present upheaval in India is essentially social and religious. It is really due to a keen conflict of two different types of civilisations".[16] In responses, Pal writes "If this be true, then it will have to be admitted that a conflict of ethical and spiritual ideals can never be overcome by any sort of political remedies".[17] Another reference of civilization we find in the text when Pal describes the "modern half-educated European" and their definition of civilization. Here he mentions "scale of civilization" that puts the critique of civilization mission theory. He notes, "The modern half-educated European is peculiarly *lacking in imagination and insight*. He cannot understand anything that does not fall into the narrow grooves of his thoughts and predilections. Inflated with the conceit of superior colour and culture, he cannot form any correct estimate of what he contemptuously brushes aside as barbarism and superstition. *Lacking to a very large extent the spirit of religion himself,* he cannot adequately assess the worth of the religious impulse, especially when expressed through unfamiliar symbols and ideas, as a motive power in human affairs. Not that he is not apprehensive of what he calls fanatical outbursts, especially among people considered *low in the scale of civilization;* but his apprehensions are very much like those of the skilful and intrepid sportsman shooting big game in the wilds of India or Africa". Thus, Pal views civilization in terms of 'religion' and criticizes the "scale of civilization" which was based on material and contextual development.

Tagore in his text *Nationalism* (1917) presents his views on civilization in a different way. He observes that "All particular civilization is the interpretation of particular human experience".[18] However, his views on civilization become more specific when he shows the contrast of Western civilization and Asiatic civilization. In his view, Western civilization is the civilization of power, therefore, it is exclusive, thus, it is naturally unwilling to open its sources of power to those whom it has selected for its purposes of exploitation. He also criticizes West's view on Asiatic civilization. "We have been repeatedly told, with some justification, that Asia lives in the past—it is like a rich mausoleum which displays all its magnificence in trying to immortalize the dead. It was said of Asia that it could never move in the path of progress, its face was so inevitably turned backwards".[19] As we know, this was the very common and prevalent colonial discourse of late nineteenth century and early twentieth century known as "Civilization mission" with which nationalists like Bipin Chandra Pal, Aurobindo and Gandhi had also to wrestle. Like Gandhi, Tagore also finds that some Indian and Asian elite are accepting these views under the "hypnotic spell" of Western ideas. Tagore challenges the colonial discourse of civilization mission arguing that "We forgot that in Asia great kingdoms were founded, philosophy, science, arts and literatures flourished, and all the great religions of the world had their cradles. Therefore, it cannot be said, that there is anything inherent in the soil and climate of Asia that produces mental inactivity and atrophies the faculties which impel men to go forward. For centuries we did hold torches of civilization in the East when the West slumbered in darkness, and that could never be the sign of sluggish mind or narrowness of vision".[20] Moreover, he appeals for a "syncretic civilization" where good part of Western civilization and Eastern civilization could meet. Thus, he warns that modern civilization cannot be accepted as full package. What we need is Eastern touch to modern means. "Therefore you cannot with a light heart accept the modern civilization with all its tendencies, methods and structures, and dream that they are inevitable. You must apply your Eastern mind, your spiritual strength, your love of simplicity, your recognition of social obligation, in order to cut out a new path for this great unwieldy car of progress, shrieking out its loud discords as it run".[21] He further mentions, "To a Western observer our civilization appears as all metaphysics, as to a deaf man piano playing appears to be mere movements of fingers and no music. He cannot think that we have found some deep basis of reality upon which we have built our institutions".[22]

He also defends Indian civilization. He notes, "it is difficult for us to prove to an unbeliever that our civilization is not a nebulous system of abstract speculations, that it has achieved something which is a positive truth—a truth that can give man's heart its shelter and sustenance. It has evolved an inner sense—a sense of vision, the vision of the infinite reality in all finite things".[23]

Further, "We also have lived for centuries, we still live, and we have our aspiration for a reality that has no end to its realization—a reality that goes beyond death, giving it a meaning, that rises above all evils of life, bringing its peace and purity, its cheerful renunciation of self. The product of this inner life is a living product".[24]

On the other hand, Savarkar in his text *Hindutva* (1923) views civilization in entriely different way. In the section of the text "What is civilization", Savarkar elaborates his views on civilization. In his definition, "Civilization is the expression of the mind of man".[25] "Civilization is the account of what man has made of matter". Further, "If matter is the creation of the Lord, then civilization is the miniature secondary creation of man". "At its best it is the perfect triumph of the soul of man over matter and man alike".[26] Locating this definition of civilization in nation he writes, "The story of the civilization of a nation is the story of its thoughts, its actions and its achievements. Literature and art tell us of its thoughts; history and social institutions of its actions and achievements".[27] It needs to be again pointed out that he views Indian civilization in terms of "Hindu civilization". He appreciates Indian civilization (Hindu civilization) in following manner, "we owe a debt of gratitude to these *Puranas* and Epics for having preserved all ancient and venerable records of our people through revolutions which had effaced the very traces of whole nations and whole civilizations elsewhere in the world."

On the basis of one *Rashtra, Jati* and *Sanskriti,* he argues that these constitute "the essence of our civilization and mark us out a cultural unit". In his words, "We Hindus are not only a *Rashtra,* a *Jati,* but as a consequence of being both, own a common *Sanskriti* expressed, preserved chiefly and originally through Sankrit, the real mother tongue of our race. Everyone who is a Hindu inherits this *Sanskriti* and owes his spiritual being to it as truly as he owes his physical one to the land and the blood of his forefathers".[28]

Now, we turn to the third question raised in the study as to how do these text define nation and offer the idea of India?

Discourse on Nation and the Idea of India

Sri Aurobindo in his text *Bhawani Mandir* (1905) defines nation in following way, "... [Nation] is not a piece of earth, nor a figure of speech, nor a fiction of the mind. It is a mighty *Shakti*, composed of the *Shaktis* of all the millions of units that make up the nation, just as *Bhawani Mahisha-Mardini* sprang into being from the *Shaktis* of all the millions of gods assembled in one mass of force and welded into unity. The *Shakti* we call India, Bhawani Bharati, is the living unity of the *Shaktis* of three hundred millions of people; but she is inactive, imprisoned in the magic circle of *tamas*, the self-indulgent inertia and ignorance of her sons. To get rid of *tamas* we have but to wake the *Brahma* within".[29]

Thus, Aurobindo claims that nation is not a territory, nor "an imagined community". Invoking the homology of *Bhawani Mahisha-Mardini*, a mythical and powerful goddess who was created by assembling the powers of many Gods—with nation, Aurobindo claims that nation is united *Shakti*, the *Shakti* what he calls India or *Bhawani Bharati* in his text. Aurobindo makes it clear that Bhawani is India and it symbolizes nation. For him, the nation is *Shakti* of its millions. It is "living unity of the *Shaktis* of three hundred millions of people of India." But he laments that she is inactive because of *tamas* or gross inertia. This *Shakti* can be revived by overcoming the *tamas* or waking up *Brahma* within.

Similarly, Gandhi in his text *Hind Swaraj* (1909) illustrates his views on nation. He notes in second chapter of the his that "As the time passes, the Nation is being forged". Further, "Nations are not formed in a day; the formation requires years". Certainly Gandhi mentions here the term nation in modern sense. He also argues that India has developed as a nation because of its "faculty of assimilation". In fact, the text makes a striking argument that India was made a "nation" much before the British came. He wrote, "We were one nation before they came to India. One thought inspired us. Our mode of life was the same. It was because we were one nation that they were able to establish one kingdom. Subsequently, they divided us".[30]

Gandhi describes, in detail, how India was a nation much before the British came to India in spite of many differences. He writes, "I do not wish to suggest that because we were one nation we had no differences, but it is submitted that *our leading men* travelled throughout India either on foot or in bullock-carts. They learned one another's languages and there was no aloofness between them. What do you think could have been the intention of those *farseeing ancestors of ours* who established *Setubandha*

(Rameshwaram) in the South, Jagannath in the East and Haridwar in the North as places of pilgrimage? You will admit they were no fools. They knew that worship of God could have been performed just as well at home. They taught us that those whose hearts were aglow with righteousness had the Ganges in their own homes. India was *one undivided land* so made by nature. They [*Acharyas*], therefore, argued that it must be one nation. Arguing thus, they established holy places in various parts of India, and fired the people with an *idea of nationality* in a manner unknown in other parts of the world. And we Indians are one as no two Englishmen are. Only you and I and others who consider ourselves civilized and superior persons imagine that we are many nations".[31]

Thus, Gandhi makes a geographical argument that India has been a nation like other modern nation for which a territory is needed. Thus for him, India not only culturally but geographically too has been a nation. In other words, for Gandhi India has been a nation because of "one undivided India", "one thought", "same mode of life", and "faculty of assimilation".

Pal in his text *The Spirit of Indian Nationalism* (1910) views nation like Aurobindo. He views nation as the mother. He clearly admits that Bunkim Chandra Chatterjee is the discoverer of this new salutation "*Bande Mataram*"; and his symbolic presentation of the "Mother" is significant. Here the essential and permanent form of the "Mother" rests eternally on the lap of *Maha-Vishnu*. "This is her real form,—*the nation eternally resting in Humanity*. And by all these means the new patriotism in India has become really a new religion to vast numbers of its people"[32].

It is important to note that Pal employs Hidnu theory of *Karma* to describe the condition of individual and nation. In his words, "He [Hindu] believes in the inexorable law of *karma*, which is only another name for the law of causation as applied in the moral world. Nations, like individuals, are equally subject to this law".[33] It is this theory of *Karma* by which Pal depicts the history of India as a nation. In his words, "They [nations], too, have to work out their respective *karmas*, both good and bad. Through their good *karma*, the Hindu came to prominence and power, colonized new regions of the earth, conquered new peoples, spread culture and civilization in the world".[34] He further views colonial rule as a result of "evil *karma*" of Indian (Hindu). He argues that people know that this phase will soon disappear with the 'another turn of the Wheel of Providence. In his logic, The sins of past generations, the evil *karma* of the nation, had not yet completely worked themselves out.[35]

However, Tagore in his text *Nationalism* (1917) views the idea of nation in a very different way. As discussed in the chapter seven, his views on nation and nationalism emerge in the context of his overall reading of Indian history, development of the modern nation and development of nationalism in Europe and its corresponding relation to the materialism. In his text, his idea of nation appears in a very discursive way when he mentions about the British presence in India and its Indian response. "In the case of British," he writes that "we had to deal, not with kings, not with human races, but with a nation—we, who are no nation ourselves". Tagore assertion that India is 'nonation' is significant. Here Tagore views nation in the term of organized politics with a specific aim. The nation and its aim that developed in Europe are different from Indian situation. Tagore writes that India has different aim and it has been devoid of politics. He points out, ".... here is India, of about fifty centuries at least, who tried to live peacefully and think deeply, the India devoid of all politics, the India of no nations, whose one ambition has been to know this world as of soul, to live here every moment of her life in the meek spirit of adoration, in the glad consciousness of an eternal and personal relationship with it".[36]

Tagore directly answers the question of what is Nation. In his view, "A nation, in the sense of the *political and economic union of a people,* is that aspect which a whole population assumes when organized for a mechanical purpose. Society as such has no ulterior purpose. It is an end in itself. It is a spontaneous self-expression of man as a social being. It is a natural regulation of human relationships, so that men can develop ideals of life in cooperation with one another. It has also a political side, but this is only for a special purpose. It is for self-preservation. It is merely the side of power, not of human ideals".[37]

This view of Tagore is radical in the sense that it makes a difference between the society and nation. As mentioned, nation, for him, is an organized mechanical entity and it is merely an economic and political union. Moreover, it is a means. While society is a "spontaneous self-expression of man" and an organization for "natural regulation of human relationships".

Tagore in his historical analysis of nation also argues that how society changed into a nation and how nation developed in due course of time. In his view, the organization of nation developed because of science and technology. Behind the development of nation there was a greed and power. He also mentions that how this development of nation has created a very inhumane world system that has created competition, mutual jealousy and supremacy. He writes, "with the help of science and the perfecting of organization this power begins to grow and brings in harvests of wealth, then it crosses its boundaries with amazing rapidity. For then it goads all its neighbouring societies with greed of material prosperity, and consequent mutual jealousy, and by the fear of each other's growth into powerfulness. The time comes when it can stop no longer, for the competition grows keener, organization grows vaster, and selfishness attains supremacy. Trading upon the greed and fear of man, it occupies more and more space in society, and at last becomes its ruling force".[38]

In a very radical way Tagore argues that power is central to the very notion of nation that has become today too abstract. He defines power as "a scientific product made in the political laboratory of the Nation, through the dissolution of the personal humanity".[39] Thus, he mentions that nation is nothing but "an organization of politics and commerce" that has become all powerful at the cost of the harmony of the higher social life, then it is an evil day for humanity".[40] Moreover, in Indian context, Tagore claims that "Nation as abstract being is ruling India".[41]

As it appears, Tagore looks the question of nation from the human point of view than political. In his view, nation represents the "organized self-interest of whole people and it is the least human and least spiritual". Like Gandhi, Tagore also looks modern nation as "soulless organization" and views nationalism as "cruel epidemic of evil". Relating the idea of nation to the spirit of nationalism he argues that "... the idea of the Nation is one of the *most powerful anesthetics* that man has invented. Under the influence of its fumes the whole people can carry out its systematic programme of the most virulent self-seeking without being in the least aware of its moral perversion—in fact feeling dangerously resentful if it is pointed out".[42]

He observes that the aim of the nation and the individual is different. He argues that Nation is abstract entity and individuality is freedom that cannot be fully realized in such abstract entity as nation. Like Gandhi who criticized modern nation because it was against the individuality, Tagore too finds the same reason against the Nation. In his words, "Those who have any faith in Man cannot but fervently hope that the tyranny of the Nation will not be restored to all its former teeth and claws, to its far-reaching iron arms and its immense inner cavity, all stomach and no heart; that man will have his new birth, in the freedom of his individuality, from the enveloping vagueness of abstraction".[43] Finally, instead of nation Tagore favours Indian tradition of "no nation" in which the individuality can be fully realized. Furthermore, he finds that India as "nonation" has potential to show the world a new way.

Unlike above mentioned nationalists, Savarkar in his text *Hindutva* (1923) views Indian nation as Hindu nation. We noted in chapter eight, Savarkar describes Hindu as a nation. He gives the idea how Hindu became the nation. "The activities of so intrepid a people as the Sindhus or Hindus could no longer be kept cooped or cabined within the narrow compass of the *Panchanad* or the Punjab." Thus, The Hindus spread "led by the consciousness of a great mission and their Sacrificial Fire that was the symbol thereof"[44] and "they soon reclaimed the vast, waste and but very thinly populated lands. Forests were felled, agriculture flourished, cities rose, kingdoms thrived,—the touch of the human hand changed the whole face of the wild and unkemp nature".[45] According to Savarkar, "Bharatakhanda" as a nation indicated "politically grander expression"—from the Himalayas to the sea—as well as "common cultural empire".[46] He quotes *Vishnu Purana* arguing that We have met with no better attempt to define our position as a people than the terse little couplet in the *Vishnu Puran*, "The land which is to the north of the sea and to the south of the Himalaya mountain is named Bharata inhabited by the descendants of are Bharata".[47] Savarkar again quotes *Bhavishya Puran, Pratisarga Parva* and writes, "The best country of the Aryans is known as Sindhusthan whereas the Mlechchha country lies beyond the Indus. This demarcation was made by the great king (Shalivahan the grandson of the great Vikramaditya). Thus, "The day on which the patriarchs of our race had crossed that stream they ceased to belong to the people they had left behind and laid the foundation of a new nation".[48] They assimilated and expanded and created "a race and a new polity that could only be most fittingly and feelingly

Yet in Savarkar's formulation Sindhusthan does not only refer to geography. In his view, "the concept expressed by this word was 'national' and not merely 'geographical'. "Sindhusthan was not merely a piece of land, but it was a nation which was ideally if not always actually a state (*rajnah-rashtram*)".[49] Further Sindhusthan refers to the culture. Sindusthan was the "Best nation of the Aryas". Elaborating it he notes, the term "is not based on any theological hair-splitting or fanaticism". The word 'Arya' expressly refers to all who "have inherited a common culture, common blood, common country and common polity," while Mlechchha also by the very fact of its being put in opposition to Sindhusthan meant foreigners nationally and racially and not necessarily religiously."

Now, we turn to fourth question; how do these texts offer the means through which divergent people within the India can construct *solidarity* across cultural and class differences?

Discourse on Means of Solidarity

Sri Aurobindo in his text *Bhawani Mandir* (1905) offers a blue print in the annexure of his text by which solidarity among Indians can be constructed. This is made through developing a cult of "political *sannyasi*" through a *math*. The last part sets the general and specific rule by which political *sannyasi* needed to observe. Strictly observing the discipline and rules of *achar* and purity, bodily and mental, prescribed by the Heads of the Order, *Math* the general rule informs us about simple living of *sannyasi*, no ranking in *Math*, no desire for personal fame, little comfort and detachments from worldly life.

Gandhi in his text *Hind Swaraj* (1909) gives the clue to achieve solidarity through *Swadeshi*, *Swaraj* and *Satyagraha*. In the last part of his text, he also provides a blue print to achieve the solidarity. *Hind Swaraj* submits the thesis that nationals tasks lay before the national elite. The most important corollary to this Gandhian theorem is that the fate of India as a nation depends on the moral character of the Indian professional classes, *i.e.* the character of its lawyers, doctors, and wealthy. It is interesting to note that Gandhi put a vehement critique of these professionals in Chapter XI and XII of his text. Gandhi laments that professional classes, who exerts tremendous influence on the general masses, are hypnotized by greed and are victims of caste, creed and status considerations, which affected the unity and integrity of the nation. To bring about this mental transformation of the Indian elite, Gandhi proposes 19 points in the final chapter of *Hind Swaraj*. Of the 19 points, three were addressed to doctors, four to lawyers, and the rest to what Gandhi calls "wealthy". Gandhi thought that only such moral transformation could give Indian elite the necessary moral strength essential for *Swaraj*.

Gandhi also puts three points that could construct solidarity among Indian: (1) Real home-rule is self-rule or self-control. (2) The way to it is passive resistance: that is soul-force or love force. (3) In order to exert this force, *Swadeshi* in every sense is necessary. Most importantly, Gandhi persuades his countrymen to make personal attempt to change for solidarity. He notes, "What we want to do should be done, not because we object to the English or that we want to retaliate, but because it is our duty to do so. You and I have nothing to do with the others. Let each do his duty. If I do my duty, that is, serve myself, I shall be able to serve others".[50]

Pal in his text *The Spirit of Indian Nationalism* (1910) finds the solidarity among Indian in *Swadeshi* movement that created a new awakening among Indians towards a new and common ideal. As noted earlier, he claims that after *Swadeshi* movement nationalism in India became at once the name of a "common ideal, a common purpose, one general spirit and impulse that moved the classes and the masses alike in more than one Indian province". He points out some programmes by which solidarity can be made. For example, he points out to the goal of "national destiny" that was to be achieved by Indian "nationalists" through the methods of Boycott. He also argues that the method of Boycott was more than the economic and political significance generally perceived. Further, what India needed was, in his view, to train people on "national lines" to realize the "national destiny". Pal in his text also calls for "National Civil Volunteering" and a "new manhood" in national life, not for narrow and selfish interest but to make "special contribution in culture and character to the larger life of universal humanity".

Thus, Pal finds that in India there is a birth of "new exegesis", which is reconstructing the old beliefs and trying to adjust them to the demands of the modern life and thought. The result is that, in his views, it has revived the faith of the educated classes of the country in national institutions and scriptures. Further, he notes that this phenomenon is rapidly bridging over the gulf between educated class and the general masses of India which was created by the foreign ideas and ideals. Pal also recognizes that "it is this religious spirit, at once so real and so conservative, which differentiates the new National Movement from the old, purely secular, political movements in British Indial".

Pal observes that this religious tone has the "messianic aspiration" since the beginning of the movement. His solidarity programme is to be understood in terms of this "messianic aspiration". Interestingly, he recognizes that this "messianic idea" exists in Hinduism which can be found in the fullest expression in the well-known verses of the *Bhagavad-Gita*. Quoting *Gita's* (IV. 8) famous verse that reads as *Dharmasamsthapanarthaya sambhavami yuge, yuge,* Pal views the nationalist movement against colonialism as the struggle between *dharma* and *adharma* in India and how Indian (Hindu) should get inspiration from the ancient religious text (Hindu text). Pal recognizes that patriotic poetry, hymes, plays, writings are playing or may play significant role in solidarity among Indians.

As mentioned earlier, Tagore's text *Nationalism* (1917) provides critique of nation and nationalism. He was basically a poet, thus we find poetic sensibility in his text not the temperament of an activist. Naturally, thus, there is no blue print in the text on the strategies or any action of the solidarity of Indian people like Gandhi, Aurobindo and Pal. However, Tagore mentions the way by which Indians have shown solidarity in their history and can show it in future also. For solidarity, he glorifies Indian past so that Indians could get confidence in them. He notes, "We forgot that in Asia great kingdoms were founded, philosophy, science, arts and literatures flourished, and all the great religions of the world had their cradles. Therefore it cannot be said, that there is anything inherent in the soil and climate of Asia that produces mental inactivity and atrophies the faculties which impel men to go forward. For centuries we did hold torches of civilization in the East when the West slumbered in darkness, and that could never be the sign of sluggish mind or narrowness of vision".[51] This is called ethno symbolic resources to solidify the nationalist sentiment. He also invokes a philosophical insight by which Indian could realize there dream not yet dreamt of. He argues that what world in general and India in particular is to realize is "simplicity and beauty" as well as "fullness of leisure". In his words, "all these have to be brought to a harmony in a manner not yet dreamt of".[52]

In Tagore's view, the constitution of India has been different. He asserts that since beginning of the history India had to suffer from a serious problem, that is the race problem. He argues that India has tried to solve this problem by making an adjustment of races and acknowledging the real differences between them. Moreover, India has tried to construct some basis of unity. "This basis has come through our saints, like Nanak, Kabir, Chaitanya and others, preaching one God to all races of India".[53]

Tagore claims that what India has been doing is worth imitating by the world as the whole world is becoming one country through scientific facility, thus what we need today is a non-political solution of the problem of racial difference. He claims that "There is only one history—the history of man. All national histories are merely chapters in the larger one. And we are content in India to suffer for such a great cause".[54] Tagore extends this point further. In his words, "The most important fact of the present age is that all the different races of men have come close together. And again we are confronted with two alternatives. The problem is whether the different groups of peoples shall go on fighting with one another or find out some true basis of reconciliation and mutual help; whether it will be interminable competition or cooperation".[55]

Like Gandhi who argued that India will perish if it follows the path of West, Tagore too argues that Europe's strength, path of lies in her history and India should not borrow the European interpretation of history. Thus, "We, in India, must make-up our minds that we cannot borrow other people's history, and that if we stifle our own, we are committing suicide. When you borrow things that do not belong to your life, they only serve to crush your life. And therefore, I believe that it does India no good to compete with Western civilization in its own field. But we shall be more than compensated if, in spite of the insults heaped upon us, we follow our own destiny".[56] "I am not for thrusting off Western civilization and becoming segregated in our independence. Let us have a deep association".[57]

Savarkar in his *Hindutva* (1923) makes an emotional appeal to Indians (read Hindu) for solidarity in the last paragraphs of his text. He emphatically claims that "the actual essentials of *Hindutva* are the ideal essentials of nationality". "Can any one of you, Oh Hindus! Whether Jain or Samaji or Sikh or any other subsection afford to cut yourselves off or fall out of the organic combination that already exists? Strengthen these ties if you can: "pull down the barriers that have survived their utility, of castes, and customs, of sects and sections:... "intermarriages between provinces and provinces, castes and castes, be encouraged where they do not exist".[58] He notes, "Let the minorities remember they would be cutting the very branch on which they stand. Strengthen every tie that binds you to the main organism, whether of blood or language or common Motherland." Blend blood, "from vein to vein, from Attock to Cuttack till at last the Hindu people get fused and welded into an indivisible whole, till our race gets consolidated and strong sharp as steel."

Again, "The ideal conditions in which a nation can attain perfect solidarity and cohesion would, other things being equal, be found in the case of those people who inhabit the land they adore, the land of whose forefathers is also the land of their Gods, the scenes of their history and mythology".[59] Offering an idea to promote solidarity, he mentions in his text, "We are trying our best, as we ought to do, to develop the consciousness of and a sense of attachment to the greater whole, whereby Hindus, Mohammedans, Parsis, Christians and Jews would feel as Indians first and every other thing afterwards. But whatever progress India may have made to that goal one thing remains almost axiomatically true – not only in India but everywhere in the world—that a nation requires a foundation to stand upon and the essence of the life of a nation is the life of that portion of its citizens whose interest and history and aspirations are most closely bound up with the land and who thus provide the real foundation to the structure of their national state."[60]

Analysis of the Discourses

These discussions lead us to make some generalizations. First of all, we noted that Indian past, which was claimed to be spiritual in nature, was glorified by all the authors in their texts considered here. However, we also saw that their version of spirituality was different from each other. The reason to portrait India as spiritual nation was to give the legitimacy of their claim that India has been civilized or, in fact, more civilized than colonials thus Indians do not need colonial presence for their development/progress what latter claimed. Second, what we noted is that in claiming legitimacy from the past, the Indian past was also made into an assemblage of what was most desired at that time. They reinterpreted Indian history and mythology for this purpose. This also permitted the growth of an impersonal Indian society where individuals were bonded through defining a shared culture and learning a shared history. Thus, the reconstruction of the past thereafter assumed a practical and utilitarian function. This proves Hobsbawm (1990) observations who, establishing a relationship between Nations and Nationalism, argued that history is reconstructed in a way that suits the ideology of nationalism and is essential to the construction of nationalism. As noted, this construction was essential to the making of a Indian state. Moreover, this process of making the Indian state incorporated not just the elite class but also the less privileged. The texts considered here, from *Bhawani Mandir* (1905) to *Essentials of Hindutva* (1923), also entails that nationalism may begin with ideas among the elite but its propagation involves having mass support. We also found that the texts find a problem of how to define Indians as citizens of a new nation. This, of course, relates to the question of identity or identities. One of the basic identities that texts reveal is the spiritual identity of citizen with humanistic and universal vision. This spiritual nature of India and Indians identity as spiritual and moral was also served to make the distinction/difference with British colonizers who were seen as materialistic and violent.

Second, on the overall reading of these texts, a significant question appears as to why the authors, from Aurobindo to Savarkar, were so aggressive in asserting that India is a nation, in spite of the fact that their versions of nation were different as discussed earlier. The answer lies in the colonial ideas that stated that India was not a nation in true sense of term (read colonial sense of the term). India's fundamental unity as a nation was denied often by prominent scholars, while its historic and cultured oneness had really never been acknowledged by the English rulers of the country. As Sir John Strachey remarked, "This is the first and most essential thing to learn about India—that there is not and never was an India, or even any country of India, possessing, according to European ideas, any sort of unity, physical, political, social, or religious; no Indian nation, no "people of India" of which we hear so much".[61] Indian nationalists subversions of such discourse is best summarized by Sri Ramchandra Guha. Guha (2011) points out, "By 1888 the British were so solidly established in India that they could anticipate, if not a thousand-year *Raj*, at least a rule that extended well beyond their own lifetimes. In that year a man who had helped put the *Raj* in place gave a series of lectures in Cambridge which were later published in book form under the simple title India. This was a primer for those who might work in India after coming down from Cambridge. But there was also a larger theoretical argument to the effect that 'India' was merely a label of convenience, "a name which we give to a great region including a multitude of different countries". In Strachey's view, the differences between the countries of Europe were much smaller than those between the 'countries' of India. Strachey's remarks were intended as a historical judgement. It is in this context the authors attempted to prove that India was a nation much before the British came".[62]

Third, we also found that all authors projected in their text that India has special mission in the world. Consider Aurobindo's *Bhawani Mandir* (1905). Aurobindo argues that India's regeneration is not only important for India, but also for the whole humanity. "India cannot perish, our race cannot become extinct, because among all the divisions of mankind it is to *India that is reserved the highest and the most splendid destiny, the most essential to the future of the human race*. It is *she* who must send forth from herself the future religion of the entire world, the Eternal religion which is to harmonise all religion, science and philosophies and make mankind one soul".[63]

One of the central themes that the texts renders is "to *aryanise* the world". The mother says Her children that by constructing Her temple, "You will be helping to create a nation, to consolidate an age, to *aryanise* the world. And that nation is your own, that age is the age of yourselves and your children, that world are no fragment of land bounded by seas and hills, but the whole earth with her teeming millions".[64] Thus, the text shows its both contextual and specific and universal meaning.

In the same way, Gandhi's *Hind Swaraj* (1905) claims India's mission in the world. Indirectly, he suggests that India is superior to any other nation and civilization and it will show a new way to the world. He notes in his text that "A nation [India] with a constitution like this is fitter to teach others than to learn from others".[65] Similarly, Bipin Chandra Pal (1910) mentions how India has special mission in the world and how it will contribute in universal humanity. Pal, in the context of "national destiny" that was to be achieved by nationalists through the methods of Boycott, mentions that ..."The end pursued by these means was essentially moral. The object was to create in the community an interest larger and higher than the narrow and more or less selfish interest of personal preferment or family advancement." These methods and works had higher objective.[66] Pal writes that 'it was really to develop a new manhood in the country, realising itself through the self-controlled activities of the national life, and gradually, through that life, making *its special contributions in culture and character to the larger life of universal humanity*".[67] Further on the occasion of criticizing the revolutionary violence he mentions India's mission in the world. He notes, "The greatest risk to India would be a further loss of her old spirit, a decadence of her revived moral and spiritual life, a diversion, for a time at least, from her *God—appointed mission as the spiritual teacher of modern humanity*".[68] In the same way, Tagore in his *Nationalism* (1917) claims that what India has been doing is worth imitating by the world as "The whole world is becoming one country through scientific facility, thus what we need today is a non-political solution of the problem of racial difference." In his words, "The most important fact of the present age is that all the different races of men have come close together. And again we are confronted with two alternatives. The problem is whether the different groups of peoples shall go on fighting with one another or find out some true basis of reconciliation and mutual help; whether it will be interminable competition or cooperation".[69] Tagore gives a solution of this problem that might be seen as role of India in modern world. He asserts that "those who are gifted with the moral power of love and vision of spiritual unity, who have the least feeling of enmity against aliens, and the sympathetic insight to place themselves in the position of others will be the fittest to take their permanent place in the age that is lying before us". Tagore argues that mere political and commercial basis of unity among races is insufficient and claims only spiritual unity would solve the differences of race.

Tagore admits that there is always a possibility to bridge the gulf between the East and the West. He argues that how the East can help the West. He asserts that "We must, however, know it is providential that the West has come to India. Yet, someone must show the East to the West, and convince the West that the East has her contribution to make in the history of civilization. India is no beggar of the West. And yet even though the West may think she is, I am not for thrusting off Western civilization and becoming segregated in our independence. Let us have a deep association".[70]

Likewise, Savarkar in his text *Hindutva* (1923) discusses the universal role of Hindu India. "We are trying our best, as we ought to do, to develop the consciousness of and a sense of attachment to the greater whole, whereby Hindus, Mohammedans, Parsis, Christians and Jews would feel as Indians first and every other thing afterwards. But whatever progress India may have made to that goal one thing remains almost axiomatically true—not only in India but everywhere in the world—that a nation requires a foundation to stand upon and the essence of the life of a nation is the life of that portion of its citizens whose interest and history and aspirations are most closely bound up with the land and who thus provide the real foundation to the structure of their national state".[71] He further mentions, "Look at America who deserted Germans during First World War. The "American State, in the last resort, must stand or fall with the fortunes of its Anglo-Saxon constituents." Hindus are India's bedrock. Therefore, even from the point of Indian nationality, must ye, O Hindus, consolidate and strengthen Hindu nationality; not to give wanton offence to any of our non-Hindu compatriots... but in just and urgent defence of our race and land".[72] In his view, "As long as competition and pan-movements compete for the world, we must have our team in order. And some day India when will be able *to dictate claims* to the whole earth they cannot do so in terms so very different from the terms which the *Gita* dictates or the Buddha lays down." In the last paragraph of his text he observes,

> "Thirty crores of people, with India for their basis of operation, for their Fatherland and for their Holyland with such a history behind them, bound together by ties of a common blood and common culture can *dictate* their terms to the whole world. A day will come when mankind will have *to face the force*. Equally certain it is that whenever the Hindu come to hold such a position whence they could

> *dictate terms to the whole world* — those terms *cannot be very different from the terms which Gita dictates" or the Buddha lays down*—A Hindu is most intensely so, when he ceases to be Hindu; and with a Shankar claims the whole earth for a Benares "Waranasi Medini !" or with a Tukaram exclaims "my country ! Oh brothers, "*the limits of the Universe — there the frontiers of my country lie !*"[73]

Problems of Nationalists Discourses

So far we have discussed that how authors of these nationalist texts constructed a difference with colonial discourse and valorized Indian civilization. Although these texts also reflect differences in their definition of spiritual essence of India, on the definitions of Indian civilization and Indian nation in particular, yet they all claim that India has special mission in the world. On the close reading of these texts, however, there emerge certain problems in their discourses. They can be discussed briefly in following manner.

First of all we find their nationalist ideology was closely based on Sanskritic, textual tradition of Vedic Brahmanism. From Aurobindo to Savarkar, all relied upon sanskrit texts for their interpretations of Indian spirituality, Indian civilization, and Indian nation. Sanskrit, especially its *dharmic* text is presumed to have preserved the cultural heritage of India. Second, we notice that the territorial spread of this cultural core was supposed to be—coexistence with the subcontinent itself. We noticed the name *Aryavart, Bharatvarsha, Hindusthan* in these texts. It is also noteworthy that Brahmanism, through religious-cultural symbolism and a consensus value system was supposed to have given unity and integrity to the subcontinent. Most importantly, the texts in hidden way seem to convey that Vedic Brahmanism can again resolve the contradiction of the India. Third, we notice that the value and principles that the texts propagates are based on the opposition of the West. Thus, the texts in a coherent way present a nationalist ideology that represents a single perspective of middle class nationalist movement to view the past, present and future of the nation.

We also notice that these texts represent a new politics of nationalism and in doing so they have "glorified India's past and tended to defend everything traditional." Moreover, all attempts to change customs and life-styles began to be seen as the aping of

Western manners and thereby regarded with suspicion. Consequently, nationalism fostered a distinctly conservative attitude towards social beliefs and practices. Thus, the national movement towards modernization was stalled by nationalist politics. Moreover, whatever reform was to be made in India it was to be occurred within the ambit of new interpretations of Brahmanism proposed by the authors of these texts. It is also interesting to note that these texts do not explicitly question the social problems of India, especially, caste issue and women problems and ignore or avoid them.

Notes and References

1. *The Complete Works of Sri Aurobindo (CWSA), Bande Mataram, Political Writings and Speeches: 1890-1908.*Vols. 06-07, Pondicherry: Sri Aurobindo Ashram Trust, 2002, p. 82.
2. Gandhi, M.K., 2008, *Hind Swaraj or Indian Home Rule,* Ahmedabad: Navajivan, p. 52.
3. Pal, Bipin Chandra. 1910, *The Spirit of Indian Nationalism.* West Kensington; London: The Hind Nationalist Agency, p. 12.
4. *Ibid.,* p. 21.
5. *Ibid.,* p. 38.
6. Tagore, Rabindranath. 1917, *Nationalism.* San Fransico USA: Macmillan, p. 16.
7. *Ibid.,* p. 17.
8. Savarkar, V.D., 1969, *Hindutva: Who is Hindu,* Bombay: Veer Savarkar Prakashan, p. 111.
9. Gandhi, *op. cit.,* p. 53.
10. *Ibid.,* p. 55.
11. *Ibid.,* p. 87.
12. *Ibid.,* p. 80.
13. *Ibid.,* p. 87.
14. *Ibid.*
15. *Ibid.*
16. Pal, *op. cit.,* p. iii.
17. *Ibid.*
18. Tagore, *op. cit.,* p. 90.
19. *Ibid.,* p. 65.
20. *Ibid.,* p. 66.
21. *Ibid.,* p. 73.

22. *Ibid.*, p. 79.
23. *Ibid.*, p. 80.
24. *Ibid.*
25. Savarkar, *op. cit.*, p. 92.
26. *Ibid.* p. 92.
27. *Ibid.*
28. *Ibid.*, p. 99.
29. *Op. cit.*, p. 83.
30. Gandhi, *Op. cit.*, p. 40.
31. *Ibid.*, p. 41.
32. Pal, *op. cit.*, pp. 13-14.
33. *Ibid.*, p. 17.
34. *Ibid.*, p. 18.
35. *Ibid.*, p. 20.
36. Tagore, *op. cit.*, p. 17.
37. *Ibid.*, pp. 19-20.
38. *Ibid.*, p. 20.
39. *Ibid.*, p. 22.
40. *Ibid.*, p. 23.
41. *Ibid.*, p. 24.
42. *Ibid.*, p. 57.
43. *Ibid.*, p. 59.
44. Savarkar, *op. cit.*, p. 10.
45. *Ibid.*, p. 11.
46. *Ibid.*, p. 13.
47. *Ibid.*
48. *Ibid.*, p. 30.
49. *Ibid.*, p. 32.
50. Gandhi, *op. cit.*, p. 90.
51. Tagore, *op. cit.*, p. 66.
52. *Ibid.*, p. 72.
53. *Ibid.*, p. 119.
54. *Ibid.*
55. *Ibid.*, p. 121.
56. *Ibid.*, p. 128.
57. *Ibid.*, p. 130.
58. Savarkar, *op. cit.*, p. 141.
59. *Ibid.*, p. 140.
60. *Ibid.*, p. 141.
61. See Ramachandra Guha. 2011. *India After Gandhi: The History of the World's Largest Democracy*. Delhi: Pan Books, p. ii.

62. *Ibid.*
63. *CWSA:* 06-07:84.
64. *Ibid.*, p. 89.
65. Gandhi, *op. cit.*, p. 54.
66. Pal, *op. cit.*, p. 3.
67. *Ibid.*
68. *Ibid.*, p. 53.
69. Tagore, *op. cit.*, p. 121.
70. *Ibid.*, p. 130.
71. Savarkar, *op. cit.*, p. 140.
72. *Ibid.*
73. *Ibid.*, p. 141.

Appendix-I

*Type of Nationalism**

Historic

(i) Pre-nineteenth century, State to nation (nation-building): *e.g.* England, Scotland, France, Portugal. Colonial nationalism (*e.g.* USA).
(ii) Nineteenth-early twentieth century. Nation to state (national unification or independence): *e.g.* Germany, Italy, Ireland.
(iii) Post-1945 anti-colonial nationalism (India, Ghana etc.).
(iv) Post-industrial Developed World nationalism (*e.g.* Scottish, Flemish, Quebecois).
(v) Post-independence, i.e. 1947-communal nationalism in Developing World (*e.g.* Kashmir, Punjab, Biafra, Sri Lanka).
(vi) Post-authoritarian regime nationalism (*e.g.* Catalan, Basque, Soviet republics).

Geographic

(i) Europe: home of classical and now post-industrial nationalism (seen in west European capitalist countries and central/east European communist/ex-communist countries).
(ii) Colonial or European settler countries' (*e.g.* Latin-America, the United States, Canada, Australia, South Africa, Israel).
(iii) Colonial/Developing World: African and Asian anti-colonial nationalism, 'pan-' movements, ethnic politics and communalism.

---

* James G. Kellas (1998). *The Politics of Nationalism and Ethnicity*, MacMillan Press Ltd., New York.

Forms and Intensity (in ascending order of violence)

(i) *Cultural:* Generally confined to intellectuals, but language conflicts can affect wider populations (especially, in Belgium, Quebec. ex-Soviet and Yugoslav republics).

(ii) *Constitutional:* In democratic systems, nationalist parties and movements which peacefully campaign for national self-determination, receiving mainly on votes in elections and referendums (*e.g.* Scotland, Catalonia, former communist countries). Also, nationalists or autonomists who accept the multinational state or consociational democracy (Belgium, Catalonia, Quebec).

(iii) *Peaceful direct action:* Conventions, plebiscites and declarations of independence outside the constitutional process (*e.g.* Ireland before 1921, Scotland, Quebec, Baltic republics).

(iv) *Violent, direct action:* (*e.g.* 'terrorist' or paramilitary groups (Quebec FLQ, Basque ETA, Corsican FNLC, Irish IRA).

(v) *Communal violence:* Especially found in Developing World countries (*e.g.* Nigeria, India, Sri Lanka, Fiji etc.) but, also in "settler" countries (South Africa, Israel), and in urban areas of industrialised countries in the form of racial violence (*e.g.* the US and Britain). "Ethnic cleansing" and genocide (universal).

Appendix-II

*Synopsis of Theory of Nationalism**

The theory is concerned to explain the **politics** of nationalism and ethnicity, that is,

1. The *positive* demand for political power for the nation, through national self-determination or other means. Autonomy or statehood is the end.
2. The *negative* reaction against rule by "foreigners", which, is seen as involving domination or exclusion and other forms of discrimination.

Each section represents a "building-block" of the theory, and each "building-block" is built upon the foundations of its predecessor. The columns are similarly linked, moving progressively from left to right to denote "necessary" and "sufficient" conditions. The relevant academic disciplines are given in brackets in the 'building-block' column.

Building-block	*Necessary condition for*	*Sufficient condition for*
1. **Human nature and political behaviour:** Instinctive behaviour (sociobiology)	Selfishness; altruism; social bonding; 'kin selection'; 'inclusive fitness'; nepotism; slavery; genocide	Ethnicity Ethnocenuism Xenophobia
(Neurophysiology, socio-linguistics)	Language	'Mother tongues' (but language divisions also require a political and social explanation).
Deliberate behaviour (social psychology)	Individual and group 'rational self-interest' Responses to displacement, frustration, etc.	'Realistic' group conflict (ingroup/outgroup) 'Irrational' ingroup/ outgroup hostility

(*Contd.*)

* James, G. Kellas, 1998, *The Politics of Nationalism and Ethnicity*, MacMillan Press Ltd., New York.

Building-block	*Necessary condition for*	*Sufficient condition for*
2. **Ideas and ideologies:** (Philosophy sociology)	The idea of the nation The idea of nationalism The idea of race	Nationalism as ideology Racism, Nazism, Fascism, anti-Semitism, white supremacy, caste systems.*
3. **Cultural, economic, social and political change:** (History, anthropology, sociology, economics, political science)		
The sovereign state	The 'nation-state' The multinational state	'Official nationalism'
Democracy/popular sovereignty Economic, cultural and political homogeneity		'Social nationalism'
Economic, social and political inequalities/ displacements in a multi-national state or colonial empire	Nationalist/ethnic/racial conflicts 'Cultural Division of Labour' Uneven development Internal Colonialism	'Ethnic nationalism' Wars of national liberation Ethnic politics
Post-industrial society	New nationalities/ ethnicities 'Post-materialist values'	National and Ethnic politics
Competitive politics	Formation of organizations and parties Voting for nationalist parties Nationalist/ethnic leaders	
Regime change	Strong capacity of nationalist and ethnic parties/movements	

(*Contd.*)

* The presence and strength of these ideologies varies with the political circumstances.

Building-block	*Necessary condition for*	*Sufficient condition for*
4. **Consociational democracy** (political science)	Political accommodation of ethnic and cultural groups	
5. **Nationalism in international relations** (Political science; international law)		
(a) state system	Nation-States	
(b) International Law	Protection of national minorities.	Nation-states
(c) Legitimacy of national self-determination in international relations.		
(d) Linkage between internal national and ethnic homogeneity and external politics:		
(i) Internal national/ ethnic tensions	Foreign policy weakly supported	Weak nationalism in state's international relations
(ii) Homogeneous nation-state, or consociational democracy	Foreign policy strongly supported internally	Strong nationalism in state's international relations
	International state system	
Patriotism and xenophobia	Relative weakness of international and supranational bodies	Loyalty and 'supreme sacrifice' in times of war.

Appendix-III

*Theories of Nationalism**

Deutsch's Theory of "Nationalism"

Karl Deutsch, the American political scientist, wrote *Nationalism and Social Communication: An Inquiry into the Foundations of Nationality* in 1953, with a 2nd edition in 1966. It has become a classic in the study of nationalism, although it has its critics (*e.g.* Smith, 1983: 100), and it has not had many imitators in subsequent writings on the subject.

Deutsch was unusual in seeking to quantify and measure the elements of nationality, looking particularly at "social communication" (common language and interpersonal transactions of all kinds). A people or nation is defined by the "complementarity or relative efficiency of communication among individuals" (Deutsch, 1966: 188). Behind the reasoning of this theory was the then-fashionable "systems theory" derived from cybernetics, with its measurement and use of "messages" which sustain a system. Deutsch also represents the school of thought which sees nations and nationalism as the product of "modernisation", the

> social mobilisation which accompanies the growth of markets, industries, and towns, and eventually of literacy and mass communication. The trends in this underlying process of social mobilization could do much to decide whether existing national trends in particular countries would be continued or reversed (Deutsch, 1966: 188).

As Deutsch admits, "this is largely a book on research and methods of research" rather than on nationalist movements. But it attracted attention to the basis of the nation as being a pattern of transactions which marked it off from other nations, thus broadening the focus from language to all kinds of social and economic data. It also asserted "modernisation" theory, which was to prove so popular in the 1960s and 1970s, but which is now largely discredited.

---

* James G. Kellas, 1998. *The Politics of Nationalism and Ethnicity*, MacMillan Press Ltd., New York.

When one looks at how particular examples of nationalism are treated by Deutsch, one sees the difficulty of relating such data to political movements. Thus, while Deutsch correctly plots the decline of the Gaelic-speaking and agricultural population of Scotland, he entirely fails to relate this convincingly to Scottish nationalism, which was based on other considerations. Nevertheless, an analysis of communication networks in Scotland, marking it off from England, would have been a good way to measure the functioning of the Scottish political system and its potentiality for nationalism.

Hechter's Theory of "Internal Colonialism"

Michael Hechter's *Internal Colonialism: The Celtic Fringe in British National Development, 1536-1966* (1975) is another landmark contribution to the study of nationalism, especially in the British context. Hechter, an American, was, like Deutsch, attracted to the research methodology of providing quantitative evidence to support his thesis. He was also influenced by "modernisation theory" or "diffusion theory" which, like that of Deutsch, posits the view that "from interaction will come commonality" and ethnic homogenisation (Hechter, 1975: 7).

Hechter, however, reacted against diffusion theory, and posited instead "internal colonialism". He maintained that modernisation and increased contact between ethnic groups within a state will not necessarily bring about ethnic unity, but will be just as likely to lead to ethnic conflict. This is because the inequalities between the regions in a country will relegate peripheral regions to an inferior position, leaving the core region dominant. The reaction to this in the peripheral regions will be hostility to the core, and if these regions are also national in character, this will take the form of nationalism. Thus, Hechter saw Scottish, Welsh and Irish nationalism as the result of internal colonialism by the English core.

Hechter's book was published before the rise of Scottish and Welsh nationalism in the late 1960s, but he has published since on the subject (Hechter, 1985). The principal change between the two publications is in the nature of his "cultural division of labour" theory. This theory states that in a situation of internal colonialism, there will be a social stratification of ethnic or oil tural groups, with the core group occupying the best class position and the peripheral groups the inferior positions. This corresponds to a "colonising" nation and "colonised" nations. Thus, in Britain, the English are the colonisers, and the Scots, Welsh and Irish the colonised.

Unfortunately for this theory, the facts seem to be at variance with such a division of labour. For example, Scots are not in practice relegated to inferior social positions in Britain, and Scotland has been as much an industrialised and imperial nation as England from the eighteenth century. This is not to say that there are not important regional inequalities in Britain, due to uneven economic development and to government and commercial policies favouring the south of England. All these have contributed to a rise in nationalism in Scotland and Wales.

Hechter took account of the criticisms levied at his theory (*e.g.* Page, 1978; Greenberg, 1980; Brand, 1985) and revised the "cultural division of labour" thesis (a hierarchical stratification) as regards Scotland to a "segmental cultural division of labour" (a vertical stratification) in which Scots occupy "occupational niches" deriving from the distinctiveness of their national institutions, such as law and education. These may not be inferior positions to those found in England, since they include high-class occupations. So, the group solidarity of 'colonised' nations and their assumed conflict with the colonisers is now called into doubt. By 1985 Hechter saw the capacity of nationalist organisations to attract support as being as important as the structure of internal colonialism (Hechter, 1985: 25). Nevertheless, his model remains a compelling one in many contexts (if not clearly in Scotland), and it will be returned to in the context of nationalisms in many parts of the world. The recurrence of a cultural division of labour in most multiethnic societies is particularly sinking.

Rokkan's Theory of Regionalism

While not strictly a theory of nationalism, Stein Rokkan's work on regionalism in Europe with Derek Urwin (Rokkan and Urwin, 1982, 1983) is relevant to "nation-building" and the problems of coreperiphery relationships. It also deals extensively with "the politicisation of peripheral predicaments" and "the central response".

Rejecting the "diffusion" model of Deutsch, but not endorsing the "internal colonial" model of Hechter, Rokkan and Urwin conclude that

> there is no simple centre-periphery polarity across culture, economics and politics. Peripheral predicaments and politicisation emerge out of the incongruity between cultural, economic and political roles, an incongruity which has existed on the continent as long as there have been states. While this remains unresolved, the potential for territorial problems remains, irrespective of the waxing and waning of individual parties or movements: (Rokkan and Urwin, 1983: 192).

It appears then, that it is a matter of degree whether the "incongruity between cultural, economic and political roles" will lead to nationalism in particular situations. Rokkan has shown that students of nationalism ought to measure the degree of harmony between such roles in a state. They should then be able to predict that a strong mismatch between these rotes will lead to nationalism.

Gellner's Theory of "Nationalism"

Ernest Gellner's *Nations and Nationalism* (Gellner, 1983) represents a type of theory which stresses the primacy of material conditions in shaping political thought and social change. In this it resembles Marxism, which Gellner nevertheless disavows. He proposes a fundamentally economic reason for the rise of nationalism. This is the development of "industrial society", which took place in certain parts of Europe at the end of the eighteenth century, and then during the nineteenth and twentieth centuries throughout most of the world.

The connection between nationalism and industrialisation is that particular forms of polity and culture are required if industrial economic growth is to occur. These forms combine in the nation-state. Once industrialisation took off, the old states were generally unable to maximise their advantages and profits until they changed both their cultural life and their state structure.

In place of the feudal or agrarian society, with its diversity of languages, cultures and ethnic groups, there had to be a homogeneous society with an educational system for all. This education would train workers and managers for industry, and provide all with a common "high culture". It was necessary to have one comcon language in a modern industrial society, for the mobility and division of labour would come from that, and from the education that all received.

Gellner, unlike many other writers on nationalism, does not believe that nationalism happened because some European thinkers invented it and forced it on political systems which would have been better off without it. Rather, he believes that nationalism "has very deep roots in our shared current condition, is not at all contingent, and will not easily be denied" (*ibid.*: 56). This means that nationalism achieved its successes because it was appropriate for the needs of the time, rather than as an ideology which could be accepted or rejected intellectually in competition with other ideologies.

At this point, attention focuses on another necessary condition for nationalism, the changing structure of the state. The medieval European state was unsuited to the task which industrialisation demanded. It was generally weak at the centre, preferring to operate through semi-independent aristocrats and churches. While some monarchies, such as those of England, France and Prussia, began to reduce the power of the barons and the church in the name of royal "sovereignty", there was little attempt to achieve a uniform culture within these countries. Indeed, several languages continued to be spoken in most contries, and often the king himself was imported from a foreign land. George I of Great Britain, for example, came to the throne in 1714 from Hanover in Germany, and spoke German, not English. There was little public education, and most education went to aspiring churchmen, lawyers and landowners. This was often in Latin a non-vernacular and pretty useless language as far as economic and social change was concerned. Only with a state education system in the vernacular, geared to the needs of industry, could progress be made. This meant a strong, centralised state, and a population free to work where it wished, without barriers of a feudal, religious or linguistic nature. The breakdown of the feudal state, and the emergence of centralised "sovcreign" authority was important for the development of nationalism, for it provided a strong state structure from which a homogeneous nation could be shaped. Control by the political authority from the centre over education, religion and law, swept away many local cultures or ethnicities, and replaced them with one large nation. In this way, "nation-states" emerged. Where these were not formed, and the principle of "one state, one culture" was denied, there was nationalist activity. While this theory applies particularly to the historic development of nationalism in Europe, it has clear relevance to new states (especially in the Developing World) which are not "nation-states" in the sense defined by Gellner.

Gellner's theory is compelling, but it has its limitations. There is little here about the primordial roots of nationalism, and its powerful emotional appeal. Why should people be prepared to die for what is in this analysis an imperative of a rational economic and social system of industrialisation? Nationalist behaviour in its contemporary form is hardly explained in this theory. It has been called "apolitical" (O' Leary, 1997) since it neglects the role of power politics in explaining nations and nationalism. It deals instead with the reasons why industrialising states adopted a national form in order to prosper, and the nationalism which was associated with that.

At one point, Gellner does address the question of the sharpness of nationalist conflict, but he relies again on a socio-economic explanation. In the early industrial age, he says, wide social chasms and the uneven diffusion of industrialisation produced social conflicts, especially when cultural (i.e. national) differences marked off these chasms. When cultural differences did not on respond to class divisions, "nothing much happened" (p. 121):

> Classes, however oppressed and exploited, did not overturn the political system when they could not define themselves "ethnically". Only when a nation became a class, a visible and unequally distributed category in an otherwise mobile system, did it become politically conscious and activist. Only when a class happened to be (more or less) a "nation" did it turn from being a dass-in-itself into a class-for-itself, or a nation-for-itself. Neither nations nor classes seem to be political catalysts: only nation-classes or class-nations are such (*Ibid.*).

In this rather obscure passage, Gellner attempts to reconcile class analysis with nationalism, something which Marxists also seek to do. The main difference between Gellner's theory and that of most Marxists is that Gellner sees nationalism as the concomitant of any type of industrialisation, while most Marxists make nationalism dependent on capitalism as such. With the arrival of proletarian rule, according to Marx, nationalism becomes redundant. Gellner, on the other hand, does not see any future situation without nationalism.

Gellner's discussion of the matching of class and national divisions has a clear parallel in Hechter's theory of internal colonialism, with its "cultural division of labour". But, in his desire to establish the nation-state as the norm for modern society, Gellner has to reject "multicultural society". For him, a homogeneous culture, at least at the level of "high culture", is necessary for modern states, although there may be room for innocuous folk cultures "in a token and cellophane-packaged form" (p. 121). There is no place in his theory for cultural pluralism and "consociational democracy", which tries to combine different national cultures within one state.

We can accept much of Gellner's historical analysis of how nation-states and nationalism emerged strongly at the time of industrialisation in Europe, when the breakdown of feudalism had taken place. It is more difficult to find in Gellner an explanation for the emergence of nationalism in pre-industrial times (*e.g.* Scotland in the Middle Ages, or England in Elizabethan times), and in non-industrialised countries in the Developing World. Moreover, nationalism arising out of post-materialist values in "post-industrial" societies (Inglehart, 1977) is clearly different from nationalism resulting from industrialisation. In all these contexts the conditions are different from those in nineteenth century nationalist Europe. Many nationalisms are found in countries which are largely agrarian, non-industrialised and non-centralised. A very important determinant of nationalism in the Developing World is the legacy of colonialism, and the independence movements directed against "white rule". Contemporary nationalisms have arisen in long-industrialised countries such as Britain, Belgium and Spain, which Gellner might have called nation-states. Something new seems to have happened there, outside Gellner's theory.

Nevertheless, Gellner's short book is a masterly study of the emergence of nationalism in history, and is a yardstick with which we can measure other writings on nationalism. It does not tell us all we want to know, but it gives us a clear theory relating nationalism to industrialisation, "high culture", and the structure of the modern state.

Walker Connor: An Ethnonationalist

Walker Connor is an American political scientist who has engaged in a vigorous debate on nationalism with fellow academics since the 1960s. A specialist on the former Soviet Union, he pointed to its fatal national divisions when other political scientists were inclined to accept the official communist view that nationalism had been transcended by socialism. In the end it appears that he was proved right, since the Soviet Union has broken up along national lines.

The best source for his work is his collected writings, *Ethnonationalism: The Question.for Understanding* (Connor, 1994), which includes his attack on American scholarship about nationalism, "Nation-building or nation-destroying?", and on the prevailing confusion in terminology ("A Nation is a Nation, Is a State, Is an Ethnić Group, Is a..."). Unlike Marxists, and most sociologists, Connor believes in the inevitable existence of nations throughout history and in the superior power of nationalism (as compared to economics, social class etc.) to shape the world. He is an almost lone primordialist in the hostile environment of the social sciences, where contextualism and constructivism rule supreme. ("Contextualism" states that nations and nationalism are the products of particular historic and social contexts, and "constructivism" states that nations and nationalism are constructs of nationalists, not "natural" (primordial phenomena). While he probably goes too far in this direction, since the actual history of nations is closely bound up in ever-changing contexts of a political and economic kind, Connor stands out as one as one of the few theorists who accept nationalism on its own terms, and as an inescapable fact of human nature. The advantage of this empathy is that he can understand and explain ethnocentrism (and its accompaniment, nationalism) wherever it occurs as a powerful force in human nature. He is not taken by surprise at its strength and recurrence, as have been so many social scientists. Unlike them, he does not reject nationalism; indeed, he favours it.

Benedict Anderson's Theory

Benedict Anderson's book, *Imagined Communities: Reflections on the Origin and Spread of Nationalism,* (Anderson, 1983), is another recent major contribution to the study of the evolution of nationalism.

Anderson is more of a "constructivist" and a 'contextualist' than a "primordialist", but, unlike Gellner, he is concerned to explore the psychological appeal of nationalism, which is close to a primordial approach: "What makes people love and die for nations, as well as hate and kill in their name?" (*Ibid.*, dustjacket). Obviously, a purely functional approach such as Gellner's will not explain the emotions engendered by nationalism, yet Anderson does not go to the other extreme of a socio-biological or primordial interpretation. He takes a historical, rather than a timeless, universalist approach, so that nationalism is seen to emerge at a specific period in European history. Anderson's originality lies in his explanation of how and why people in certain circumstances come to 'imagine' themselves part of a nation, and why such an "imagined community" has such a powerful attraction for them.

He first builds up a set of necessary conditions for the emergence of nationalism. These are partly material, and partly joychic. More subtly, he analyses the "pilgrimages" which people make in their social and economic lives. It is these pilgrimages which define the boundaries of the nation, and lead people to identify with it and not with another social or political entity. Such pilgrimages may thus be taken to be the sufficient condition for particular nations to be "imagined" and form the focus of nationalism. This seems to be a combination of Deutsch's community of communication, and Hechter's cultural division of labour.

The principal material precondition for nationalism, according to Anderson, is what he calls "print-capitalism", meaning commercial printing on a widespread scale. It is this which spreads the idea of the nation and the ideology of nationalism, not only within one nation, but throughout the world. Through print-capitalism, vernacular languages are strengthened by the publishing of dictionaries and literature generally. In this way,

Millions are "imagined" by many people, and linguistic nationalisms take root. Printing standardises languages, and also aids the development of capitalism and the centralised state. A sense of nationality flows from the common language and education which printing facilitates. But the emergence of nationalism also depended on some other "modernising" processes, such as scientific discoveries and the exploration of the world. These broke down old ways of looking at society, and also broke the unity of Christendom and the Moslem world, with their associated international languages, Latin and Arabic. The monarchical state too, with its "divine right of kings" and hierarchical authority structure, gradually gave way to rule "by the people".

At this point, Anderson links up with Gellner's theory, which connects nationalism with modernisation and the needs of the industrial state. But he goes further than Gellner by explaining the emotional power of nationalism. He draws attention to nationalism's appeal as a faith in an everlasting life through membership of a continuing nation.. The nation represents the continuity of the extended family from one generation to the next. In an age of declining religion, with its belief in an afterlife, nationalism has a special appeal as a "secular transformation of fatality into continuity, contingency into meaning" (p. 19). Anderson stresses the character of nationalism, not as a political ideology self-consciously followed, but as a cultural system with religious characteristics.

By pursuing the notion of "pilgrimages"—essentially, the pattern of social communication and "life chances" of different peoples—Anderson is able to explain why nationalism has been found in every type of society in the modern world. The nation is often the social grouping which represents the boundary for mobility, both geographic and economic. This may be a matter of sharing a common language, or of being the object of differential treatment by the state. If an individual is identified as the member of a particular nation, this may give access to power and wealth, or conversely, discrimination and deprivation.

In the first instance, it is the state which determines which "pilgrimages" can be made by members of different nations within it. Indeed, the state may decide who the members of the nations are. It does this to protect the interests of the powerful, and to keep other groups in a subordinate position. This is not necessarily anything to do with industrialisation (as in Gellner's theory), but is much more about political and social power generally. [(For an extended treatment of the role of the state in shaping nationalism and the character of ethnicity, *see* Paul Brass (ed.), *Ethnic Groups and the State,* 1985; John Breuilly, *Nationalism and the State,* 1982, 1985, 1993)].

This means that the development of nationalism can be analysed in almost any society, and not just in industrial society. For wherever a system of status and power divisions is based on nationality, nationalism is likely to flourish. This was the case in the multinational empires of Europe, and in the European colonies in America, Asia and Africa. In these areas, the imperial system confined the life chances or "pilgrimages" of natives (including Europeans born there, known as "creoles" in Latin America) to the colonies. Eventually, these natives saw themselves as members of a nation in rebellion against the imperial country. In this way, nationalism was born in the colonies, it was led by two groups, called by Anderson, "pilgrim creole functionaries and provincial creole printmen". The former were administrators and businessmen of native or creole origins, and the latter native/creole intellectuals and writers whose publications inspired national consciousness. Because of the policies of imperialism, they were cut off from advancement, in the imperial home country and followed their 'pilgrimages', or careers, in the colonies, which they came to perceive as separate nations in rebellion against the imperial country.

A later refinement of the concept of "pilgrimages" relates to "official nationialism". which reacts against the new vernacular (in this, book "social" or "ethnic") nationalisms. Fearing the break-up of the state through nationalist separatism, the old dynastic states begin a nationalism of their own. They try to impose a particular national culture on the whole state, and make that the condition for advancement, socially, politically and economically. Thus, the Russian Empire of the Czars instituted the policy of "Russification", making the use of the Russian language obligatory throughout the Empire (this policy was also followed by the communists in the USSR). In the ex-colonies in Africa and Asia which gained independence after 1950, similar official nationalisms can be found, linking successful "pilgrimages" in their societies to the adoption of a national language and culture sponsored by the state.

The title *Imagined Communities* points to the mental processes involved in nationalism. Members of even the smallest nation can never know most of their fellow nationals, "yet in the minds of each lives the image of their communion" (p. 15). This is not a question of "false consciousness", for there are, Anderson says, no "true" communities larger than face-to-face primordial villages. All other communities are imagined.

Anderson introduces new perspectives into the study of how nationalism has evolved. But there is ambiguity in his definition of a nation and in his account of the conditions for the emergence of nationalism. Nations are no more "imagined" than other social categories and identities, such as class, and defining what is 'real' rather than "imagined" in social affairs is a cul-de-sac. And the social preconditions for nationalism are ambiguous. Printing could destroy nations as well as create them. Many languages and nations (or ethnic groups) have died or been weakened in competition with literary languages and nations possessing printing resources.

As for religion, it seems that it is not always replaced by nationalism, but may go hand in hand with it. We have seen that churches have reinforced nationalism in such countries as Ireland, Poland, Armenia, Israel and Iran. It is difficult, therefore, to relate the rise of nationalism to the decline of religion, except perhaps in some mainly secular societies. In some cases, religion and nationalism thrive together; in others, where a church is strongly supranational (as the Roman Catholic Church or Islam), there may be tension between loyalty to religion and loyalty to the state or nation. However, even supranational churches can underpin nationalist movements against oppressive states which deny nationalism its free expression. Thus, the Roman Catholic Church and Islam are closely involved with nationalism in eastern Europe and Asia.

Anderson's use of the idea of "pilgrimages", points to the pattern of communication and social mobility as a powerful binding force in the consciousness and action of social groups (as Karl Deutsch did earlier). But there seems to be *a priori* question here why do ethnic or national groups crop up so often in social stratification? Why do people seem to prefer their fellow nationals as companions on their pilgrimages, and why do states use nationality as a method of dividing power? Can there be something special about nationality which is not present in other social, economic and political divisions? Our final theorist. Anthony Smith, focuses on this in the ethnic origins of nationalism, and its special characteristics.

Anthony Smith's Theory of Nationalism

Anthony D. Smith's book *The Ethnic Origins of Nations* (1986) focuses on ethnicity as the precursor of nationalism, and gives an explanation of the transition from ethnic identities and loyalties to those relating to nations. For Smith, "modern nations simply extend, deepen and streamline the ways in which members of *ethnie* [Smith's term for ethnic groups] associated and communicated. They do not introduce startlingly novel elements, or change the goals of human association and communication" (p. 215).

He is thus concerned to emphasise the continuity between ethnic identities and loyalties on the one hand and nationhood and nationalism on the other. In contrast, both Gellner and Anderson stress the essential *novelty* and *modernity* of nationalism. Smith does acknowledge the changes which made ethnicity into nationalism, and his explanations are similar to Gellner's and Anderson's. For example, the decline of religion, the rise of the centralised and bureaucratic state, as well as the pressures of the industrial economy are necessary for "ethnie" to be mobilised and politicised into nations. But the "new imaginings" and new thoughts (clearly a reference to Anderson's *Imagined Communities)* which lead people into national consciousness and nationalism are not really so new. Their essence can be found in pre-national communities at least as far back as Ancient Greece and Rome, although there was an ambivalence at that time about "the masses' and their claim to be included in the "ethnie". Apart from this, Smith concludes:

> it is clear that modern nations and nationalism have only extended and deepened the meanings and scope of older ethnic concepts and structures. Nationalism has certainly universalized these structures and ideals, but modern 'civic' nations have not in practice really transcended ethnicity or national sentiments... In terms of ends, as

> opposed to means, there is a remarkable continuity between nations and *ethnie,* nationalism and ethnicism; continuity but not identity (p. 216).

Smith moves the study of nationalism back to the pre-modern period, as Hans Kohn did in *The Idea of Nationalism* (1944). But Smith sees more in common between modern nations and their precursors than Kohn did. At the same time, Smith talks of "continuity", but not identity, between "ethnicism" and nationalism. Nationalism is more concerned with statehood or some form of self-government than "ethnicism", which to less clearly political. Nevertheless, "nationalism... does more effectively what pre-modern ethnicists tried to do, that is, keep out foreigners and diffuse to their kinsmen the traditions and myths of their ancestors, using the modern mass education system" (p. 216).

Smith here echoes Gellner's theory of nationalism, where the latter speaks of the nation's education system and "high culture" engendering cultural homogeneity. But Gellner saw this in functional terms: the means to economic efficiency in a developed industrial state. Smith, on the other hand, dwells on the traditional or pre-modern content to national culture, which has little to do with industrialisation. National myths, old languages, and so on, are the substance of nationalism as much as modernising communications and education, and Smith's theory is better able to cope with these than Gellner's (Smith and Gellner debated nationalism in public, shortly before Gellner died. *See* "The Warwick Debate", *Nations and Nationalism,* Vol. 2, part 3 (November 1996), pp. 357-88.

Where Smith seems to leave questions unanswered is regarding the transition from ethnicity to nationalism, and in the strength or weakness of particular nationalisms. "Continuity, but not identity" between ethnicity and nationalism opens up as many problems as it solves, similar to those involving the connection between human nature and nationalism, or between ethnocentrism and nationalism.

Eric Hobsbawm: A Marxist Historian of Nationalism

Hobsbawm's name is very well-known throughout the world as a historian of social movements. He has also paid particular attention to nationalism, which he detests. He attacks the views of fellow-Marxist Tom Nairn, who favours nationalism, especially in his native Scotland. In 1990 Hobsbawm published *Nations and Nationalism since 1780: Programme, Myth, Reality* (2nd edn., 1992), in which he supports the classic Marxist view of nationalism as "false consciousness", and a "bourgeois" construction, doomed to extinction along with that class. Indeed, he believes that the late twentieth century has witnessed the beginning of nationalism's final demise. Although, he is no longer clearly an old-style communist, he certainly supports a non-nationalist, left-wing social and political system. Hobsbawm takes a cosmopolitan view society, in which nations and nationalism have no positive role. He is anti-nationalist, having witnessed what he considers its evil ways in twentieth century Europe (in later books, *Age of Extremes* (1994) and *On History* (1997), he continues the attack).

The problem with Hobsbawm's approach is its *a priori* reasoning from Marxist principles. This makes it difficult for him to accept the facts. The end of the twentieth century has seen a revival of nationalism, and the collapse of communism. So, on two major counts, Hobsbawm seems to have got it wrong. But it would require a longer-term perspective, from the next century, to provide the proof of that.

Tom Nairn and the "Break-up of Britain"

Tom Nairn published his book *The Break-Up of Britain* in 1977 (2nd edn., 1981). Nairn is (or was) a committed Marxist, who nevertheless considers nationalism progressive in Marxist terms, especially in Britain. He supports Scottish nationalism, if not necessarily the Scottish National Party (SNP), and predicted that it was going to break up the British state. He provides a wealth of theoretical and factual evidence for this view. His approach is mainly materialist, in that he explains nationalism as the result of uneven capitalist development, and Scottish nationalism in particular he attributes to the end of the British Empire and the discovery of North Sea oil. These gave She Scots a rational economic motive for going independent.

He was immediately attacked by Eric Hobsbawm in the pages of the *New Left Review* (1977) for the nationalist heresy in socialist! thinking. Hobsbawm believed that socialism and nationalism were incompatible, in line with Marx. In fact, both Nairn and Hobsbawm got it wrong at the time of writing. Britain did not break up as predicted by Nairn, and nationalism remained a progressive force, at least in Britain, despite Hobsbawm. The debate between Hobsbawm and Nairn is of particular interest to those who want to study the treatment of nationalism in Marxism. It is conducted at a high level of theoretical abstraction, as well as political commitment, but with a rather remote connection to actual political events (*e.g.* the relative failure of both the Communist Party and the SNP in electoral terms).

Liah Greenfeld's "Five Roads to Modernity"

Greenfeld's book, *Nationalism: Five Roads to Modernity* (Greenfeld, 1992), is often referred to in sociological discussions of nationalism. She maintains that "nationalism lies at the basis of the world", because it is the "constitutive principle of modernity" (p. 491). This is because modernity breaks down the old "society of orders" and replaces it with an open, socially mobile one. In that society, nation and nationalism are essential ingredients, since they provide status and dignify, where previously these were based on aristocracy, the church, and wealth.

Greenfeld examines England, France, Russia, Germany and the United States of America (USA) for the development of national identity and consciousness over 500 years. She gives a very detailed "sociological history", but not a Marxist nor other materialist one. Her book can be compared to another well-known work by the historian Linda Colley: *Britons, Forging the Nation, 1707-1837* (1992). Greenfeld is strong on social psychology and cultural history, but rather obscure as a describer of events. The terms "modernity" and "post-modernity" are slippery concepts, and nationalism does not necessarily belong with either. One writer who places nationalism in a "post-modern" or "post-materialist" context is Ronald Inglehart (Inglehart, 1977). Both Inglehart and Greenfeld agree that a desire for status lies at the root of nationalism. The *politics* of nationalism and ethnicity do not emerge clearly from Greenfeld's book. But it is a marker in the literature on nationalism, nevertheless.

The theories discussed here are important to an understanding of nationalism, because they seek to explain how nationalism came to dominate world politics in the modern period. In comparison to the study of human nature and the study of political ideas, they stress the periodisation of history, and the particular contexts in which nationalism arose. They locate nationalism in time and place, rather than in the universals of "ethnocentrism" and the "idea of nationalism". In the theories discussed in this chapter, it is apparent that developments in history are closely related to the emergence of nationalism in different parts of the world at different periods.

However, we are still some way from explaining these particular nationalisms. Once more, the "necessary" conditions for nationalism in general are not the "sufficient" conditions for nationalist movements to emerge and thrive. This means that we must go beyond the theories discussed so far to look for other explanations for the strengths and weaknesses of nationalist movements. We have to look at a variety of theories or explanations which locus not so much on the historical emergence of nationalism on the world scene as on contemporary nationalist political behaviour and the politics of cultural pluralism.

Bibliography

Aloysius, G., 1997. *Nationalism Without A Nation in New India.* New Delhi: Oxford University Press.

Bruce Robertson (ed.) 1999. *The Essential Writings of Raja Rammohan* Ray. New Delhi: Oxford University Press.

Chadha, Yogesh. 1999. *Gandhi: A Life.* New York: John Wiley & Sons.

Chatterjee, Parth. 1986. *Nationalist thought and the Colonial world: A Derivative Discourses?* London: Zed Books.

Chatterjee, Partha. 1993. *The Nation and its Fragments: Colonial and Postcolonial Histories.* Princeton, NJ: Princeton University Press.

Chattopadhyay, Bankimchandra. 1992. *Ananda math.* Trans. and adapt. Basanta Koomar Ray. Bombay and Delhi: Vision.

Collins, Michael. 2012. *Empire, Nationalism and the Postcolonial World. Rabindranath Tagore's Writings on History, Politics, and Society.* London and New York: Routledge.

Encyclopedia of Indian War of Independence 1857-1947 (Vols. 1 to 19). 2009. New Delhi: Anmol Publisher.

Gandhi, M.K., 1927. *An Autobiography or My Experiments With Truth.* Ahmedabad: Navajivan Publishing House.

Gandhi, M.K., 2008. *Hind Swaraj or Indian Home Rule,* Ahmedabad: Navajivan Publishing House.

Guha, Ramachandra (ed.) 2009. *Nationalism.* India: Penguin Books.

Guha, Ramachandra. 2011. *India After Gandhi: The History of the World's Largest Democracy.* Delhi : Pan Books.

Godbole, V.S., 2004. *Rationalism of Veer Savarkar.* Thane: Itihas Patrika Prakashan.

Gupta, Kalyan Sen. 2005. *The Philosophy of Rabindranath Tagore.* Aldershot: Ashgate.

Hans Kohn. 1944. *The Idea of Nationalism.* Mumbai: MacMillan Publications. 1944.

Hugh B. Urban. 2007. *Tantra: Sex, Secrecy, Politics, and Power in the Study of Religion.* Delhi: Motilal Banarsidass.

Iyer, Raghavan, N., 1983. *Utilitarianism and All That*, Santa Barbara, CA, U.S.A.: Concord Grove Press.

Lederle, Mathew, 1976. *Philosophical Trends in Modern Maharashtra*. Mumbai: Popular Prakashan.

Mehta, V.R., 1992. *Foundation of Indian Political Thought*, New Delhi: Manohar Publishers.

Pal, Bipin Chandra. 1910. *The Spirit of Indian Nationalism*. West Kensington; London: The Hind Nationalist Agency.

Parel, A.J., 1997. *Hind Swaraj and other Writings*. New Delhi: Foundation Books.

Penderal Moon. 1999. *The British Conquest and Domination of India*, New Delhi: India Research Press.

Keer, Dhananjay. 1988. *Veer Savarkar*. Mumbai: Popular Prakashan,1988.

Rainee and Kumar, *International Journal of English and Literature* (IJEL)ISSN(P): 2249-6912; ISSN(E): 2249-8028, Vol. 3, Issue 5, December 2013, 21-26.

Samagra Savarkar Vangamaya (Vols. 1-8). Pune: Prakashan Samiti, Maharashtra Prantik Hindu Sabha, 1963-65.

Savarkar, V.D., 1969. *Hindutva: Who is Hindu*, Mumbai: Veer Savarkar Prakashan.

Sharma, Jiotirmaya. 2003. *Hindutva: Exploring the Idea of Hindu Nationalism*. New Delhi: Viking/Penguin Books.

Stephen Hey. 1992. *Source of Indian Tradition*, vol. 2, New Delhi: Penguin Books.

Tagore, Rabindranath. 1917. *Nationalism*. San Fransico, USA: MacMillan.

The Complete Works of Swami Vivekananda, (CW), Vols. I-VI, 1962. Kolkata: Advaita Ashrama.

The Complete Works of Sri Aurobindo (CWSA), Bande Mataram, Political Writings and Speeches: 1890–1908.Vols. 06-07, 2002. Pondicherry: Sri Aurobindo Ashrama Trust.

The Collected Works of Mahatma Gandhi (CWMG, Vols. 1-95). 1999. New Delhi: Publication Division, Government of India.

Verma, V.P., 1980. *Modern Indian Political Thought*, New Delhi: Sterling.

Webb Miller. 1938. *I Found No Peace*, New York: Garden City. 1938.

Webliography

archiv.ub.uni-heidelberg.de/voll text server/.../HPSACP_Wolf.pdf,

http://www.gktoday.in/indian-councils-act-1909-morley-minto-reforms-communal-representation/

www.facts-about-india.com/

https://cultural.maharashtra.gov.in/english/.../VOL.../HOME_RULE_MOVEMENT.pd.

http://www.gktoday.in/non-cooperation-movement-1920/.

Index